Read SAP PRESS online also

With booksonline we offer you online access to leading SAP experts' knowledge. Whether you use it as a beneficial supplement or as an alternative to the printed book – with booksonline you can:

- Access any book at any time
- Quickly look up and find what you need
- Compile your own SAP library

Your advantage as the reader of this book

Register your book on our website and obtain an exclusive and free test access to its online version. You're convinced you like the online book? Then you can purchase it at a preferential price!

And here's how to make use of your advantage

1. Visit www.sap-press.com
2. Click on the link for SAP PRESS booksonline
3. Enter your free trial license key
4. Test-drive your online book with full access for a limited time!

Your personal **license key** for your test access including the preferential offer

zx7n-pbmc-j5i4-gus6

Official ABAP™ Programming Guidelines

 **PRESS**

SAP PRESS is a joint initiative of SAP and Galileo Press. The know-how offered by SAP specialists combined with the expertise of the Galileo Press publishing house offers the reader expert books in the field. SAP PRESS features first-hand information and expert advice, and provides useful skills for professional decision-making.

SAP PRESS offers a variety of books on technical and business related topics for the SAP user. For further information, please visit our website: *www.sap-press.com*.

Hermann Gahm
ABAP Performance Tuning
2010, 348 pp.
978-1-59229-289-9

Thomas Schneider
SAP Performance Optimization Guide
2008, 638 pp.
978-1-59229-202-8

Horst Keller, Sascha Krüger
ABAP Objects
2007, 1059 pp.
978-1-59229-079-6

James Wood
Object-Oriented Programming with ABAP Objects
2009, 357 pp.
978-1-59229-235-6

Horst Keller, Wolf Hagen Thümmel

Official ABAP™ Programming Guidelines

Galileo Press

Bonn • Boston

Galileo Press is named after the Italian physicist, mathematician and philosopher Galileo Galilei (1564–1642). He is known as one of the founders of modern science and an advocate of our contemporary, heliocentric worldview. His words *Eppur se muove* (And yet it moves) have become legendary. The Galileo Press logo depicts Jupiter orbited by the four Galilean moons, which were discovered by Galileo in 1610.

Editor Stefan Proksch
Assistant Developmental Editor Justin Lowry
Translation Lemoine International, Inc., Salt Lake City, UT
Copyeditor Julie McNamee
Cover Design Jill Winitzer
Photo Credit Masterfile/Ric Frazier
Layout Design Vera Brauner
Production Editor Kelly O'Callaghan
Assistant Production Editor Graham Geary
Typesetting Publishers' Design and Production Services, Inc.
Printed and bound in Canada

ISBN 978-1-59229-290-5

© 2010 by Galileo Press Inc., Boston (MA)

1st Edition 2010
1st German edition published 2009 by Galileo Press, Bonn Germany

Library of Congress Cataloging-in-Publication Data
Keller, Horst, 1960-
  [ABAP-Programmierrichtlinien. English]
  Official ABAP programming guidelines / Horst Keller, Wolf Hagen Thümmel. -- 1st ed.
      p. cm.
  ISBN-13: 978-1-59229-290-5 (alk. paper)
  ISBN-10: 1-59229-290-9
  1. ABAP/4 (Computer program language) I. Thümmel, Wolf Hagen. II. Title.
  QA76.73.A12K4613 2010
  005.1'17--dc22   2009032614

Contents at a Glance

1   Introduction 17

2   General Basic Rules 23

3   ABAP-Specific Basic Rules 41

4   Structure and Style 79

5   Architecture 155

6   Secure and Robust ABAP 217

A   Obsolete Language Constructs 341

B   Automatic Check of Naming Conventions 365

C   Table of Rules 373

D   Recommended Reading 377

E   The Authors 379

Contents

Foreword 13

Acknowledgments 15

1 Introduction **17**

1.1 What Are Programming Guidelines? 17
1.2 Why Programming Guidelines? 18
1.3 Which Guidelines Are Involved Here? 18
1.4 Target Audience 19
1.5 How to Use This Book 20

2 General Basic Rules **23**

2.1 Separation of Concerns 23
2.2 KISS Principle 32
2.3 Correctness and Quality 34

3 ABAP-Specific Basic Rules **41**

3.1 ABAP Objects as a Programming Model 41
3.2 Program Type and Program Attributes 50
    3.2.1 Program Type 51
    3.2.2 Program Attributes 55
    3.2.3 Original Language 60
3.3 Modern ABAP 62
3.4 Checks for Correctness 65
    3.4.1 Syntax Check 65
    3.4.2 Extended Program Check 69
    3.4.3 Code Inspector 72
    3.4.4 ABAP Test Cockpit 76

4	**Structure and Style**	**79**
4.1	Source Code Formatting	80
4.1.1	Case Sensitivity	80
4.1.2	Statements per Program Line	83
4.1.3	Using the Pretty Printer	86
4.1.4	Line Width	89
4.2	Naming	91
4.2.1	Selecting the Language	92
4.2.2	Descriptive Names	94
4.2.3	Names of Repository Objects	101
4.2.4	Program-Internal Names	106
4.3	Comments	115
4.3.1	Selecting the Language	115
4.3.2	Content	117
4.3.3	Arrangement in the Source Code	120
4.4	Program and Procedure Structure	123
4.4.1	Global Declarations of a Program	124
4.4.2	Local Declarations	127
4.5	Source Code Organization	130
4.5.1	Source Code Modularization	130
4.5.2	Multiple Use of Include Programs	132
4.6	Alternative Notations	135
4.6.1	Alternative Language Constructs in Statements	135
4.6.2	Chained Statements	137
4.6.3	Method Calls	141
4.6.4	Assignments and Calculations	143
4.6.5	Calculation Expressions	145
4.7	Complexity	146
4.7.1	Expressions	147
4.7.2	Nesting Depth	149
4.7.3	Procedure Volume	150
4.7.4	Class Size	151
4.7.5	Dead Code	153
5	**Architecture**	**155**
5.1	Object-Oriented Programming	155
5.1.1	Encapsulation	156

	5.1.2	Modularization	157
	5.1.3	Static Classes and Singletons	161
	5.1.4	Inheritance	166
	5.1.5	Class References and Interface References	167
	5.1.6	Local Types for Global Classes	169
	5.1.7	Instance Constructor	171
5.2	Error Handling		172
	5.2.1	Reaction to Error Situations	172
	5.2.2	Classical and Class-Based Exceptions	174
	5.2.3	Exception Categories	178
	5.2.4	Exception Texts	180
	5.2.5	Using Exception Classes	183
	5.2.6	Handling and Propagating Exceptions	185
	5.2.7	Cleanup After Exceptions	186
	5.2.8	Catchable Runtime Errors	188
	5.2.9	Assertions	190
	5.2.10	Messages	191
5.3	User Interfaces		195
	5.3.1	Selecting the User Interface Technology	195
	5.3.2	Encapsulating Classical User Interfaces	199
	5.3.3	Lists	204
	5.3.4	Accessibility	207
5.4	Data Storage		208
	5.4.1	Persistent Data Storage	208
	5.4.2	Database Accesses	210
	5.4.3	Client Handling	211
	5.4.4	Using the Shared Memory	213

6   Secure and Robust ABAP   **217**

6.1	Data Types and Data Objects		217
	6.1.1	Bound and Standalone Data Types	218
	6.1.2	Declaration of Data Types and Constants	220
	6.1.3	Declaration of Variables	224
	6.1.4	Including Structures	226
	6.1.5	Using Types	228
	6.1.6	Referring to Data Types or Data Objects	230
	6.1.7	Table Work Areas	232
	6.1.8	Literals	233

	6.1.9	Strings	236
	6.1.10	Start Values	238
	6.1.11	Data Objects for Truth Values	239
6.2		Assignments, Calculations, and Other Accesses to Data	241
	6.2.1	Assignments Between Different Types	241
	6.2.2	Avoiding Invalid Values	243
	6.2.3	Using Conversion Rules	245
	6.2.4	Specification of Numbers	247
	6.2.5	Selecting the Numeric Type	249
	6.2.6	Rounding Errors	253
	6.2.7	Division by Zero	255
	6.2.8	Casting	255
	6.2.9	Runtime Errors When Accessing Data Objects	257
	6.2.10	Anonymous Containers	259
	6.2.11	Passing Global Data by Reference	260
6.3		System Fields	262
	6.3.1	Access	262
	6.3.2	Obsolete and Internal System Fields	264
	6.3.3	Evaluation	265
	6.3.4	Return Value	267
	6.3.5	Using System Fields as Actual Parameters	268
	6.3.6	Using System Fields on the User Interface	270
	6.3.7	Using System Fields in Operand Positions	272
6.4		Internal Tables	273
	6.4.1	Selecting the Table Category	274
	6.4.2	Secondary Keys	276
	6.4.3	Initial Memory Allocation	280
	6.4.4	Sorted Filling	281
	6.4.5	Aggregated Filling	283
	6.4.6	Output Behavior	284
	6.4.7	Loop Processing	286
6.5		Modularization Units	287
	6.5.1	Function Modules and Subroutines	288
	6.5.2	Type of the Formal Parameters of Procedures	289
	6.5.3	Transfer Type of Formal Parameters	292
	6.5.4	Passing Output Parameters by Reference	294
	6.5.5	Typing of Formal Parameters	296
	6.5.6	Internal and External Procedure Calls	298
	6.5.7	Exiting Procedures	302

	6.5.8	Dialog Modules and Event Blocks	304
	6.5.9	Macros	306
6.6	Dynamic Programming Techniques		309
	6.6.1	Using Dynamic Programming Techniques	309
	6.6.2	Runtime Errors During Dynamic Processing	311
	6.6.3	Using Dynamic Data Objects	313
	6.6.4	Memory Consumption of Dynamic Memory Objects	315
	6.6.5	Administration Costs of Dynamic Memory Objects	318
	6.6.6	Accessing Data Objects Dynamically	321
	6.6.7	Generic Programming	324
6.7	Internationalization		329
	6.7.1	Storing System Texts	329
	6.7.2	Translation-Friendly Message Texts	331
	6.7.3	Text Environment	333
	6.7.4	Character Set of Source Code	335
	6.7.5	Splitting Texts	336
	6.7.6	Codepages for Files	337

Appendices 339

A	Obsolete Language Constructs	341
	A.1	Procedures	342
	A.2	Declarations	343
	A.3	Object Generation	347
	A.4	Calls and Exits	347
	A.5	Program Flow Control	349
	A.6	Assignments	350
	A.7	Calculation Statements	352
	A.8	Processing Character and Byte Strings	353
	A.9	Internal Tables	355
	A.10	Dynpro Flow Logic	357
	A.11	Classical List Processing	358
	A.12	Data Storage	360
	A.13	Contexts	362
	A.14	External Interfaces	363
B	Automatic Check of Naming Conventions	365
	B.1	Naming Conventions in the Code Inspector	365
	B.2	Type-Specific Prefix Components	366
	B.3	Prefixes for Procedure-Local Declarations	367

	B.4	Structured Programming	....	369
	B.5	Object-Oriented Programming	....	370
	B.6	Assessment of the Naming Conventions	....	371
C	Table of Rules	....	373
D	Recommended Reading	....	377
E	The Authors	....	379
	Index	....	381

Foreword

Beauty is in the eye of the beholder. This proverb was the motto of an internal SAP project to increase the efficiency of the interplay of development, maintenance, and support. This project was started as a joint action of the respective executive areas in the summer of 2006.

In the course of this project, it was determined that the good legibility and simple understanding of program code were very important factors with regard to this goal. The original requirement for the project mainly derived from the maintenance organizations that have to use a highly maintainable product to efficiently carry out their tasks. True to the project's motto, the main focus was supposed to be on a specific beholder, that is, the user who doesn't develop the program but has to read and understand it as an employee of a maintenance department.

But as you know, the real meaning of this proverb is that beauty can be interpreted in various ways or that everyone can perceive beauty differently. So the question inevitably arises why only one perspective, that is, the maintenance perspective, should define a legible or "beautiful" program. It should also be nice for other users of a program. For this reason, the goal of the original project was set as follows: An ABAP program must be legible and understandable not only for the maintenance department but also for all those who come in contact with it. Not least, the program's developers must feel comfortable with the code to really work efficiently.

In the early years of ABAP, however, concepts such as legibility and maintainability certainly weren't declared development goals. Instead, functionality and performance were the primary concerns. In addition, the individual development departments had their own programming style, which resulted in myriad individual programming guidelines both within SAP and at the customer. On closer inspection, these programming guidelines turned out to be a mere collection of naming conventions. Of course, this only works out as long as the development and maintenance of closed program units are carried out within a closed team, if code is transferred to other developers only marginally, and if there are only a few alternative solutions to implement the programming task.

In the meantime, this approach has changed decisively. Because software is developed at different locations and the responsibilities of development and maintenance are distributed across different organizational units, the transfer of code has become a standard task. Moreover, the continuous growth of ABAP's functional scope leads to the consequence that there are many different ways to achieve a given goal. For the latter, the coexistence of classical procedural ABAP — the good old ABAP/4 — and the modern class-based ABAP Objects is an excellent example.

All of this suggested that it was finally time to stipulate highly universal ABAP programming guidelines as a sound basis for the efficient creation, further development, and maintenance of ABAP programs in all organizational units involved, which also include the original requirements of the maintenance organizations. Here, it proved as a happenstance that the ABAP language group, that is, the makers of ABAP, defined a set of general ABAP programming guidelines almost at the same time and for similar reasons. These guidelines were published in early 2006 in *SAP Professional Journal* and focused on, besides the maintainability of ABAP programs, also on their robustness as another important quality characteristic.

Within the scope of the mentioned project, the rules of these programming guidelines, which are partly based on notes of the ABAP keyword documentation, were compiled in an internal SAP list of recommended rules for ABAP programming, including some further rules on code complexity and a list of naming conventions. To make this rather plain list more appealing, to address a wider audience, and to achieve a better implementation of the programming guidelines — and ultimately because more and more partners and customers of SAP ask for generally available programming guidelines — SAP decided to publish the created guidelines in the form of this book. This book enables all ABAP developers within and outside of SAP to benefit from the formerly SAP-internal ABAP programming guidelines without any restrictions.

For all of these reasons, it is a great pleasure for me to present this book as the first version of the official ABAP programming guidelines since the ABAP language has been developed. I would like to thank everyone who contributed to these guidelines and particularly the two authors from the ABAP language group who met this responsible task.

Beauty is in the eye of the beholder — so please let us know about your opinion of the ABAP programming guidelines. I look forward to receiving your comments, concerns, and possibly praise in order to improve subsequent editions of these programming guidelines!

Jim Hagemann Snabe
Member of the Board of SAP

Acknowledgments

The authors would like to thank everyone who contributed to the creation of these ABAP programming guidelines. Due to the large number of people who provided us with remarks, we kindly ask for your understanding that we cannot mention every single person. Concrete suggestions for improvement for our manuscript, which were incorporated in this book, come from the following SAP co-workers: Ulrich Brink, Thomas Demmig, Randolf Eilenberger, Rasmus Faust, Herrmann Gahm, Michael Gutfleisch, Rolf Hammer, Christiane Kettschau, Udo Klein, Thomas Rohmann, Lindsay Russell, Dirk Troltenier, Doris Vielsack, and Sigrid Wortmann.

Special thanks go to Sebastian Wagner, the project lead of the programming guidelines project, who unremittingly and constantly promoted this project and ensured that our idea of a book became reality. We would also like to thank Andreas Blumenthal, Vice President of the TD Core AS&DM ABAP department, the driving force behind the programming guidelines in our working group — without his support, the ABAP programming guidelines would probably never have evolved in this form and in this book. Furthermore, we feel particularly honored that Jim Hagemann Snabe, a member of the board of SAP, contributed the foreword of this book and thus emphasizes the importance of programming guidelines.

At Galileo Press, we would like to thank Stefan Proksch from the editorial office and Iris Warkus from production for their unfailingly good and professional support — and for sparing us too much bureaucracy in this project. Additionally, we thank Osseline Fenner for the careful linguistic revision of the German manuscript. For the English manuscript, thanks go to Julie McNamee, who did the final copy editing.

I, Horst Keller, would like to thank my wife Ute for her understanding and her patience because once again a lot of our spare time had to be sacrificed for this book project. I, Wolf Hagen Thümmel, would like to thank my family for their patience during the creation of this book.

Horst Keller
Knowledge Architect, TD Core AS&DM ABAP

Wolf Hagen Thümmel
Senior Developer, TD Core AS&DM ABAP

"The basics of common sense follow the same rules among all nations around the world."
– Wilhelm Heinrich Wackenroder

1 Introduction

Right now, you are holding the official ABAP programming guidelines in your hands. Official — to what extent? These guidelines emerged from a joint action of the ABAP language group and the various development and maintenance organizations within SAP. Who should know better than the makers themselves how the ABAP language is supposed to be used and where possible pitfalls are hidden? And who can understand the maintainability of ABAP programs better than the maintenance organizations of SAP that support the large number of existing ABAP applications?

You can therefore be assured that these programming guidelines are based on profound detailed technical knowledge of the ABAP language and the associated development tools as well as on the broad experience in the development and maintenance of comprehensive ABAP applications.

But what are programming guidelines?

1.1 What Are Programming Guidelines?

It is indisputable that there are advantageous and less advantageous programming practices. The general goal of programming guidelines is to promote the advantageous practices and force back the disadvantageous ones.

Interestingly enough, many developers, and perhaps even more project leads and IT managers, think of naming conventions when they hear the term programming guidelines. But programming guidelines are not just naming rules (which are sometimes rightly considered random). In fact, they also provide rules for the program structure and modularization and for the use of problematic or obsolete language constructs among other things. For this reason, programming guidelines inevitably consist of two different components: specifications on the programming style, which are language-independent to a large extent, and specifications on the use or prevention of certain language constructs that strongly depend on the programming language.

1.2   Why Programming Guidelines?

Guidelines on the programming style are based on the knowledge that source code must be read and understood again and again by different persons during the software lifecycle. It should therefore be designed in such a way that the human reader can comprehend it easily and quickly, even if this is completely irrelevant for the processing by the computer. There are numerous scientific studies on the human-readable design of source codes whose results are summarized in various books, for instance, in *Code Complete* (Microsoft Press, 2004).

An important aspect when reading source code is the recognition value. For this reason, the programming guidelines are used to ensure uniform source code standards within a project or an entire organization. Such uniform standards facilitate the collaboration of multiple developers of a piece of software, the transfer of development or maintenance responsibility to other persons, or the involvement of third parties, for instance, within the scope of code reviews. In general, the meaning of such uniform standards increases with the number of persons that participate in a software project.

But also the individual developer, who maintains and further develops his own programs in the long term, can achieve higher efficiency and program quality by adhering to advantageous programming practices.

1.3   Which Guidelines Are Involved Here?

The main problem of programming guidelines is often that they are too comprehensive and possibly too difficult to understand so that a developer cannot know them all by heart. We try to motivate the individual rules established here and to illustrate them in examples wherever reasonable so that they can be memorized more easily and always retraced. For the rules on the programming style, we focus on the basic aspects that are really helpful from our point of view.

Programming guidelines are aimed at increasing the productivity in development and maintenance. By contrast, excessive specifications, for instance, for naming, which developers cannot learn by heart due to their volume, are rather suited to sustainably derogate the productivity. So, the guidelines in this book are aimed at being reasonable but not dogmatic, profound but not fundamentalist. The compliance with these guidelines should be a given for a developer and not understood as a formalistic necessity.

In software development, there are many aspects that must be considered if the product is to comply with professional requirements and possible legal requirements. Such aspects include, for example, usability, documentation, throughput, response time behavior, functional correctness, and so on. In each development organization, there will be corresponding product standards for these aspects to consistently ensure the quality of the software product. The ABAP guidelines presented in this book are deliberately limited to such partial aspects that are directly linked with the use of the ABAP programming language. These are recommendations and specifications that are supposed to ensure that the ABAP code is comprehensible, is understandable, and reliably carries out the tasks that the developers intended. So in these partial aspects, the ABAP programming guidelines support the different product standards or are derived from them. The remaining partial aspects that are also critical but not directly associated with the use of the ABAP programming language are not discussed in this book.

1.4 Target Audience

The goal of the guidelines presented here is to provide internal and external SAP developers with support for the use of the ABAP language. ABAP is a living programming language that is continuously further developed. In this ongoing development, great importance is attached to downward compatibility in order to not invalidate the large number of custom developments of SAP customers. For this reason, in many places ABAP provides modern solution options in parallel to the previous ones. Possibly, ABAP developers sometimes find it hard to determine which of the offered technologies can be used advantageously and why others are no longer recommended. This guide establishes clarity and security in such situations.

This book is not an introduction to ABAP and ABAP Objects; instead, it is aimed at experienced ABAP developers. Beginners in the area of ABAP programming should first refer to the introduction, *ABAP Objects* (SAP PRESS, 2007), and the comprehensive *The Official ABAP Reference* (SAP PRESS, 2005) or the ABAP keyword documentation. The introduction already includes the present guidelines to a large extent and gives instructions for modern and robust ABAP programming.

The target group of these guidelines is ABAP developers who learned this language at a time when concepts were up-to-date that are now considered obsolete; this particularly applies to those who learned ABAP/4. Of course, we also hope to address developers who already develop with ABAP Objects. The latter will surely find many new aspects or maybe a confirmation for their own programming style — which would be the ideal case from the program quality perspective.

1.5 How to Use This Book

The present ABAP programming guidelines comprise recommendations from different subject areas. **Chapter 2**, General Basic Rules, and **Chapter 3**, ABAP-Specific Basic Rules, start with the general principles that must be taken into account when creating new programs and classes. **Chapter 4**, Structure and Style, discusses questions on style, for instance, naming, commentation, and structure of programs and procedures. **Chapter 5**, Architecture, answers individual questions on the architecture, such as the programming model or troubleshooting. Another large part of the ABAP programming guidelines relate to the secure and robust usage of the ABAP programming language. **Chapter 6**, Secure and Robust ABAP, deals with this topic.

Appendix A, Obsolete Language Constructs, lists all obsolete ABAP language elements that must no longer be used according to our programming guidelines and of which most are syntactically prohibited in ABAP Objects anyway. **Appendix B**, Automatic Check of Naming Conventions, discusses a proposal for a prefix-based naming convention that is predefined as a standard setting in the Code Inspector.

The recommendations provided in Chapters 2 to 6 are formulated as rules. There are four different categories that each address different partial aspects of ABAP programming and are each labeled with a separate pictogram. All of these partial aspects are equally important and therefore the categories are listed at random:

▶ **Legible programs**

Basically, these rules ensure that the source code is oriented toward the human reader. For programs that are consequently particularly well legible and clear, these rules ensure that they can be maintained with a reasonable effort and that they can be further developed if required.

▶ **ABAP specifics**

The rules of this category are derived from special technical features of the ABAP language and the ABAP Workbench, which simply cannot be bypassed.

▶ **Correct and robust programs**

This category includes rules that are used to ensure a correct and robust use of the ABAP language to protect against unpleasant surprises, as well as general rules in the sense of a functionally correct and successfully usable software product.

▶ **Programming model**

Today's manifold requirements for a commercial software product can only be met reasonably and with a justifiable effort based on a suitable modern programming model. The rules of this category include only a few but rather fundamental specifications.

Of course, there are also overlaps between the mentioned categories. For example, Rule 4.15, Do Not Use Include Programs Multiple Times, could be assigned to all four categories. However, a multiple assignment is omitted here, and exactly one category is selected instead. **Appendix C,** Table of Rules, includes an overview of all rules.

Benefit from the many years of experience of the ABAP group and the many persons, who have contributed directly or indirectly to the creation of these guidelines, by considering the rules of all four categories and the notes in the individual chapters in your daily work.

"Every man is the architect of his own fortune — unfortunately, only very few understand the basic rules of architecture."
– Walter Boveri

2 General Basic Rules

This chapter introduces some general basic rules in the context of the ABAP programming guidelines. Although these basic rules are presented according to ABAP programming requirements here, they apply to any kind of (business) application programming and are not ABAP-specific. Many of the rules in the next chapters are derived from or support these general basic rules.

2.1 Separation of Concerns

Background

The concept *Separation of Concerns* (SoC) originates from the article *"On the Role of Scientific Thought"* by Edsger W. Dijkstra in 1974:

> *"... But nothing is gained — on the contrary! — by tackling these various aspects simultaneously. It is what I sometimes have called 'the separation of concerns', which, even if not perfectly possible, is yet the only available technique for effective ordering of one's thoughts, that I know of. This is what I mean by 'focusing one's attention upon some aspect': it does not mean ignoring the other aspects, it is just doing justice to the fact that from this aspect's point of view, the other is irrelevant." (Springer-Verlag, 1982)*

In programming, SoC is a principle according to which an application is split into separate units whose functions overlap as little as possible. SoC is achieved by modularization and encapsulation as well as arrangement in software layers.

Although the common three-layer architecture of the SAP system — today referred to as SAP NetWeaver Application Server ABAP (SAP NetWeaver AS ABAP) — is almost predestined for ABAP programming according to the SoC principle, SoC has hardly been used previously. Application programs, that is, *dialog programs* in *module pools* or *reports* in *executable programs*, were usually monolithic blocks that simultaneously respond to user actions of the presentation layer, execute the application logic, and access data of the persistence layer. This type of programming is no longer contemporary in times in which keywords, such as *Service-Oriented Architecture* (SOA), take center stage.

Rule

[■] **Rule 2.1: Adhere to the SoC Principle**

Adhere to the principle of SoC. Model your applications in a strictly service-oriented manner. Always separate the logic of the application layer from the logic of the presentation layer and the persistence layer and from the logic for the communication with external systems. Encapsulate the repository objects of the individual concerns in separate packages.

Details

The SoC principle identifies the parts of an application that serve specific purposes and encapsulates them within self-contained units that communicate with each other only via well-defined interfaces. This way, usually complex software is split into manageable components. Software thus becomes

- more stable
- easier to understand
- easier to reuse
- easier to transport
- easier to maintain
- easier to test

You can even add to the last aspect that the adherence of the SoC principle is nothing less than the prerequisite for executing isolated automated module tests (see Section 2.3, Correctness and Quality).

Bad Example

Figure 2.1 shows two aspects of the ABAP application development that don't use the SoC principle.

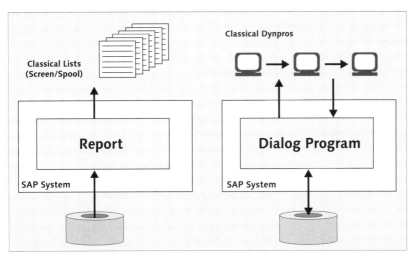

Figure 2.1 Classical ABAP Programming — Reporting and Dialog Programming

This bad example is nothing more than the programming models of report and dialog programming, which have been propagated by SAP for a long time! This may be surprising for you, but as already mentioned, our programming guidelines strive to be more than an introduction of naming conventions.

Strictly speaking, of course, we do not want to use reporting or the programming of transactions itself as bad examples but the way that such applications were usually implemented. Already the mini report in Listing 2.1 is a typical example of how various concerns are combined in one programming unit. This applies both to the data declaration and to the implementation of the functionality. The access to persistent data, the data processing, and the presentation of the data as well as the related declarations are implemented in one unit.

```
REPORT z_non_soc_report.

PARAMETERS p_carrid TYPE spfli-carrid.

DATA: spfli_tab   TYPE STANDARD TABLE OF spfli,
      alv         TYPE REF TO cl_salv_table,
      alv_exc     TYPE REF TO cx_salv_msg.

SELECT *
      FROM spfli
      INTO TABLE spfli_tab
      WHERE carrid = p_carrid.
```

```
IF sy-subrc = 0.
  SORT spfli_tab BY cityfrom cityto.
  TRY.
      cl_salv_table=>factory(
        IMPORTING r_salv_table = alv
        CHANGING  t_table      = spfli_tab ).
      alv->display( ).
    CATCH cx_salv_msg INTO alv_exc.
      MESSAGE alv_exc TYPE 'I' DISPLAY LIKE 'E'.
  ENDTRY.
ENDIF.
```

Listing 2.1 Simple Classical Report Without Separation of Concerns

Of course, it is a little over-the-top to enforce a strict SoC for such small programs as shown in Listing 2.1. However, real applications are in most cases very large ABAP programs (executable programs, module pools) in which all concerns are addressed simultaneously. Modularization was usually restricted to the reuse of functional units and rarely adapted to the actually existing layers. Moreover, large amounts of global data were created that were used across various procedures and layers. Consequently, all program parts inherently depend on each other and cannot be tested separately. We are convinced that the quality of such programs cannot be improved just by adhering to naming conventions but that a paradigm shift is actually necessary to approach programming tasks.

Listing 2.2 demonstrates that you can handle the SoC principle already with the procedural means of classical ABAP — in this case, by means of subroutines. Listing 2.2 has the same function as Listing 2.1, but all concerns are implemented in separate procedures, which are assigned to layers. As already mentioned, this seems to be over-the-top for simple programs; however, if the concerns of Listing 2.1 need to be tested separately and independently of each other, changing to the approach used in Listing 2.2 would be the only option. Only now you can easily add test methods in ABAP Unit test classes to the program of Listing 2.2 that test the individual procedures.

```
REPORT z_soc_report.

SELECTION-SCREEN BEGIN OF SCREEN 100.
PARAMETERS p_carrid TYPE spfli-carrid.
SELECTION-SCREEN END OF SCREEN 100.

TYPES spfli_tab TYPE STANDARD TABLE OF spfli.
```

```abap
DATA: carrid TYPE spfli-carrid,
      table  TYPE spfli_tab,
      rc     TYPE sy-subrc.

START-OF-SELECTION.
  PERFORM get_carrid CHANGING carrid.
  PERFORM get_table  USING    carrid
                     CHANGING table
                              rc.

  IF rc = 0
    PERFORM sort_table    CHANGING table.
    PERFORM display_table USING    table.
  ENDIF.

* Presentation layer

FORM get_carrid
     CHANGING value(carrid) TYPE spfli-carrid.
  CALL SELECTION-SCREEN 100.
  IF sy-subrc = 0.
    carrid = p_carrid.
  ENDIF.
ENDFORM.

FORM display_table
     USING table TYPE spfli_tab.
  DATA: alv     TYPE REF TO cl_salv_table,
        alv_exc TYPE REF TO cx_salv_msg.
  TRY.
      cl_salv_table=>factory(
        IMPORTING r_salv_table = alv
        CHANGING  t_table      = table ).
      alv->display( ).
    CATCH cx_salv_msg INTO alv_exc.
      MESSAGE alv_exc TYPE 'I' DISPLAY LIKE 'E'.
  ENDTRY.
ENDFORM.

* Application layer

FORM sort_table
     CHANGING table TYPE spfli_tab.
  SORT table BY cityfrom cityto.
ENDFORM.

* Persistency layer
```

```
FORM get_table
    USING    carrid   TYPE spfli-carrid
    CHANGING table    TYPE spfli_tab
             rc       TYPE sy-subrc.
  SELECT *
        FROM spfli
        INTO TABLE table
        WHERE carrid = carrid.
  rc = sy-subrc.
ENDFORM.
```

Listing 2.2 Classical Report with a Procedural Separation of Concerns

The SoC via subroutines shown in Listing 2.2 gives an insufficient impression with good reason. Listing 2.3, coming up in the next section, is an example of how you're supposed to implement the SoC using methods in concern-specific classes.

Good Example

Figure 2.2 shows a diagram of how an ABAP application development that adheres to the SoC is supposed to look.

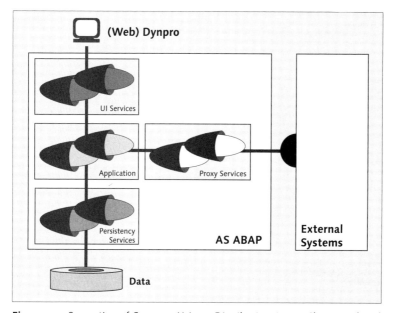

Figure 2.2 Separation of Concerns Using a Distribution Across Classes and Packages

After the concerns have been identified, they are implemented in ABAP Objects classes. The concerns that are shown in Figure 2.2 are general tasks that usually always need to be performed in application programming with ABAP:

▶ The communication with a user interface (UI) via UI services

▶ The actual application logic

▶ The access to persistent data via persistency services

▶ The communication with external services via proxy services

Of course, you can and usually need to further differentiate between these basic concerns.

The boxes that map the individual concerns in Figure 2.2 symbolize packages. All repository objects (classes, data types, database tables, etc.) that belong to one concern are supposed to be included in corresponding packages. As of SAP NetWeaver AS ABAP Release 7.2, an operational package concept will be delivered that supports this SoC with encapsulated packages. In encapsulated packages, the access from repository objects of a package to those of another package is only possible via package interfaces. This is checked during the syntax check. A package can further restrict the usability of its repository objects using access control lists. Subpackages support a further separation of the concerns within a package.

For example, an encapsulation of all database tables of an application in the package for persistency services prevents all programs that do not belong to this package from having access to these database tables. In contrast, for instance, programs of the persistency layer cannot directly communicate with components of the presentation layer, for example, with a Web Dynpro ABAP application. Prior to Release 7.2, the encapsulation of the packages should already be prepared by selecting PACKAGE CHECK AS SERVER in the package properties. Such packages already have package interfaces, and a package check is made during the extended program check. When changing to Release 7.2, such packages are migrated in encapsulated packages.

Listing 2.3 shows the change of the SoC from Listing 2.2 to program-local classes.

```
REPORT z_soc_class_report.

SELECTION-SCREEN BEGIN OF SCREEN 100.
PARAMETERS p_carrid TYPE spfli-carrid.
SELECTION-SCREEN END OF SCREEN 100.
```

```
TYPES spfli_tab TYPE STANDARD TABLE OF spfli.

CLASS presentation_server DEFINITION.
  PUBLIC SECTION.
    CLASS-METHODS:
      get_carrid RETURNING VALUE(carrid) TYPE spfli-carrid,
      display_table IMPORTING VALUE(table) TYPE spfli_tab.
ENDCLASS.

CLASS presentation_server IMPLEMENTATION.
  METHOD get_carrid.
    CALL SELECTION-SCREEN 100.
    IF sy-subrc = 0.
      carrid = p_carrid.
    ENDIF.
  ENDMETHOD.
  METHOD display_table.
    DATA: alv     TYPE REF TO cl_salv_table,
          alv_exc TYPE REF TO cx_salv_msg.
    TRY.
        cl_salv_table=>factory(
          IMPORTING r_salv_table = alv
          CHANGING  t_table      = table ).
        alv->display( ).
      CATCH cx_salv_msg INTO alv_exc.
        MESSAGE alv_exc TYPE 'I' DISPLAY LIKE 'E'.
    ENDTRY.
  ENDMETHOD.
ENDCLASS.

CLASS application_server DEFINITION.
  PUBLIC SECTION.
    CLASS-METHODS
      sort_table CHANGING table TYPE spfli_tab.
ENDCLASS.

CLASS application_server IMPLEMENTATION.
  METHOD sort_table.
    SORT table BY cityfrom cityto.
  ENDMETHOD.
ENDCLASS.

CLASS persistency_server DEFINITION.
  PUBLIC SECTION.
    CLASS-METHODS
```

```
      get_table IMPORTING carrid TYPE spfli-carrid
                EXPORTING table  TYPE spfli_tab
                          rc     TYPE sy-subrc.
ENDCLASS.

CLASS persistency_server IMPLEMENTATION.
  METHOD get_table.
    SELECT *
           FROM spfli
           INTO TABLE table
           WHERE carrid = carrid.
    rc = sy-subrc.
  ENDMETHOD.
ENDCLASS.

CLASS report DEFINITION.
  PUBLIC SECTION.
    CLASS-METHODS main.
ENDCLASS.

CLASS report IMPLEMENTATION.
  METHOD main.
    DATA: carrid TYPE spfli-carrid,
          table  TYPE spfli_tab,
          rc     TYPE sy-subrc.
    carrid = presentation_server=>get_carrid( ).
    persistency_server=>get_table( EXPORTING carrid = carrid
                                   IMPORTING table  = table
                                             rc     = rc ).

    IF rc = 0.
      application_server=>sort_table(
         CHANGING table = table ).
      presentation_server=>display_table( table ).
    ENDIF.
  ENDMETHOD.
ENDCLASS.

START-OF-SELECTION.
  report=>main( ).
```

Listing 2.3 Class-Based Report with Separation of Concerns

Compared to Listing 2.1, Listing 2.3 first seems to be even more overdone, but only at first glance. A real application program commonly doesn't consist of only

31

25 lines. The larger and more realistic the application program, the smaller the overhead that results from the encapsulation of concerns in classes. If you properly use the reusability options in ABAP Objects, you can make the code even leaner (see examples in Chapter 3, in Section 3.1, ABAP Objects as a Programming Model).

Furthermore, in contrast to Listing 2.2, the individual layers are now encapsulated in classes, that is, in real program-based units. In real life, this encapsulation is not implemented within one program but in global classes that are assigned to different packages depending on the layer. These packages, in turn, are connected via package interfaces. Only this way can you benefit from the other mentioned advantages of the SoC — in addition to the testability, which is already achieved in Listing 2.2.

2.2   KISS Principle

Background

The KISS principle says that you should always choose the simplest solution for a problem. KISS can have the following meanings (this list is not complete):

▶ Keep it simple, stupid.

▶ Keep it small and simple.

▶ Keep it sweet and simple.

▶ Keep it simple and straightforward.

▶ Keep it short and simple.

▶ Keep it simple and smart.

▶ Keep it strictly simple.

The basic statement of the KISS principle is similar to Occam's razor, which says that the theory that is preferred in science is the one that makes fewer assumptions to explain observable predictions (see Wikipedia entry on the KISS principle).

Rule

Rule 2.2: Adhere to the KISS Principle

Adhere to the KISS principle, and limit the complexity of your programs as much as possible.

Details

A problem's solution that is as simple, minimalist, and easy to understand as possible is usually the best solution — also considering stability, understanding, and maintainability in addition to functional correctness.

There are a lot of bad examples for the KISS principle. Why?

▸ The programs are too complex right from the start. Reasons for this can be a poor design or simply a rash, undisciplined programming style.

▸ The programs are maintained for lengthy periods. New functions are added — usually via IF control structures — to old functions instead of newly implementing old and new functions together. Programs that were first quite simple become thus more and more complex, although this is not justified by the complexity of the task to be executed.

To develop according to the KISS principle, you should ensure right from the start that the complexity of the program remains manageable. Chapter 4, Structure and Style, and particularly Chapter 4, Sections 4.3, Comments, and 4.7, Complexity, list rules that support this approach.

Tip

If existing programs don't adhere to the KISS principle, and these programs must be further developed, you should implement appropriate refactoring. Refactoring refers to the process of manually or automatically improving the structure of programs while retaining the observable program behavior. It improves the legibility, understandability, maintainability, and extensibility, as well as considerably reducing the related effort for troubleshooting and functional extensions (see Wikipedia entry on code refactoring). The (incremental) refactoring of an existing program is not only useful for the adherence of Rule 2.2, Adhere to the KISS Principle, but also for all following rules.

The refactoring of existing code is supported by a coverage with module tests, which is requested in Section 2.3, Correctness and Quality. Comprehensive module tests can ensure that a program still has the same behavior after the refactoring process.

Example

On the left side, Figure 2.3 shows the structure of a method that doesn't adhere to the KISS principle. The method consists of approximately 160 statements and reaches a nesting depth of 12 levels (in Chapter 4, see Section 4.7.2, Nesting Depth). The method, which is only schematically illustrated, is a real example from a live ABAP program, which has reached the status shown on the left by being continuously developed further. Because the reached complexity made required changes nearly impossible, the developer was even forced to implement the corresponding refactoring according to the KISS principle.

The result is illustrated on the right in Figure 2.3. Because method M was split into three methods with less than 100 statements each and a maximum nesting depth of 5 levels, manageable modularization units were generated, which follow the rules from Chapter 4, in Section 4.7, Complexity, and allow for the required modification. Ideally, however, the status shown on the left side of Figure 2.3 should never occur.

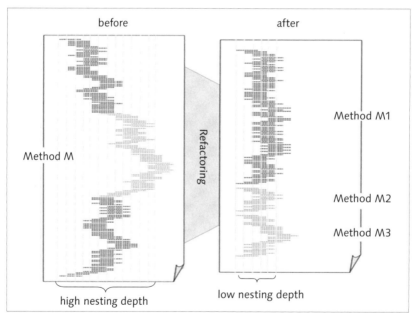

Figure 2.3 Refactoring of a Complex Method (Left) into Three Simpler Methods (Right)

2.3   Correctness and Quality

Background

In most organizations in which professional software is developed, there are usually product standards that must be met. These product standards define what correctness and quality mean for programs. SAP itself has a wealth of such standards that the development departments have to follow. The following lists the most critical common product standards for developers:

▶ **Accessibility**
Within the scope of information technology, accessibility means that any person — including handicapped persons — can access and use the products of information technology. To make products, such as software or websites, accessible to all users, they must be designed in such a way that they can also be used if some capabilities are missing (e.g., the ability to see or the ability to differentiate between colors) and they must be compatible with utilities, such as screen readers or screen magnifiers.

▶ **Documentation**
A product standard on documentation usually defines which documents must be provided to the customer and ensures that the delivered documentation is consistent, correct, and up-to-date across all product areas.

▶ **Functional correctness**
The functional correctness of software is generally considered its most important quality characteristic. Software that isn't functionally correct is in most cases useless. A product standard on the functional correctness usually requires absolute absence of errors and also defines the stability of interfaces and the behavior of programs in the case of upgrades. To achieve these goals, you can require an appropriate test coverage of the software.

▶ **Globalization**
For software that is used worldwide, you usually require a product standard on globalization. It includes internationalization (in Chapter 6, see also Section 6.7, Internationalization) and localization.

  ▶ **Internationalization**
  Internationalization comprises the technical aspects of globalization, such as Unicode capability, word processing, screen display, printing, data exchange, times zones, translatability, and so on, and consequently lays the technical foundation for localization. A critical internationalization aspect is the translation of the UIs and other texts.

  ▶ **Localization**
  Localization is required if globally used software needs to be adapted to local (usually country-specific) requirements, such as legal stipulations and specific business processes.

▶ **Performance**

A program that is functionally correct but cannot be executed within an acceptable time is as useless for the user as an incorrect program. A performance product standard ensures that this aspect is not neglected. It can include rules for efficient database access and the scalability of the application logic.

▶ **Security**

For security-critical software — which should actually apply to any kind of business software — a product standard on security defines all security-relevant aspects of a product by referring to possible security gaps or legal stipulations and also includes related instructions for meeting the standard.

▶ **Usability**

Usability of software refers to the adaptation of UIs to the requirements of human end users and their tasks. A product standard on usability is supposed to ensure that end users can perform their tasks efficiently and effectively. Usability keywords include concepts such as consistency of UIs, operational simplicity, intuitive task-specific and role-specific UIs, individual adaptability, error tolerance, and so on.

These standards may also correspond to legal stipulations, but they mainly emerge from the natural and fundamental goal to ensure the correctness and quality of software that is delivered to customers. In this context, programming guidelines assume a critical role. Many of the guidelines in this book directly or indirectly support one of the listed standards or are derived from one. Consequently, they serve to support and adhere to such standards and thus enable you to write correct programs of high quality. On the other hand, programming guidelines might even be promoted to an obligatory product standard.

However, because the programming guidelines cannot completely include all possible product standards, such as all rules of a performance or security standard, the following basic rule is introduced.

Rule

[✓] **Rule 2.3: Adhere to Existing Product Standards or Check Their Adherence**

Follow the product standards that exist in your organization, and ensure the correctness and quality of your programs by testing them with all of the available test tools, both during and after the development process.

Details

It is obvious and doesn't have to be further explained that product standards must be adhered to. But it is often neglected that the static and dynamic analysis tools that are available in the ABAP environment provide valuable help for meeting important product standards — particularly the standards on functional correctness and performance. With this basic rule, you should therefore use all available tools to a large extent that help you ensure the correctness and quality of ABAP programs:

- Regularly perform the extended program check (Transaction SLIN), and remove all messages (in Chapter 3, see Section 3.4.2, Extended Program Check).

- Regularly execute the Code Inspector (Transaction SCI) with the default check variant, and remove all messages (see Section 3.4.3, Code Inspector).

- Check the usability and accessibility of your UI elements with the corresponding tools (integrated with Workbench tools and as of Release 7.0 EhP2 in the ABAP Test Cockpit (ATC), see Section 3.4.4, ABAP Test Cockpit).

- Completely cover the functions of your procedural units by module tests with ABAP Unit (integrated with the ABAP Workbench, the Code Inspector, and as of Releases 7.0 EhP2 and 7.2, in the ATC).

- Completely cover the functions of your applications by scenario tests with eCATT (Transaction SECATT).

- Check the memory consumption of your programs using the ABAP Memory Inspector (Transaction S_MEMORY_INSPECTOR and integrated as the MEMORY ANALYSIS function in the ABAP Debugger).

- Check the runtime behavior and the performance using the ABAP runtime analysis (prior to Release 7.0 EhP2 with Transactions SE30 and ATRA; as of Releases 7.0 EhP2 and 7.2 replaced by Transaction SAT).

- Check the test coverage using the Coverage Analyzer (Transaction SCOV, and as of Release 7.0 EhP2, integrated with the ABAP Unit Browser of the ABAP Workbench).

- Document your programs and services with all available means. From comments (see Section 4.3, Comments, in Chapter 4), to simple data element documentations for context-sensitive input help, to class and method documentations for the documentation of APIs, to an explanation of the concepts and the creation of tutorials in different locations, such as SAP Knowledge Warehouse, or on the Internet, such as SAP Developer Network (SDN, *http://sdn.sap.com*).

Since Release 7.0 EhP2, the ABAP Test Cockpit (ATC), which is integrated with the ABAP Workbench and the SAP transport system, considerably supports the execution and evaluation of the most important tests (in Chapter 3, see Section 3.4.4, ABAP Test Cockpit). Some of these tests also check the adherence to some of the rules of the ABAP programming guidelines that are introduced later in this book.

Tip

In case of doubt, the product standards override the guidelines and recommendations in this book. For example, if performance or security aspects disallow some of the programming practices mentioned here, you must always adhere to the standards.

Example

Figure 2.4 illustrates the test coverage of procedures of a package before (top) or after (bottom) the implementation of module tests with ABAP Unit Browser.

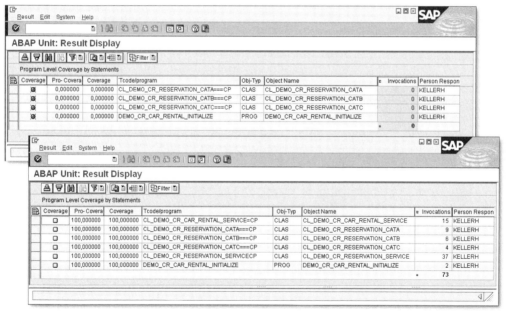

Figure 2.4 Poor and Good Test Coverage with Module Tests in the ABAP Unit Browser of the Object Navigator

The display of the test coverage shown here is possible as of Releases 7.0 EhP2 and 7.2 in the ABAP Unit Browser of the Object Navigator in which functions of the Coverage Analyzer are integrated. The example shown here comprises the classes of the SABAP_DEMOS_CAR_RENTAL_APPL package, which is also available with Releases 7.0 EhP2 and 7.2 as a subpackage for the application layer of a small sample application that demonstrates the strict adherence to the SoC (see Section 2.1, Separation of Concerns), their package structure, as well as the complete coverage by module tests.

"If you wanted to know how much I loved you, you would have to invent a completely new language."
—Friedrich von Schiller

3   ABAP-Specific Basic Rules

Besides the rules specified in Chapter 2, General Basic Rules, this chapter additionally introduces you to a set of ABAP-specific basic rules that result from the special technical conditions of the ABAP language, the ABAP runtime environment, and its history. These basic rules also determine many of the more specific rules that follow this chapter.

3.1   ABAP Objects as a Programming Model

Background

ABAP is a hybrid programming language that supports both a procedural and an object-oriented programming model. The procedural programming model is based on the modularization of programs in classical processing blocks, that is, event blocks, dialog modules, function modules, and subroutines. In ABAP Objects, the class conceptually supersedes the classical program,[1] and the modularization is implemented through its methods.

Both models are interoperable in such a way that you can access classes in classical processing blocks and call classical programs and procedures within methods. The hybrid nature of the language is mainly due to the downward compatibility because ABAP has procedural roots and because both entire programs and reusable procedures (primarily function modules) were still supposed to be reuseable with the implementation of the object-oriented programming model in the late 1990s.

---

1   From the technical point of view, classes are still declared and implemented in programs.

Rule

[■] **Rule 3.1: Use ABAP Objects**

Use ABAP Objects wherever possible for new and further developments. Classical processing blocks may be newly created in exceptional cases only.

Details

The demand for the separation of concerns (SoC) (see Rule 2.1, Adhere to the SoC Principle) is ideally supported by using ABAP Objects as much as possible. The scope of this book doesn't include a detailed comparison of ABAP Objects and the procedural programming model. An article in *SAP Professional Journal* ("Not Yet Using ABAP Objects? Eight Reasons Why Every ABAP Developer Should Give It a Second Look") illustrated that the object-oriented programming — and here particularly ABAP Objects in comparison to classical procedural ABAP — is better suited to meet the requirements of modern programming. This article mentioned eight reasons to use ABAP Objects, which are summarized here:

1. **Data encapsulation**

   ABAP Objects enables an advanced way of data encapsulation. In classical procedural programming, the state of an application is determined by the content of the global variables of a program. In object-oriented programming, the state is encapsulated in classes or objects as instances of classes. The distribution of data across the different visibility sections of a class — public, protected, package-visible (as of Release 7.2), and private — enables a clear differentiation between externally and internally usable data. Even without an in-depth object-oriented modeling, application programs benefit from these attributes with regard to stability and maintainability.

2. **Explicit instantiation**

   ABAP Objects enables the multiple instantiation of a class via an explicit object creation using the CREATE OBJECT statement. Each instance of a class (object) has its own state that is determined via the values of its attributes and can be changed via the methods of the class. Automatic garbage collection ensures that objects that are no longer required are deleted from the memory. Procedural models do not provide multiple instantiation, which is why they oblige you to apply stateless functions on separately stored data.

3. **Inheritance**

   ABAP Objects enables the reuse of classes through inheritance, where classes with special behaviors are derived from more general classes, and only the differences must be implemented anew. In the procedural model, you can use existing functions only as available, or you must create new ones.

4. **Interfaces**
   In ABAP Objects, you can address objects via standalone interfaces. This way, developers don't need to take care of the implementation details of the class behind the interface. This way, the provider of an interface can change the underlying implementations without having to modify the programs that the interface uses. The procedural model does not have such a concept of stand-alone interfaces.

5. **Events**
   ABAP Objects makes it easier to implement event-driven program flows. A publish-and-subscribe mechanism can loosely couple applications, without the trigger of an event having to know anything about any possible handlers. This allows greater flexibility than the procedural approach, in which the programs are much stronger coupled, and the program flow is usually much more strictly defined.

6. **Explicit orthogonal concepts**
   ABAP Objects contains a small number of closely defined, mutually orthogonal, fundamental concepts, which makes it more reliable and less error-prone than classical ABAP. Classical procedural ABAP is dominated by implicit behaviors in which programs are controlled by implicit events of the runtime environment and via global data. The concepts of ABAP Objects, however, are explicitly shown in a program. ABAP Objects is easier to learn and use than classical procedural ABAP.

7. **Cleansed syntax**
   ABAP Objects contains cleansed syntax and semantics rules. Classical procedural ABAP is a language that has evolved over time, and contains several obsolete and overlapping concepts. With the implementation of ABAP Objects, classes and methods provided a field for cleansed syntax and semantics rules, which was completely unaffected by the requirements on the downward compatibility. This way, in ABAP Objects, that is, within classes and methods, most obsolete and error-prone language constructs were syntactically forbidden. Also, questionable and potentially faulty data accesses are checked more closely and may also be forbidden. The syntax cleansing enforces the use of the ABAP language in classes, which can only be claimed through guidelines outside of classes (see Section 3.3, Modern ABAP).

8. **Access to new technologies**

Often, ABAP Objects is the only way of using new ABAP technologies. For example, GUI controls, Web Dynpro ABAP, Runtime Type Services (RTTS), or the Internet Communication Framework (ICF) provide exclusively class-based interfaces. If programs that use such services would still be implemented purely procedurally, this would result in an unnecessary mix of programming models and a correspondingly increased complexity.

So the urgent recommendation to use ABAP Objects has aspects both in form and content:

▶ As detailed in reasons 1 through 5, the object-oriented programming model is better suited to keep the complexity of software manageable through principles, such as encapsulation and inheritance. Admittedly, a good object-oriented design is not an easy task, and there are still developers with little experience in this area even today. Against this background, those who still think about approaching a new development in the classical procedural way have to bring to mind that even the procedural event-driven ABAP programming model with its system events is not easy to understand.

▶ Reasons 6 through 8 describe rather formal aspects suggesting that you should create procedures only in the form of methods today, even if no real object-oriented design is present. Function modules and subroutines should be created only in exceptional cases in which ABAP Objects doesn't provide any alternatives yet.

In Chapter 5, Section 5.1, Object-Oriented Programming, provides notes and recommendations on the successful use of ABAP Objects.

Exception

In the current state (Releases 7.0 EhP2 and 7.2), the following attributes are still missing in ABAP Objects to replace classical processing blocks with methods:

▶ Remote Method Invocation (RMI) as a replacement for Remote Function Call (RFC)

▶ A replacement for the call of update function modules (`CALL FUNCTION IN UPDATE TASK`)

▶ A replacement for the call of subroutines during `COMMIT WORK` and `ROLLBACK WORK` (`PERFORM ON COMMIT/ROLLBACK`)

- Object-oriented handling of classical dynpros, including selection screens as a replacement for dialog transactions, CALL SCREEN and CALL SELECTION-SCREEN

- Dynamic generation of classes as a replacement for the classical dynamic program generation (GENERATE SUBROUTINE POOL)

- Direct support of background processing as a replacement for the call of executable programs (SUBMIT VIA JOB)

Exactly for such cases, the following classical processing blocks may still be created in new programs:

- Function modules are still required for RFC and the update and are recommended for the call of classical dynpros and selection screens (see Rule 5.19, Encapsulate Classical Dynpros and Selection Screens).

- Subroutines are still required for PERFORM ON COMMIT/ROLLBACK and in dynamically generated subroutine pools (GENERATE SUBROUTINE POOL).

- Dialog modules and event blocks for selection screen events are still required in function groups that wrap the classical dynpros and selection screens (see Rule 3.2, Select the Appropriate Program Type).

- The START-OF-SELECTION event block is still required in executable programs that are intended for background processing.

Within such a processing block, however, you should immediately delegate the execution to a suitable method (see Rule 6.37, No Implementations in Function Modules and Subroutines, and Rule 6.44, No Implementations in Dialog Modules and Event Blocks). This doesn't need to be a method of a global class but can absolutely be located within the associated main program within the scope of a local class. To ensure that the system implements the same stricter check in such processing blocks as in the methods, you can activate the OBSOLETE STATEMENTS (OO CONTEXT) check in the extended program check (see Section 3.4.2, Extended Program Check).

Bad Example

Listing 3.1 contains a rudimentary implementation of handling different types of bank accounts in a function group and their use in a program, whereas only the "withdrawal of an amount" function is shown. The function modules of the function group work on external data that are loaded into a global internal table in the LOAD-OF-PROGRAM event. The control for whether a checking account or savings

45

account is handled is carried out via an input parameter, and the different handling is delegated to various subroutines via a CASE WHEN control structure, whereas no reuse takes place. The subroutines access the global internal table. The withdraw function module is called for different accounts in an application program. The exception handling is carried out classically using further CASE WHEN control structures for querying sy-subrc.

```abap
FUNCTION-POOL account.

DATA account_tab TYPE SORTED TABLE OF accounts
                 WITH UNIQUE KEY id.

LOAD-OF-PROGRAM.
  "fetch amount for all accounts into account_tab
  ...

...

FUNCTION withdraw.
*"----------------------------------------------------
*"  IMPORTING
*"     REFERENCE(id) TYPE accounts-id
*"     REFERENCE(kind) TYPE c DEFAULT 'C'
*"     REFERENCE(amount) TYPE accounts-amount
*"  EXCEPTIONS
*"      negative_amount
*"      unknown_account_type
*"----------------------------------------------------
  CASE kind.
    WHEN 'C'.
      PERFORM withdraw_from_checking_account
        USING id amount.
    WHEN 'S'.
      PERFORM withdraw_from_savings_account
        USING id amount.
    WHEN OTHERS.
      RAISE unknown_account_type.
  ENDCASE.
ENDFUNCTION.

FORM withdraw_from_checking_account
  USING l_id     TYPE accounts-id
        l_amount TYPE accounts-amount.
  FIELD-SYMBOLS <account> TYPE accounts.
  READ TABLE account_tab ASSIGNING <account>
```

```
      WITH TABLE KEY id = l_id.
    <account> = <account> - l_amount.
    IF <account> < 0.
      "Handle debit balance
      ...
    ENDIF.
ENDFORM.

FORM withdraw_from_savings_account
    USING l_id      TYPE accounts-id
          l_amount TYPE accounts-amount.
    FIELD-SYMBOLS <account> TYPE accounts.
    READ TABLE account_tab ASSIGNING <account>
      WITH TABLE KEY id = l_id.
    IF <account>_wa-amount > l_amount.
      <account>-amount = <account>-amount - l_amount.
    ELSE.
      RAISE negative_amount.
    ENDIF.
ENDFORM.

***********************************************************

PROGRAM bank_application.

...

CALL FUNCTION 'WITHDRAW'
  EXPORTING
    id                  = ...
    kind                = 'C'
    amount              = ...
  EXCEPTIONS
    unknown_account_type = 2
    negative_amount     = 4.
CASE sy-subrc.
  WHEN 2.
    ...
  WHEN 4.
    ...
ENDCASE.

...

CALL FUNCTION 'WITHDRAW'
  EXPORTING
```

```
      id                    = ...
      kind                  = 'S'
      amount                = ...
   EXCEPTIONS
      unknown_account_type  = 2
      negative_amount       = 4.
CASE sy-subrc.
   WHEN 2.
      ...
   WHEN 4.
      ...
ENDCASE.
```

Listing 3.1 Modeling of Bank Accounts in Function Groups

Good Example

Listing 3.2 contains a rudimentary implementation of handling different types of bank accounts in classes and their use in a class, whereas only the "withdrawal of an amount" function is shown again.

The different types of accounts are implemented in subclasses of an abstract class for accounts. Each instance of an account is provided with the required data in its constructor. If required, the application class generates instances of accounts of the desired type and uses their methods polymorphically via a superclass reference variable. The exception handling is carried out via class-based exceptions. CASE WHEN control structures are not required any more. As already announced in the description of the examples in Chapter 2, Section 2.1, Separation of Concerns, no overhead of code is generated here any longer for the use of classes in comparison to the procedural programming.

```
CLASS cx_negative_amount DEFINITION PUBLIC
                         INHERITING FROM cx_static_check.
ENDCLASS.

CLASS cl_account DEFINITION ABSTRACT PUBLIC.
  PUBLIC SECTION.
    METHODS: constructor IMPORTING id     TYPE string,
             withdraw    IMPORTING amount TYPE i
                         RAISING   cx_negative_amount.
  PROTECTED SECTION.
    DATA amount TYPE accounts-amount.
ENDCLASS.
```

```
CLASS cl_account IMPLEMENTATION.
  METHOD constructor.
    "fetch amount for one account into attribute amount
    ...
  ENDMETHOD.
  METHOD withdraw.
    me->amount = me->amount - amount.
  ENDMETHOD.
ENDCLASS.

CLASS cl_checking_account DEFINITION PUBLIC
                          INHERITING FROM cl_account.
  PUBLIC SECTION.
    METHODS withdraw REDEFINITION.
ENDCLASS.

CLASS cl_checking_account IMPLEMENTATION.
  METHOD withdraw.
    super->withdraw( amount ).
    IF me->amount < 0.
      "Handle debit balance
      ...
    ENDIF.
  ENDMETHOD.
ENDCLASS.

CLASS cl_savings_account DEFINITION PUBLIC
                         INHERITING FROM cl_account.
  PUBLIC SECTION.
    METHODS withdraw REDEFINITION.
ENDCLASS.

CLASS cl_savings_account IMPLEMENTATION.
  METHOD withdraw.
    IF me->amount > amount.
      super->withdraw( amount ).
    ELSE.
      RAISE EXCEPTION TYPE cx_negative_amount.
    ENDIF.
  ENDMETHOD.
ENDCLASS.

**********************************************************

CLASS bank_application DEFINITION PUBLIC.
```

```
   PUBLIC SECTION.
     CLASS-METHODS main.
 ENDCLASS.

 CLASS bank_application IMPLEMENTATION.
   METHOD main.
     DATA: account1 TYPE REF TO cl_account,
           account2 TYPE REF TO cl_account.

   ...

     CREATE OBJECT account1 TYPE cl_checking_account
       EXPORTING
         id = ...

     CREATE OBJECT account2 TYPE cl_savings_account
       EXPORTING
         id = ...

   ...

     TRY.
         account1->withdraw( ... ).
         account2->withdraw( ... ).
       CATCH cx_negative_amount.
         ...
     ENDTRY.
   ENDMETHOD.
 ENDCLASS.
```

Listing 3.2 Modeling of Bank Accounts in Classes

3.2 Program Type and Program Attributes

Already when you create an ABAP program, you determine the stability and maintainability by selecting the program type and the program attributes. Among other things, the program type and the program attributes specify the severity of the syntax check. Another important attribute of programs (like all other development objects) is their original language.

3.2.1   Program Type

Background

Each ABAP program has a program type that specifies the declarations and processing blocks a program can contain and how it can be executed via the ABAP runtime environment. The possible program types in ABAP are as follows:

▶ **Executable program**
An executable program can contain all possible declarative statements. All processing blocks are possible except for function modules. It supports classical dynpros as well as selection screens and can be executed both using the SUBMIT statement and transaction codes. You can create an executable program using the ABAP Editor.

▶ **Class pool**
A class pool always contains declarative statements for a global class and can also include declarative statements for local types, interfaces, and classes. Only methods are possible as processing blocks. It doesn't support classical dynpros or selection screens. You can call the methods of the global class from the outside depending on the visibility and execute the public methods of the global class using transaction codes. You can create a class pool using the Class Builder.

▶ **Interface pool**
An interface pool can only contain the declarative statements for a global interface. Processing blocks and classical dynpros or selection screens are not possible. You cannot call or execute an interface pool, and you create it using the Class Builder.

▶ **Function group (function pool)**
A function group can contain all types of declarative statements. All processing blocks are supported except for the reporting event blocks. They support classical dynpros as well as selection screens. You can call their function modules, but you can also access the dynpro processing of the function group using transaction codes. You can create a function group using the Function Builder.

▶ **Module pool**
A module pool can contain all possible declarative statements. All processing blocks are supported except for the reporting event blocks and function modules. It supports classical dynpros as well as selection screens, and you can

execute it using transaction codes. You can create a module pool using the ABAP Editor.

▶ **Subroutine pool**
A subroutine pool can contain all possible declarative statements. The LOAD-OF-PROGRAM event block as well as subroutines and methods are possible as processing blocks. It doesn't support classical dynpros or selection screens. You can call the subroutines, but you can also execute methods using transaction codes. You can create a subroutine pool using the ABAP Editor.

▶ **Type group (type pool)**
A type group can contain the declarative statements, TYPES and CONSTANTS. Processing blocks and classical dynpros or selection screens are not possible. You cannot call or execute a type group. You create a type group using the ABAP Dictionary.

In addition to the mentioned compilation units, that is, programs that can be compiled independently, there are also *include programs,* which will be discussed separately in Chapter 4, Section 4.5, Source Code Organization.

In ABAP, a program execution means that the system loads a program into the memory and executes one or more of its processing blocks. Here, you differentiate between independent and called program execution:

▶ **Standalone program execution**
In the standalone program execution, you start the program either using a transaction code (CALL TRANSACTION and LEAVE TO TRANSACTION statements) or using the SUBMIT statement for an executable program. The SUBMIT statement also allows for the execution in a background process.

▶ **Called program execution**
In the called program execution, a running program calls a procedure (method, function module, or subroutine) of another program that is loaded into the internal session of the caller if required (see Chapter 6, Section 6.5.6, Internal and External Procedure Calls).

The program flow within the standalone program execution depends on the selected program type and the type of the program call:

▶ In a program call via a transaction, you must differentiate between *object-oriented (OO transaction)* and *dialog transactions.* For object-oriented transactions, the transaction code is linked with a method of a local or global class. The program flow is determined by this method. Dialog transactions, however, are linked with a classical dynpro of the program. Here, the program flow is determined by the associated dynpro flow logic.

▶ The program flow of an *executable program* that was started using SUBMIT is determined by the reporting process of the ABAP runtime environment. Here, the runtime environment calls the different reporting event blocks, START-OF-SELECTION, GET and END-OF-SELECTION, of the program.

You must select the program type taking into account the technical attributes of a program mentioned here and the requirements on the program execution. Not all mentioned program types can still be used reasonably for new developments.

Rule

Rule 3.2: Select the Appropriate Program Type [⚙]

To select the program type, proceed as follows:

▶ The program type, class pool or interface pool, automatically arises for global classes and interfaces.

▶ For the implementation of completed functionality that is not supposed to be displayed in the class library, you can use the program type, subroutine pool, for local classes.[2]

▶ If you require function modules, this automatically results in the function group program type. Furthermore, you must use function groups to wrap classical dynpros or selection screens.

▶ If an execution is required within the scope of a background processing, this automatically results in the executable program type.

▶ No new module pools and type groups are supposed to be created any longer.

Details

The hierarchy provided in Rule 3.2 for selecting the program type results from the basic rule described in Section 3.1, ABAP Objects as a Programming Model, which stipulates the use of ABAP Objects. The following list further describes the specific aspects:

---

2 As of Release 7.2, you can use the operational package concept to restrict the usability of global classes to one package so that this role of subroutine pools becomes less important.

- If functionality will be provided across the whole package or system in the context of ABAP Objects, this is done via the global classes or interfaces that implicitly have the program type, class pool, or interface pool. The call is done either via a method call or an OO transaction if you want a standalone program execution.

- To implement closed functionality that is not supposed to be called via a method call but instead by using a transaction code, which additionally neither requires a parameter transfer nor has a user interface (UI), you can use the subroutine pool program type. The implementation will be carried out only via local classes, and the program call will be carried out via an OO transaction. Subroutine pools were — as the name suggests — originally intended for subroutines that were called from other programs. Because subroutines, and particularly their external call, are declared as obsolete within these programming guidelines, this intended use for subroutine pools is no longer given. Instead, subroutine pools are proposed as independent containers for local classes because they are hardly impacted by implicit processes of the ABAP runtime environment otherwise.

- Remote-enabled Function Modules (RFM), which provide functionality via the RFC interface either across servers or across systems or are used for parallelization, can only be created in a function group. The implementation of the actual functionality, however, is to be carried out in a class, for example, in a local class within the function group (see Rule 6.37, No Implementations in Function Modules and Subroutines).

- For update function modules, which are called within the update using CALL FUNCTION IN UPDATE TASK, the same applies as for RFMs.

- Programs with a classical dynpro interface or selection screens (as far as they should still be required; see Rule 5.18, Use Web Dynpro ABAP) should also be created as a function group, which only implements the UI but doesn't contain its own application logic (see Rule 2.1, Adhere to the SoC Principle, and Rule 5.19, Encapsulate Classical Dynpros and Selection Screens). This program type is suitable because it can contain both classical dynpros and an external functional interface in the form of function modules. The dialog modules of the function group called by the dynpro flow logic should basically contain method calls only, for instance, for methods of local classes.

- An executable program includes several event blocks that are executed when the various reporting events occur. This form of event control is largely obsolete and should no longer be used. Executable programs should only be used where they are technically required, thus mainly for background processing. In this case, too, the actual implementation should be carried out in methods, for example, via methods of a local class within the executable program. The event block of the initial event, START-OF-SELECTION, should only include a method call (see Rule 6.44, No Implementations in Dialog Modules and Event Blocks), and other event blocks should no longer occur.

▶ The module pool used to be the program type, which was traditionally used for the classical dialog programming with dynpros. As discussed in Chapter 2, Section 2.1, Separation of Concerns, the concept of SoC is not sufficiently supported through module pools. For this reason you should not create any new module pools. Instead, you should encapsulate classical dynpros in function groups if they still need to be used.

▶ The type group program type was initially implemented as a workaround because occasionally it was not possible to define any types for internal tables in the ABAP Dictionary. The same applied to the global storage of constants. Both gaps have been closed in the meantime. In the ABAP Dictionary, you can define any types, and in global classes and interfaces, it is possible to create both types and constants for package-wide or system-wide use. For this reason, the type group program type is obsolete, and no new type groups are supposed to be created any longer (in Chapter 6, see Section 6.1.2, Declaration of Data Types and Constants).

Note

In cases in which you still use program types other than class and interface pools, you should activate the check OBSOLETE STATEMENTS (OO Context) in the extended program check (see Section 3.4.2, Extended Program Check) to implement the same more stringent syntax check for the program components, which are not implemented in local classes, as within classes.

3.2.2   Program Attributes

Background

In addition to further, less important properties, each ABAP program has a set of program attributes that control specific aspects of the program behavior and the syntax check severity. This includes:

- **Unicode checks active**
  For creating a Unicode program.

- **Fixed point arithmetic**
  For considering the decimal separator in operations with packed numbers.

- **Logical database**
  For connecting an executable program with a logical database.

You define the program attributes when you create a program using the corresponding tool (Class Builder, Function Builder, ABAP Editor), and it is technically possible to change them later.

Rule

[⚙] **Rule 3.3: Accept the Standard Settings for Program Attributes**

Set the program attributes for new programs as follows:
- UNICODE CHECKS ACTIVE activated
- FIXED POINT ARITHMETIC activated
- No assignment to a logical database

These settings correspond to the default values when you create a new program, so you can keep them without any changes. Once the program attributes are set, you should not change them retroactively.

Details

Different behaviors or check severities are only provided for compatibility reasons to keep existing programs compilable and executable. New programs should not use obsolete settings by any means.

- When you create a new program, the UNICODE CHECKS ACTIVE attribute is already set as a default setting. This attribute must never be reset. Only when the Unicode checks are activated can you ensure that the program can be executed both in Unicode systems and in non-Unicode systems and that it provides the same results, respectively.[3] When you prepare a non-Unicode system for

---

3 A program with activated Unicode checks is referred to as a *Unicode program*. A *Unicode system* represents an SAP system in which the characters are displayed in Unicode format (ISO/IEC 10646) (currently UTF-16 with platform-dependent byte order). On a Unicode system, you can only execute Unicode programs; Unicode programs, however, can also be executed on non-Unicode systems. The programs provided by SAP are usually Unicode programs.

the migration to Unicode, all existing non-Unicode programs must be converted into Unicode programs. The activation of the Unicode checks only provides benefits for the developer, for instance, in the form of a more stringent static type check and a stricter separation of byte and character string processing.

▸ When you create a new program, the FIXED POINT ARITHMETIC attribute is already set as a default setting. This attribute must never be reset. If the fixed point arithmetic is deactivated, the position of the decimal separator of packed numbers (type p) is only considered for the display in a classical dynpro or for the formatting using WRITE TO but not for calculations. Today, such behavior meets the developer's expectations only in rare cases. If the calculation is supposed to be carried out with packed numbers without any decimal places, this must be specified by adding DECIMALS 0 in the declaration.

▸ When you create a new executable program, the LOGICAL DATABASE attribute is empty. Via this attribute, the executable programs are assigned to a logical database,[4] which combines the selection screen and the flow of the program with the selection screen and the flow of the logical database. Logical databases should no longer be used because they are based on the cross-program use of global data, implicit subroutine calls, and the reporting event control, and are therefore contrary to modern concepts. Existing logical databases can be accessed using the LDB_PROCESS function module if required, which can be called from a method, for example. You should no longer create new logical databases. Instead, you should provide a corresponding service via a global class.

Because a subsequent change to the program attributes potentially involves change-over effort, you should set the correct attributes right from the start and not change them later on. Particularly for attributes that influence the syntax check (currently the Unicode check) you should always decide for the highest possible check severity to be well prepared for subsequent, possibly requested changeovers.

The following sections assume that you only work with the activated Unicode check and the fixed point arithmetic and without the logical databases. For obsolete or problematic language constructs, which are only available if the Unicode

---

4 A logical database is a special development object that is processed in the *Logical Database Builder* and provides other ABAP programs with data from the nodes of a hierarchical tree structure. A logical database includes a hierarchical structure, a database program written in ABAP, and its own standard selection screen.

checks are switched off, no special rule is created in these guidelines any longer. They are only mentioned briefly within the list of the obsolete language elements (see Appendix A, Obsolete Language Constructs).

Bad Example

Figure 3.1 shows an ABAP program in which UNICODE CHECKS ACTIVE is not selected in the program attributes contrary to the recommendation of Rule 3.3, Accept the Standard Settings for Program Attributes.

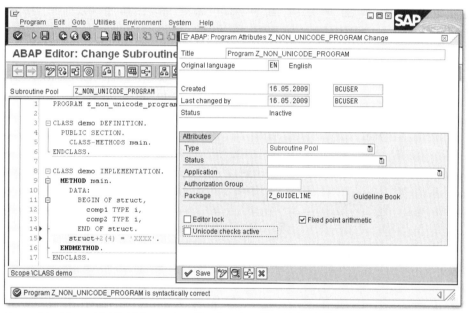

Figure 3.1 Allowed Subfield Access to a Structure in a Non-Unicode Program

In the non-Unicode program shown in Figure 3.1, you can readily execute a write access to a subfield across two numeric components of a structure, whereas an implicit casting (see Chapter 6, Section 6.2.8, Casting) of the subarea takes place for the type c. The result in the components depends on the alignment gaps, the internal presentation of the numeric values (byte order), and the used code page, and it is therefore extremely platform-dependent. A live program must not contain such code by any means. This usually results in erroneous data or runtime errors that are difficult to reproduce.

Good Example

Figure 3.2 shows an ABAP program in which the UNICODE CHECKS ACTIVE attribute is selected in the program attributes in accordance with Rule 3.3, Accept the Standard Settings for Program Attributes.

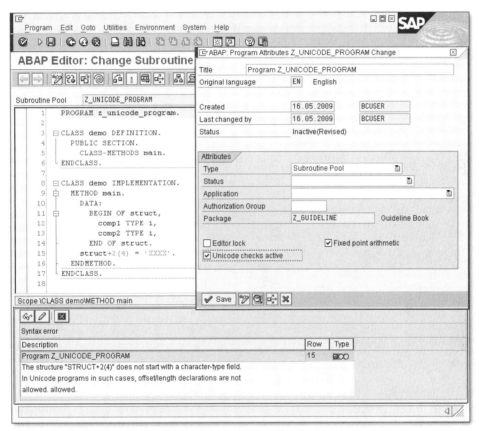

Figure 3.2 Syntax Error During the Subfield Access to a Structure in a Unicode Program

In the Unicode program of Figure 3.2, the code of Figure 3.1 results in a syntax error. Unwanted subfield accesses are prohibited just like any other unwanted accesses to structures or other parts of the working memory. If it is possible to statically determine them, this results in a syntax error similar to the one in the example shown here. Otherwise, a runtime error occurs with a meaningful short dump while the program is executed.

3.2.3   Original Language

Background

When you create a new repository object (e.g., a program, a class, or a database table in the ABAP Dictionary), you must specify its original language. This is done implicitly using the current logon language. All texts of the development object, which are created during the development and can be translated, such as descriptive short and long texts, text elements of a program, and also the documentation of data types or interfaces, are assigned to the specified original language. The creation of the texts in other languages is implemented in a translation process, which is detached from development, from the original language into the target languages.

Currently, there is no technical support for the project-wide replacement of the previously selected original language with another language.

Rule

[⚙]   **Rule 3.4: Determine Original Language at Project Level**

Before you start the implementation, determine a carefully selected original language for the repository objects at project level. Developers may create their development objects only in the original language determined for the respective project (or for a subproject in exceptional cases).

Details

When you determine the original language, you should proceed as follows:

▶ In case of a unilingual staff assignment of all development groups that participate in a project, the original language of all development objects is the native language of all developers involved (unilingual development).

▶ In case of a multilingual staff assignment of the development groups,

  ▶ the original language of all development objects is either a language that all people involved understand, which is usually English (unilingual development),

  ▶ or the original language of the development objects in individual parts of the project is based on the native language of the developers that mainly work on these parts (multilingual development).

Unilingual development groups normally represent the ideal case but cannot always be formed today. The two possible settings for multilingual developer groups — unilingual or multilingual development — meet two different requirements, which are contradictory:

▶ When a user logs on to a system in a language different from the original language, it is usually not possible to reasonably work with a product that is still being developed or newly developed until the relevant texts are available in the respective target language. The translation is usually carried out in a downstream translation system and then transported back into the development system. For this reason, an efficient development, particularly in internationally staffed development groups (that are possibly distributed across multiple locations), is only possible if a uniform original language is determined for the entire project at the beginning. This original language then enables all persons involved in the development and validation process to use the product at least for testing. In case of a unilingual development in multilingual development groups, some or even all developers of a project must create texts in a language that is not their native language.

▶ Usually, there is no support provided in the form of tools or defined processes for linguistic or stylistic checks of the UI texts and documentations, which developers create in languages that are not their native language. Therefore, it is desirable that the developers that participate in the development of user dialogs and documentations work in their native language and that trained translators translate these texts into their native language based on specified terminology.

The latter is the reason why English is not claimed as the comprehensive uniform original language of all development projects. Instead, unilingual development groups should definitely work in their native language with a possibly downstream translation.

In multilingual development groups, it ultimately depends on the case to specify the original language for each development object. The first reason usually outweighs so that a unilingual development must be implemented in international development to use the development resources of a project as effectively as possible. In individual cases, it can absolutely make sense to specify the native language of the developers as the original language in subprojects in which a high quantity of text must be created.[5]

---

5 This particularly concerns the SAP-internal development in which large parts are still implemented by German-speaking developers.

In multilingual projects, functions that are related to one business case should be developed in one language only, at least at package level. Table contents should also be created in a uniform language.

Tip

Because the original language is determined by the logon language when a repository object is created, you must deliberately decide on a logon language when creating and processing repository objects.

Note

Irrespective of whether you implement a unilingual or multilingual development with a project, you must always create a uniform *terminology* for all texts created in the project before you start a development and adhere to it consistently. In a multilingual development, you should implement the translation of the terminology into the languages used, preferably before the development starts so that the developers can use it. In addition, you must always comply with the existing standards for UI texts and documentation (in Chapter 2, see Section 2.3, Correctness and Quality).

3.3   Modern ABAP

Background

ABAP is a living programming language that is continually being developed. Since the implementation of ABAP some 30 years ago, new ABAP programs are continuously being developed, while the ABAP language itself is advanced at the same time. Further developments of the ABAP language are either extensions of the existing language attributes to implement new functionality or to replace existing functionality with more advanced concepts. The replacement of existing language elements with new ones usually makes the existing language elements superfluous or obsolete. The most prominent example of a further development of the ABAP language is still the implementation of ABAP Objects for Release 4.6.

With regard to the ABAP language, SAP has committed itself to a policy of strict downward compatibility. This means, on the one hand, that an ABAP program written for SAP R/3 Release 3.0 can be executed on SAP NetWeaver AS ABAP in Release 7.2 without any modifications, at least as long as it is a non-Unicode system. On the other hand, this also means

- An experienced developer has hardly ever been forced to break with old habits and to engage in new concepts. The only exception is the changeover to Unicode systems for which the ABAP programs must be converted into Unicode programs with slightly changed syntax rules.

- ABAP beginners get confused by the multitude of options available to do one and the same thing. If in doubt, older programs serve as templates, and the obsolete concepts are frequently used instead of the new ones.

To remedy these problems, you can use the following simple rule.

Rule

Rule 3.5: Do Not Use Obsolete Language Elements

Do not use obsolete language elements for new developments. It is also recommended to incrementally change over to newer concepts as they are available.

Details

Newer language elements are always the better language elements. Obsolete language elements are only provided for downward compatibility reasons. A statement or statement addition is declared as obsolete only when a more powerful alternative exists or when the language element is determined as prone to errors (in the sense that it invites insecure and nonrobust programming). For this reason, secure and robust programming is not possible if obsolete language elements are used, which makes the use of such obsolete language elements out of the question for new developments.

If ABAP Objects is used, the majority of the obsolete statements and additions are already prohibited syntactically. For this reason among others, it is strongly recommended to use ABAP Objects (see Rule 3.1, Use ABAP Objects). Outside of ABAP Objects, that is, in cases that are still allowed according to Section 3.1, ABAP Objects as a Programming Model, you must make sure no obsolete language elements are used. For this purpose, Appendix A, Obsolete Language Constructs, provides an overview of the obsolete statements and statement additions.

Bad Example

Listing 3.3 shows the solution of a task using obsolete language elements. A procedure is supposed to replace all occurrences of a `substring` in a `text` with a new character string `new` if the substring is not at the end of a word.

```
FORM bad_example USING      substring  TYPE csequence
                            new         TYPE csequence
                 CHANGING text          TYPE csequence.
  DATA: pattern TYPE string,
        subrc   TYPE sy-subrc.
  CONCATENATE '*' substring INTO pattern.
  SEARCH text FOR pattern.
  IF sy-subrc <> 0.
    CLEAR subrc.
    WHILE subrc = 0.
      REPLACE substring WITH new INTO text.
      subrc = sy-subrc.
    ENDWHILE.
  ENDIF.
ENDFORM.
```

Listing 3.3 Use of Obsolete Language Elements

In Listing 3.3, aside from the modularization with FORM-ENDFORM, the statement SEARCH and the used variant of REPLACE are obsolete as of Release 7.0. Furthermore, as of Releases 7.0 EhP2 and 7.2, a character string operator && is available as a replacement for CONCATENATE.

Good Example

Listing 3.4 executes the same task as Listing 3.3; however, it uses the latest available language elements.

```
METHOD good_example.
  FIND REGEX substring && `\b` IN text.
  IF sy-subrc <> 0.
    REPLACE ALL OCCURRENCES OF substring IN text WITH new.
  ENDIF.
ENDMETHOD.
```

Listing 3.4 Use of Modern Language Elements

The subroutine is replaced with a method. By using FIND in connection with a regular expression, which is composed using the character string operator &&, you no longer require any helper variable. The WHILE loop is replaced with REPLACE ALL OCCURRENCES, whereas another helper variable is omitted, and the control flow is moved to the ABAP runtime environment. The latter increases the execution speed and is also helpful to meet Rule 4.22, Restrict the Nesting Depth of Control Structures, on limiting the maximum nesting depth.

Note

In connection with Rule 3.5, Do Not Use Obsolete Language Elements, the question on the coexistence of old and new concepts within a program unit arises. There is only one area in which this is clearly syntactically defined, that is, the use of the classical and the class-based exception concept (in Chapter 5, see Section 5.2.2, Classical and Class-Based Exceptions) in processing blocks. Else, obsolete language elements can be directly next to new language elements in a program part. In this context, it is recommended to design the use as consistently as possible within a context, that is, to not use different statements, such as FIND and SEARCH, in parallel for the same purpose.

However, this does not mean that if already existing procedures are extended, you should still use obsolete language elements for consistency reasons just because they already exist there. You should rather use the opportunity and directly change the entire procedure to the corresponding new language elements. By covering the procedures to be changed with module tests, you can ensure that no surprises occur during such a changeover.

3.4   Checks for Correctness

In Chapter 2, Section 2.3, Correctness and Quality, we already discussed the correctness and quality of programs in general and briefly presented the tools that are available for their check. This section now particularly discusses the syntactic correctness of ABAP programs, which is controlled using the syntax check and the extended program check as well as the standard check of the Code Inspector and the new ABAP Test Cockpit (ATC).

3.4.1   Syntax Check

Background

The syntax check provides syntax errors and syntax warnings:

▸ As soon as a syntax error occurs, the system ends the check and displays a corresponding error message. In many cases, the system proposes a correction that you can accept. Programs with syntax errors can be activated, but they cannot be generated and therefore executed. In the extended program check, the syntax errors are reported as fatal errors. Syntax errors must be remedied by all means.

▶ If a syntax warning occurs, the syntax check is not terminated, and the program can be executed in principle. The syntax warnings are displayed in the ABAP Editor after an execution of the syntax check and the extended program check (see Section 3.4.2, Extended Program Check).[6] When a program is activated, the system only generates syntax warnings if there are syntax errors at the same time.

The warnings notified by the syntax check are subdivided into three priorities that are only displayed by the extended program check, however:

▶ **Priority 1**
Errors that apparently will lead to a program termination if the ABAP program is executed. This priority also contains all constructs that should not be used at all because they suggest program errors and very likely lead to incorrect behavior.

▶ **Priority 2**
This priority refers to all constructs that do not necessarily lead to error behavior but are obsolete and supposed to be replaced with current constructs, for example. Errors of priority 2 can become errors of priority 1 or syntax errors in future releases.

▶ **Priority 3**
Summarizes all errors whose correction is desirable, but not necessarily required for the current release. However, a tightening of the priority in future releases is not excluded.

The severity of the ABAP syntax check is determined by the decisions that were made when the program was created (see Section 3.2, Program Type and Program Attributes). As a result, program constructs that only lead to syntax warnings outside of classes or in non-Unicode programs can represent real syntax errors within

---

6 Of course, testing tools that include the checks of the extended program check, such as the Code Inspector and the SAP-internal ABAP Test Cockpit (as of Releases 7.0 EhP2 and 7.2), also display syntax warnings.

classes or in Unicode programs. As of Releases 7.0 EhP2 and 7.2, you can suppress selected syntax warnings using pragmas.[7]

With the implementation of the operational package concept as of Release 7.2, the syntax check also checks package violations. Here, it depends on the encapsulation level that was set for the corresponding package whether a syntax error or only a syntax warning occurs.

Rule

Rule 3.6: Consider Syntax Warnings	[✓]
Take all warnings of the ABAP syntax check seriously. No syntax warnings may occur in a completed program.

Details

You must always correct the causes of syntax warnings because they generally lead to unpredictable errors. Such warnings are frequently promoted to errors by SAP in a subsequent release of SAP NetWeaver AS ABAP. In this case, a program that initially only included syntax warnings is syntactically incorrect and can no longer be used after an upgrade. The same applies to the changeover from non-Unicode programs to Unicode programs or to the migration of older program parts to ABAP Objects.

With regard to the package check, the consistent use of the package concept that is already available before Release 7.2 (select PACKAGE CHECK AS SERVER in the Package Builder) or the specification of a weak encapsulation as of Release 7.2 represents an initial step on the way to real encapsulation. It enables the users of development objects to adapt their usage locations even before hard syntax errors occur. For this reason, particularly all warnings of the package check both before and after Release 7.2 must be taken seriously and be corrected, so that the program remains syntactically correct even after an intensified encapsulation of the used packages.

---

7 A pragma is a program directive that doesn't influence the program flow but impacts certain checks.

Bad Example

Figure 3.3 shows a section of a non-Unicode program in a non-Unicode system in which a `VALUE` specification leads to a syntax warning because an improper initial value is set for a structure.

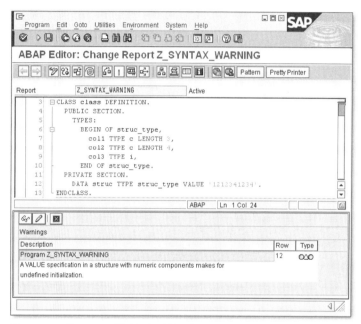

Figure 3.3   Program with Syntax Warning

Note

In a Unicode program, that is, a program for which the UNICODE CHECKS ACTIVE program attribute is set, the statement that solely leads to a warning in Figure 3.3 results in a syntax error.

Good Example

Figure 3.4 shows the corrected program of Figure 3.3. The components of the structure are provided with type-specific initial values in the instance constructor. The program has no syntax warnings and is correct also as a Unicode program.

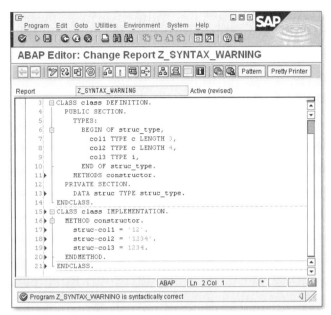

```
    3  ⊟ CLASS class DEFINITION.
    4  │    PUBLIC SECTION.
    5  │      TYPES:
    6  ├        BEGIN OF struc_type,
    7  │          col1 TYPE c LENGTH 3,
    8  │          col2 TYPE c LENGTH 4,
    9  │          col3 TYPE i,
   10  ┴        END OF struc_type.
   11▶ │      METHODS constructor.
   12  │    PRIVATE SECTION.
   13▶ │      DATA struc TYPE struc_type.
   14  └  ENDCLASS.
   15 ⊟ CLASS class IMPLEMENTATION.
   16▶ ├   METHOD constructor.
   17▶ │      struc-col1 = '12'.
   18▶ │      struc-col2 = '1234'.
   19▶ │      struc-col3 = 1234.
   20▶ │    ENDMETHOD.
   21▶ └ ENDCLASS.
```

Figure 3.4 Correct Program Without Syntax Warning

3.4.2 Extended Program Check

Background

You can call the extended program check for activated programs either from the ABAP Workbench or using Transaction SLIN. It performs static checks that are too involved for a normal syntax check. You can execute either individual or multiple partial tests or a standard check that includes the most critical partial tests.

The extended program check outputs errors, warnings, and messages. The standard check notifies you of the errors and warnings that are particularly critical.[8] Furthermore, the extended program check also displays the errors and warnings of the syntax check.

Since Releases 7.0 EhP2 and 7.2, in the initial screen of the extended program check, you can also select a check of PROGRAMMING GUIDELINES that checks the adherence to some of the rules presented in this book that can be verified statically.

---

8 The classification of the individual results as error, warning, or message may vary depending on whether you execute a standard check or explicitly selected individual checks.

The messages of the extended program check, which are inapplicable in some special cases, can be hidden using pseudo comments and, since Releases 7.0 EhP2 and 7.2, using pragmas. Messages that directly arise from a normal syntax check could not be hidden before Releases 7.0 EhP2 and 7.2.

Rule

[✓]   **Rule 3.7: Use the Extended Program Check**

Use the extended program check, and take its results seriously. No messages of the standard check may occur for a completed program.

Details

The errors, warnings, and messages output by the extended program check are as important as the syntax errors and syntax warnings of the syntax check (see Section 3.4.1, Syntax Check). For example, an error notified by the extended program check can indicate that a program will definitely lead to a runtime error when it is executed. Warnings and messages usually refer to a questionable use of language elements, which most likely result in unexpected program behavior.

In rare cases in which a check result provided by the extended program check is not justified, this must be documented using an appropriate pseudo comment or a pragma (since Releases 7.0 EhP2 and 7.2). The appropriate pseudo comment or the pragma is indicated in the message. This way, the system suppresses the message of the extended program check. Ideally, in less obvious situations, an additional comment should describe why the message is not applicable here.

Tip

The extended program check is a valuable help for writing correct ABAP programs. This advantage must not be undone by using unspecific pseudo comments or pragmas. You should never use the

```
SET EXTENDED CHECK OFF.
```

statement, which suppresses all messages of the extended program check for an entire source code section.

If the ABAP program is submitted to a code review, the results of the extended program check should be used to evaluate the quality.

Bad Example

Figure 3.5 shows the result of a partial check of the extended program check, which is implemented since Releases 7.0 EhP2 and 7.2. It indicates a particularly questionable query of the content of sy-subrc (in Chapter 6, see Section 6.3.4, Return Value).

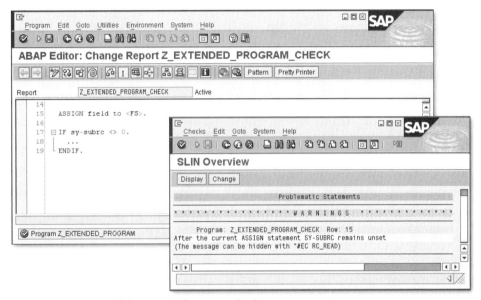

Figure 3.5 Warning of the Extended Program Check

The program section shows a typical error in a syntactically correct program. The developer wrongly assumes that the static form of the ASSIGN statement sets the sy-subrc system field, which is not the case. This entails that the developer falsely believes that he secured his program and that an incorrect program behavior occurs if sy-subrc has a value that is unequal zero due to previous statements. Therefore, the big advantage of the extended program check is that the system examines not only individual statements for syntactic correctness but entire program sections for semantic errors.

Good Example

Figure 3.6 shows the corrected version of the program of Figure 3.5. Instead of the wrong query of sy-subrc, the logical expression IS ASSIGNED, as recommended in the documentation, is used. The message of the extended program check could also be hidden using a pseudo comment, "#EC RC_READ, or a pragma, ##SUBRC_READ (as of Releases 7.0 EhP2 and 7.2), but this is not recommended in this case because the extended program check indicates a real problem.

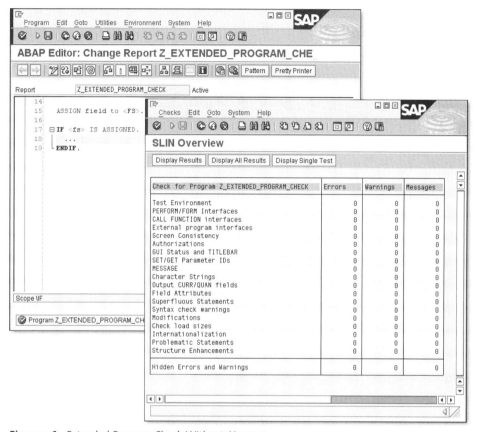

Figure 3.6   Extended Program Check Without Message

3.4.3   Code Inspector

Background

The Code Inspector is a tool to statically check repository objects in terms of performance, security, syntax, and adherence to naming conventions. You can use the full functional scope of the Code Inspector using Transaction SCI to implement complex static checks as well as regular mass tests for large quantities of development objects.

You can also call the Code Inspector from the ABAP Workbench to carry out a standard set of checks for your current object, for instance, using the PROGRAM • CHECK • CODE INSPECTOR menu path of the ABAP Editor. The default check variant used here contains most of the checks of the extended program check (see Section 3.4.2, Extended Program Check) as well as some additional security and performance checks. Beyond that, you can integrate the Code Inspector in the release of transports.

Like in the extended program check, the results of the Code Inspector are subdivided into the three categories of error, warnings, and simple messages and can be hidden using special pseudo comments.

Rule

Rule 3.8: Use Default Check Variant of the Code Inspector	[✓]
Execute the default check variant of the Code Inspector prior to releasing a program, and remove all error messages.	

Details

If you observe Rule 3.7, Use the Extended Program Check, the default check variant of the Code Inspector only indicates messages of checks that go beyond the extended program check. These messages basically concern possible performance or security risks in programs. Examples are messages on unfavorable WHERE conditions in SELECT, the pass by value instead of the pass by reference, or insecure program calls.

Compared to the messages of the extended program check, the cause of these problems cannot be corrected always so easily, for example, because there is no other option for a selection or because the clarity or robustness of a construct is considered as more important than a possible minor performance loss.

In such cases, you can suppress the messages using the appropriate pseudo comments. Such a pseudo comment clearly indicates for the reader of the program that the program author executed corresponding checks and that he suppressed the message intentionally and for good reasons. The latter can be further confirmed using additional normal comments if required (see Chapter 4, Section 4.3, Comments).

Bad Example

Figure 3.7 shows the result of a Code Inspector run for a sample class. Warnings are issued because an internal table is passed by value, and an inner join is used for database tables with activated SAP buffering in the SELECT statement.

Figure 3.7 Warnings of the Code Inspector

Good Example

Figure 3.8 shows the corrected version of the program of Figure 3.7 in which the Code Inspector no longer issues any messages.

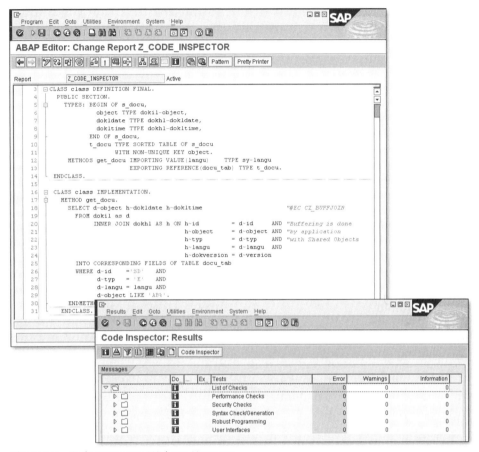

Figure 3.8 Code Inspection Without Messages

The pass by value of the internal tables was replaced with a pass by reference. For passing the elementary parameter langu, the pass by value was kept for reasons of robustness. In the standard check used here, it didn't generate any warning anyhow. If the Code Inspector displays a warning in such as case, it can be hidden using the pseudo comment, "#EC CI_VALPAR.

The inner join of the `SELECT` statement bypasses the SAP buffering, which would result in performance problems if the method was called frequently. But if you assume for the example displayed here that the method is part of a larger application, in which a buffering of the selected data is ensured via Shared Objects, you should preferably use the inner join instead of other constructs with lower performance, such as a nested `SELECT` loop. Therefore, the warning of the Code Inspector is hidden using the pseudo comment "`#EC CI_BUFFJOIN`, and the reasons are described in a normal comment.

3.4.4 ABAP Test Cockpit

Background

As of Releases 7.0 EhP2 and 7.2, the ABAP Test Cockpit (ATC) is integrated with the ABAP Workbench for internal SAP use. This framework considerably facilitates the development-oriented handling of the required tests. The ATC allows for the execution and results display of different tests for development objects, such as

- Extended program checks
- Static performance tests
- Module tests with ABAP Unit Browser
- Static usability tests
- Package checks

While the Code Inspector is only integrated with the development environment via the standard check, which is detailed in Section 3.4.3, and can otherwise only be operated using a dedicated transaction, the ATC is completely integrated with the Object Navigator and the Transport Organizer and is readily available for tests during development. After development and transport, quality managers can use the ATC to implement mass tests. For now, however, the ATC is only available at SAP and possibly at SAP partners for the development of SAP programs.

Rule

[✓] | **Rule 3.9: Configure and Use the ABAP Test Cockpit Correctly**

If the ATC is available in your system, make sure that an ATC run for all development objects involved no longer displays any messages before a transport is released. For this purpose, you should integrate the ATC check directly into the release of transports.

Details

The ATC is the first tool that can be used both by SAP developers and within the framework of a central quality assurance. For example, if a developer checks all development objects of a package in the development system using the same ATC configuration that the quality manager uses within the framework of a mass run in a consolidation system, he can directly avoid all messages without having to wait for the quality manager's feedback.

If the ATC is available and configured correctly, Rule 3.9 includes the preceding Rules 3.6, 3.7, and 3.8.

Exception

At the moment, the ATC is not yet available for developments in customer systems.

Bad Example

Figure 3.9 shows the result of an ATC run implemented in the Transport Organizer. The checked transport request still contains erroneous objects.

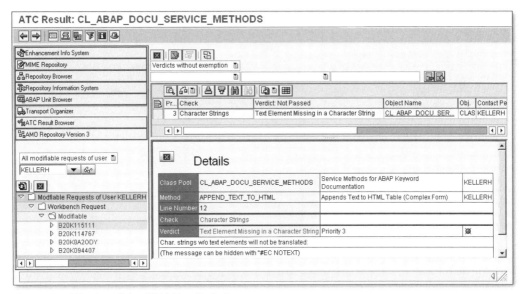

Figure 3.9 Warning of the ABAP Test Cockpit

Good Example

Figure 3.10 shows the result of an ATC run in the Transport Organizer after the error shown in Figure 3.9 has been remedied. The transport can be released now.

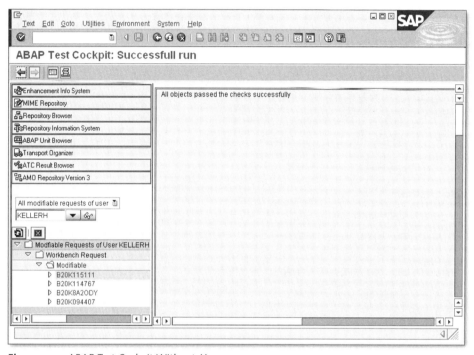

Figure 3.10 ABAP Test Cockpit Without Messages

"The proper words in the proper places are the true definition of style."
– Jonathan Swift

4   Structure and Style

Structure and style summarize all aspects of a program that have no direct influence on its functionality. These aspects remain hidden to the user when he uses the program. However, the structure and style are very significant for the traceability of the program flow by a human viewer. The source code must be designed in such a way that a person other than the program developer can work with it reasonably. There are many situations in which this is necessary, for example:

- A review or code inspection takes place.

- Another developer must check the program while processing an error message (hotline, development support).

- The program was completely transferred from the development department to the maintenance department where it is maintained and possibly further developed.

- A program that was delivered by an organization (e.g., SAP) is supposed to be modified or further developed in other organizations (e.g., at SAP partners or customers).

A sound program structure and programming style is highly significant also beyond the mentioned situations because the developer himself should be able to quickly orient himself in his code even after not working on it for a long period..

All of this is based on the knowledge that source code must be read and understood again and again during the software lifecycle. Source code that is delivered once and then runs without any maintenance does not exist in real life for realistic programs that contain more than just a few lines. In addition to adhering to general standards, such as functional correctness or performance (see Section 2.3, Correctness and Quality), for a program the rule applies that its source code must always be adapted to the requirements of the human reader.

Therefore, this chapter discusses guidelines that help provide comprehensible and traceable ABAP source codes. It is clear, of course, that questions on style are always assessed individually by the different viewers true to the motto "beauty is in the eye of the beholder" and that they are discussed controversially. So the following sections are restricted to a core of recommendations that are indisputable to a large extent. The goal of this chapter is not to dictate a specific programming style but rather to provide a reasonable programming style. A developer must feel comfortable in his own sources so that he can work really efficiently. Occasionally, excessive style specifications can do more harm than good.

The following sections mainly discuss generally accepted guidelines that also often apply independently of the programming language. Cases in which the recommendations deviate from the generally accepted guidelines due to ABAP specifics are explicitly indicated in the following.

4.1 Source Code Formatting

A formatting that emphasizes the logical structure of the source code is decisive for the legibility of the source code. Such a formatting is obtained with an appropriate case sensitivity, an appropriate arrangement of statements in lines, suitable insertion of blank characters and blank lines, and a properly selected line width.

4.1.1 Case Sensitivity

Background

In contrast to many other modern programming languages, ABAP is not case-sensitive for ABAP words[1] nor for operators and names of operands. Dynamic programming is the only exception here (see Section 6.6, Dynamic Programming Techniques) where the names of operands must usually be specified in uppercase.

---

[1] An ABAP word is a token of an ABAP statement that expresses its semantics. ABAP words are either ABAP keywords or additions. Tokens are the elementary parts of an ABAP statement into which it is split by the Compiler. Other tokens are: operands, operators, and some special characters.

Rule

Rule 4.1: No Mixed Uppercase and Lowercase in Names [✿]

Use only lowercase or uppercase in an individual token. Use uppercase for keywords and lowercase for operands.

Details

Writing tokens, that is ABAP words and names, in upper or lower case used to be a very important aspect for the formatting of the source code. A uniform adherence to upper and lower case made it easier for the reader to differentiate keywords and names. Due to the syntactic source code coloring in the ABAP Editor,[2] this aspect has become less important; however, Rule 4.1 still makes sense because usually there is no syntactic source code coloring available in a printed source code. Therefore, a uniform rule for using upper and lower case is useful that emphasizes the difference between keywords and names.

Because the usage of upper and lower case in ABAP source code has no syntactic significance outside of character literals — that is, text field literals in inverted commas (') and string literals in back quotes (`) and, since 7.0 EhP2 and 7.2, character string templates in vertical lines (|) — the ABAP development environment is not designed to maintain it permanently outside the mentioned constructs. The *Pretty Printer* only offers the alternatives to use only lowercase or only uppercase or to use either uppercase or lowercase for keywords and respectively the opposite for names in operand positions.

Because of the latter, it doesn't make sense in ABAP to use upper and lower case as a self-defined means of style. In other words, the names should not be based on the *mixed case style* (also referred to as *camel case style*; see the following example), which is very popular in languages where case sensitivity is taken into account. A consistent notation cannot be ensured due to the missing syntactic relevance. A mixed notation will be lost sooner or later when the Pretty Printer is used — even if this is unintentional. Moreover, it possibly prevents other developers from using the Pretty Printer after changes have been made to the source code. However, the use of the Pretty Printer is explicitly recommended (see Rule 4.3).

---

2 The new ABAP Editor with source code coloring is available as of Release 6.20 — assuming an appropriate current basis support package and SAP GUI — and can be selected via the Utilities - Settings menu item in the ABAP Workbench. In newer Releases as of 7.0, it is the default setting.

Bad Example

Listing 4.1 shows the declaration of a class with names in mixed case style or camel case style.

Here, the respective beginning of a word is indicated with an uppercase within a combined name.

```
CLASS ClDemoCrReservationService DEFINITION ABSTRACT.
  PROTECTED SECTION.
    DATA carTab TYPE demoCrCarsTt.
    CONSTANTS basisRate TYPE demoCrBasisRate VALUE 20.
    METHODS makeReservation
      IMPORTING
        iCustomerId TYPE DemoCrCustomerId
        iDateFrom   TYPE DemoCrDateFrom
        iDateTo     TYPE DemoCrDateTo
      RAISING
        CxDemoCrNoCustomer
        CxDemoCrLock
        CxDemoCrReservation.
    METHODS computePrice
      IMPORTING
        iDateFrom TYPE DemoCrDateFrom
        iDateTo   TYPE DemocrDateTo
      RETURNING
        VALUE(rPrice) TYPE DemoCrPrice.
ENDCLASS.
```

Listing 4.1 Mixed Case Style or Camel Case Style

This code provided as a bad example approximately follows the Java convention, and in the eyes of many beholders it might look more beautiful than the following good example. Whether it is beautiful or not is less important than the mentioned technical restrictions, which don't allow for such a naming at the moment. Executing the Pretty Printer would undo beauty irreversibly because the names would appear very illegible subsequently, for example, `cldemocrreservationservice`.

Good Example

Listing 4.2 shows the declaration of a class in *ABAP style* in which words of combined names are separated by underscores (_). These separations cannot get lost when you use the Pretty Printer.

```abap
CLASS cl_demo_cr_reservation_service DEFINITION ABSTRACT.
  PROTECTED SECTION.
    DATA car_tab TYPE demo_cr_cars_tt.
    CONSTANTS basis_rate TYPE demo_cr_basis_rate VALUE 20.
    METHODS make_reservation
      IMPORTING
        i_customer_id TYPE demo_cr_customer_id
        i_date_from   TYPE demo_cr_date_from
        i_date_to     TYPE demo_cr_date_to
      RAISING
        cx_demo_cr_no_customer
        cx_demo_cr_lock
        cx_demo_cr_reservation.
    METHODS compute_price
      IMPORTING
        i_date_from TYPE demo_cr_date_from
        i_date_to   TYPE demo_cr_date_to
      RETURNING
        VALUE(r_price) TYPE demo_cr_price.
ENDCLASS.
```

Listing 4.2 ABAP Style

The example is formatted according to the Pretty Printer setting that is proposed in Section 4.1.3, Using the Pretty Printer. In this setting, ABAP words are in uppercase and operands in lowercase. Irrespective of its configuration, the separation of the words in the names would remain after each execution of the Pretty Printer.

Tip

As of Releases 7.0 EhP2 and 7.2, the built-in character string functions, to_mixed and from_mixed, are available that allow for the conversion between names in ABAP style with underscores and names in mixed case style or camel case style, which can be helpful for the data exchange with external systems.

4.1.2   Statements per Program Line

Background

An ABAP statement, whether a declaration or an executable statement, ends with a period. Then, further statements can follow within the same line. In addition, you can distribute statements across multiple lines.

Rule

> **Rule 4.2: One Statement at Most per Program Line**
>
> At most, put one statement in each source code line. Long statements can and should be wrapped at suitable positions and thus be distributed across consecutive lines.

Details

Multiple statements in one line impair the legibility of the source code. Particularly if entire control structures are in one line, it is not easy to keep an overview of the logical structure due to missing indentations. Therefore, you should not use the option to put several statements into one program line.

Besides the worse legibility, multiple statements within one line can also lead to a decreased debugging function. Up to and including Releases 7.0 EhP2 and 7.2, even with the single step option, the ABAP Debugger stops only once for each executable program line.[3] Therefore, it is disruptive for debugging if a line includes more than one statement.

When a statement is distributed across several lines (see Rule 4.4, Do Not Use Full Line Width) — which happens quite often considering the possible size of complex ABAP statements[4] — there should be no blank lines between the parts of the statement. The line breaks should be done at semantically suitable positions so that groups with similar semantic meaning stand together if possible. Indentations should be arranged in such a way that the statement is well structured and legible.

---

3   As of Releases 7.0 EhP2 and 7.2, the ABAP Debugger can also stop at each single statement within a line or at individual partial expressions during the evaluation of an expression. This behavior can be set using the Debugger function Step Size.

4   Sometimes the use of several pseudo comments (see Section 3.4.2, Extended Program Check, and Section 3.4.3, Code Inspector) for a statement even requires the distribution across multiple lines.

Bad Example

Listing 4.3 shows a syntactically correct program section that hardly any beholder would consider beautiful, let alone understand quickly. Even the Pretty Printer (see Section 4.1.3) is unable to turn the code shown here into something beautiful.

```
CLASS class DEFINITION.
  PUBLIC SECTION. METHODS meth. ENDCLASS.

CLASS class IMPLEMENTATION. METHOD meth.
  DATA: itab TYPE TABLE OF dbtab, wa TYPE dbtab.
  SELECT * FROM dbtab INTO TABLE itab WHERE column = ' '.
  IF sy-subrc <> 0. RETURN. ENDIF.
  LOOP AT itab INTO wa. ... ENDLOOP.
  ENDMETHOD. ENDCLASS.
```

Listing 4.3 Several Statements per Program Line

Good Example

Listing 4.4 shows the same code as in Listing 4.3; here, however, the recommended arrangement of one statement per line is considered. The complex SELECT statement is distributed across multiple consecutive lines according to its clauses.

```
CLASS class DEFINITION.
  PUBLIC SECTION.
    METHODS meth.
ENDCLASS.

CLASS class IMPLEMENTATION.
  METHOD meth.
    DATA: itab TYPE TABLE OF dbtab,
          wa   TYPE dbtab.
    SELECT *
           FROM dbtab
           INTO TABLE itab
           WHERE column = ' '.
    IF sy-subrc <> 0.
      RETURN.
    ENDIF.
    LOOP AT itab INTO wa.
      ...
    ENDLOOP.
  ENDMETHOD.
ENDCLASS.
```

Listing 4.4 One Statement at Most per Program Line

4.1.3   Using the Pretty Printer

Background

The arrangement of ABAP statements in the source code is not specified syntactically. According to Rule 4.2, there should be a maximum of one statement per line, which can be arbitrarily indented and wrapped from the technical point of view.[5] This way, you can make the control structures visible, and by inserting blank lines, you can optically group related source code sections.

While languages with a C-like syntax, in which statement blocks within control structures are delimited by curly brackets, provide an inexhaustible source for discussions on how to best make indentations, for ABAP this is obvious: For each introductory statement (e.g., IF), there is a corresponding concluding statement[6] (in this case, ENDIF). Introductory and concluding statements are arranged at the same level; the block content is indented.

The Pretty Printer can adapt the source code at any time (even in display mode) with regard to the indentation of control structures and case sensitivity of keywords and names.

Rule

Rule 4.3: Use the Pretty Printer Consistently and Universally

Use the Pretty Printer to format your source code consistently. If the Pretty Printer is not sufficient, you must make manual adaptations accordingly.

---

5 But note that in ABAP statements, blank characters cannot be added or left out totally at random. For example, tokens must be separated with at least one blank character (in particular operands and operators), whereas in a method call, there must not be any blank characters between the name of the method and the left bracket.

6 Event blocks for events of the ABAP runtime environment are the only exception here. They are started with a statement (e.g., START-OF-SELECTION) but are not concluded with the corresponding concluding statement; instead, they are concluded with the next processing block. However, event blocks should only be used in exceptional cases (see Section 3.1, ABAP Objects as a Programming Model).

Details

It is recommended to use the Pretty Printer to make the indentations that are indispensable for the legibility of the source code. This way, you ensure that the indentation is consistently based on the logical control structure and that the indentation depth is identical for each program. A purely manual formatting is error-prone and not useful.

Even though you can adapt the source code to any other style (within the setting options provided) using the Pretty Printer, you should select a consistent and universal style. The reason for this is that the version management and the correction workbench are not designed to ignore pure style differences between source code versions. Therefore, the following Pretty Printer settings are recommended for a consistent source code formatting, which cover the expectations and habits of most ABAP developers:

▶ **Indent**
Indispensable to make the logical structure of the program visible. Rule 4.2, One Statement at Most per Program Line, must be adhered to.

▶ **Do Not Insert Standard Comment**
The standard comment only contains redundant information and is not adapted if the source code is changed. This setting is available as of Releases 7.0 EhP2 and 7.2.

▶ **Keyword Uppercase**
Enables a better understanding of the source code also in printed form where syntax colorings are usually not available (see Section 4.1.1, Case Sensitivity).

The indentation of entire statements using the Pretty Printer is usually satisfactory and reliable; prior to Releases 7.0 EhP2 and 7.2, however, problems can occur with regard to indentations and statements that are distributed across several lines. These deficiencies have been removed to a large extent as of these releases, but in earlier releases, you need to perform some manual processing to align parts of the statements one below the other.

Additionally, you must ensure the correct use of blank lines between the boundaries of blocks of related source code manually. Syntactic units, such as classes, methods, control blocks, or semantic units of a program, should be separated from one another with one or two blank lines depending on their size and their meaning. However, there should not be more than two blank lines in succession.

Note

For reasons of beauty, we rather would like to recommended to use the KEYWORD LOWERCASE setting for the Pretty Printer. The reason is, that in all tools that are required for the ABAP development, the names of the repository objects and also the names of the data objects in the ABAP Debugger are displayed in uppercase. If you used the KEYWORD LOWERCASE setting, the format of the source codes would match these displays, for instance, when reading COLUMN columns form a DBTAB database table:

```
select COLUMN1 COLUMN2 ...
       from DBTAB
       into corresponding fields of ITAB
       where COLUMN = FIELD.
```

Moreover, the display of names in uppercase would better correspond to the fact that many dynamic operand positions in ABAP still require uppercase. A prominent example is the quasi static call of function modules. Using the KEYWORD LOWERCASE setting, the call of a function module FUNCTION_MODULE would be as follows:

```
call function 'FUNCTION_MODULE' exporting PARAMETER = FIELD.
```

However, the KEYWORD LOWERCASE setting was implemented in the Pretty Printer only relatively late and could not stand up against the generally used setting, KEYWORD UPPERCASE. Moreover, the ABAP syntax diagrams and the sample programs of the ABAP documentations as well as all relevant publications are formatted using the KEYWORD UPPERCASE setting so that a recommendation to use the KEYWORD LOWERCASE setting would rather lead to confusions and would not be helpful for the acceptance of the programming guidelines.

Bad Example

Listing 4.5 shows the example from Listing 4.4 without indentations and only with lowercase. The highlighting of the ABAP words, which are bold here and in color in the ABAP Editor, could get lost in a program printout, which would make the program even less legible.

```
class class definition.
public section.
methods meth.
```

```
endclass.
class class implementation.
method meth.
data: itab type table of dbtab,
wa type dbtab.
select *
from dbtab
into table itab
where column = ' '.
if sy-subrc <> 0.
return.
endif.
loop at itab into wa.
...
endloop.
endmethod.
endclass.
```

Listing 4.5 Source Code Without Indentations and Without Keyword Uppercase

Good Example

See Listing 4.4.

4.1.4 Line Width

Background

Before Release 6.10, the maximum line width of an ABAP program was restricted to 72 characters. Since Release 7.0, it is 255 characters. The Editor allows for more than 255 characters; however, it breaks a line that contains more than 255 characters between two tokens in case of an ENTER.

Rule

Rule 4.4: Do Not Use Full Line Width

Limit the width of a line in the source code to a reasonable size. As a rule of thumb, you should be able to print a program on common paper formats without truncation or line breaks.

Details

Whereas the old restriction to 72 characters was too strict, the full utilization of the 255 characters that are now available would not enhance the legibility of a program. Although today very large monitors are available, it can still be necessary, for example, for code inspections or reviews to print a program or program section. It is therefore advisable to break long statements at suitable positions (see Section 4.1.2, Statements per Program Line) and to distribute long literals across multiple lines using the literal operator (&) or the concatenation operator (&&) (as of Releases 7.0 EhP2 and 7.2).

Note

The sample programs in the documentations and books like this one are restricted in width in a natural way, which makes them legible at the same time.[7] You should keep this in mind even if you have more space available.

Bad Example

Figure 4.1 shows a method in which a very long literal is assigned to the return value. The literal is not displayed completely even on very wide screens, and in the printout it will be broken or even truncated.

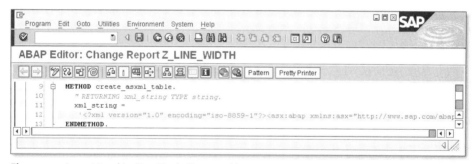

Figure 4.1 Long Literal in One Single Program Line

Good Example

The method shown in Figure 4.2 uses a literal whose content is identical to the one of the method in Figure 4.1; here, however, it is composed of multiple shorter

---

7 Unfortunately, this also partly constrains to names that are shorter than would actually be possible, which infringes Rule 4.6, Assign Descriptive Names, to some extent.

literals using the literal operator (&). The literal is split at appropriate positions, and the method becomes more legible both on the screen and the printout.

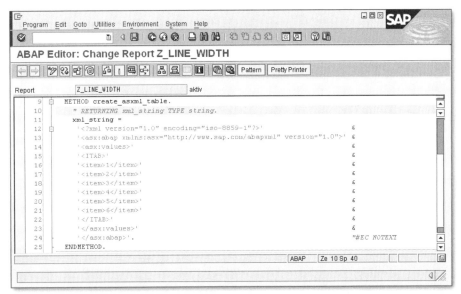

Figure 4.2 Long Literal Distributed Across Multiple Lines

4.2 Naming

A suitable naming for the repository objects defined outside the program and for the entities declared within the program, such as data types, data objects, and procedures, is of paramount importance for tracing and comprehending a program. Primarily, all names used must be legible, catchy, and suitable. These requirements are met by selecting descriptive names. Moreover, it is necessary to prevent naming conflicts.

In the literature you can find a detailed assessment of the advantages and disadvantages of certain naming specifications. Here, we have a different opinion in some cases, which can be traced back to the specifics of ABAP and the ABAP Workbench. It is not our goal to establish cross-language rules. Due to the fundamental difference of the programming languages ABAP and Java that are used within the SAP environment (particularly the different behavior with regard to uppercase and lowercase, see Section 4.1.1), it doesn't make sense to have common naming specifications.

Note

We intentionally use the concept *naming* and not *naming conventions*. Even though the term *programming guidelines* is frequently equated with *naming conventions* and many existing programming guidelines mainly include the definition of more or less meaningful prefixes and suffixes, we pursue a different approach here. In this book, the discussion of meaningful names is given its due space, but it definitely doesn't represent the core of the guidelines.

From the perspective of a maintenance organization, whose task it is to maintain monolithic ABAP applications that have evolved over time and that possibly include complex procedures without a clearly defined task, large quantities of global data objects, or cryptic and even misleading names, the request for strict naming conventions with standardized prefixes and suffixes may be understandable.[8] The present programming guidelines, however, particularly aim for the new development of robust ABAP programs that can be developed and maintained cost-efficiently. Against this background, it would be wrong to claim a naming for new developments that basically addresses problems of older code, which are excluded from the outset if the programming meets current standards.

The rules on naming that are listed in the following are in line with the requirements of a modern ABAP development.[9] Concerning older code, however, it is recommended to implement a refactoring according to the basic guidelines presented here. This way, you can get down to the root of maintenance problems. If you do nothing else but retroactively adapt the names of technical naming conventions, you will only be attempting to cure the symptoms.

4.2.1 Selecting the Language

Background

The natural language that has established itself globally for writing computer programs is English because the language elements of all important programming

---

8   Appendix B, Automatic Check of Naming Conventions, presents a *Code Inspector check*, which you can use to monitor the adherence to such a naming convention. For new developments, however, this procedure is not recommended.

9   The only disadvantage is that the adherence cannot be monitored easily using automatic checks. Our rules address the human viewer who wants to understand an ABAP program as quickly as possible and unambiguously — and not an automated test tool.

languages are taken from the English language, and their syntax is based on English grammar. ABAP forms no exception here. More than this: To achieve correct English, equivalent additions for related statements were given different names. Famous examples are the additions, VARYING and VARY, which are obsolete by now, to the statements, DO or WHILE (see Section A.5.5, Loops for Memory Content). ABAP can be considered a subset of English so to speak.

Rule

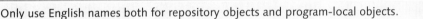

Rule 4.5: Use English Names
Only use English names both for repository objects and program-local objects.

Details

The use of names in a language other than English is unnatural in a programming language whose language elements are taken from the English language and may be considered not beautiful by virtually all beholders. Moreover, the use of English names enables a large group of persons to understand the source code. The consistent use of another language would not be possible anyway in the IT environment because of the large number of English technical terms.

When there are differences between British and American English, the American spelling should be used. It is usually shorter and more common in the IT environment.

Note

This rule is independent of the selection of the original language (see Rule 3.4, Determine Original Language at Project Level).

Bad Example

Figure 4.3 shows one of the most notorious examples for a non-English name in the ABAP environment, that is, the UZEIT component of the SYST system structure and its data element, SYUZEIT. All other components — except for the equally notorious components DATUM and MANDT (for the German word *Mandant* [client]) — are English terms or abbreviations.

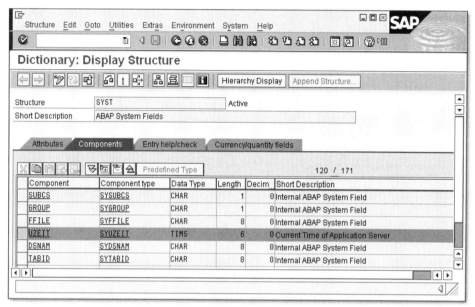

Figure 4.3 Non-English Names in the ABAP Dictionary

Good Example

All good example programs of this book, of the *ABAP Objects* (SAP PRESS, 2007) book, the ABAP keyword documentation, and so on.

4.2.2   Descriptive Names

Background

A name can include both technical and semantic information:

▸ Technical information can be very versatile. Examples for the options in a data object include the data type, the context of the declaration whether a procedure parameter is passed by value or by reference, and so on.

▸ The semantic information indicates the purpose of classes or data types, the content of data objects, the functionality of methods, and so on.

The technical information on a repository object or a program-internal entity can be viewed directly in the ABAP Workbench, are displayed in a tooltip, or are just a double-click away. In contrast to purely technical type information, however, the semantics of a variable are more difficult to identify without the corresponding information in the name.

Rule

Rule 4.6: Assign Descriptive Names	

Define all names so that they include the semantic information that is required for their context and are comprehensible at the same time.

Details

The goal of naming is to assign descriptive and self-documenting names. Here, you should always follow a problem-oriented approach instead of an implementation-oriented approach. For example, a truth value should not have the name `flag`, but a name that indicates its meaning, for instance, `is_checked`.

When you select a descriptive, problem-oriented name, you should particularly consider the following aspects:

- Suitable selection of nouns, verbs, and adjectives

- Reasonable use of abbreviations

- Suitable separation of name components

All of these aspects are discussed in detail in the following sections. Because you can usually view the purely technical information for a named object in the ABAP Workbench easily and quickly using the double-click navigation, they can be omitted as name components in favor of semantic information.[10]

The selection of nouns, verbs, and adjectives for naming depends on the entity to be described:

- **Package and package interfaces**
  A package comprises a collection of repository objects of a specific subject area. The name of the package can either consist of one or several nouns in singular that describe the subject area, for instance, `sabp_compiler`, or of one or several nouns in plural that name the objects contained, such as in `sabp_analyze_`

---

[10] Organizations, whether SAP-internal or SAP-external, that want to specify technical information in addition to semantic information in names, can define them in own naming conventions that are based on our semantic rules. However, we are convinced that the coding of technical attributes in names is not suited to increase the traceability or maintainability of ABAP programs that have been developed according to the present guidelines. This may be different in the context of other programming languages with a lower versatility of types and less powerful development environments.

`tools`. Subpackages start with the name of the super package and contain suffixes that indicate the specialization. The name of a package interface starts with the name of the package. Information on the visibility or the restriction to certain users are attached optionally as a suffix, for example, `_PUBLIC`, which stands for *public interface* or `_VERIFICATION` for *interface to verification tools*.

▶ **Data types, classes, and interfaces**
They denote *categories of things* and are therefore named with *nouns*, for instance, `cl_abap_codepage`. The higher the degree of specialization, the higher the number of nouns required for description. This can lead to longer, combined names, for instance, `if_abap_string_writer` or `cl_abap_xml_name_converter`. If required, the name can also be further specified with an additional adjective, as in `if_serializable_object` and `cl_abap_weak_reference`. The name of a category is usually in singular, which is why a class name should generally consist of nouns in singular.[11]

▶ **Variable data objects and procedure parameters**
They describe *properties* and are therefore named with a *noun*, for instance, `cl_abap_regex->pattern`. Analogous to the natural language use, truth values are labeled by prefixing an `is_`. If the property to be described is a set (in ABAP, usually an internal table), this should be expressed using the plural, for example, the `matches` parameter of the `cl_abap_matcher->find_all` method.

▶ **Constants**
From a technical point of view, these are data objects whose values are unchangeable at program runtime. They describe special, unchangeable *properties*. Their values to be described with *nouns* distinguish them with a specific property (e.g., minimum size, start value, etc.), which are expressed by one or several additional *adjectives*. Examples are `cl_abap_exceptional_values=>decfloat34_max` and `cl_abap_format=>o_extended_monetary`.[12]

▶ **Events**
They are named with an expression in *present perfect* that describes their occurrence, for instance, `cl_dd_form_element->button_clicked` and `cl_gui_alv_tree->selection_changed`.

---

11 However, there are many examples for deviations from this rule, for instance, `cl_abap_memory_utilities`. Such classes often don't model a category but provide a hodgepodge of loosely coupled functionality, usually in the form of exclusively static methods.

12 In this example, the noun is abbreviated considerably (`o` for *output format*). You are provided with more information on useful abbreviations later on.

▶ **Procedures**

New procedures are methods according to Rule 3.1, Use ABAP Objects. Here, you must differentiate different cases:

▶ *Event handlers* are named after the corresponding event and additionally obtain a prefix that identifies them as handler methods. In ABAP, the on_ prefix has established itself, which follows the natural language use and clearly labels a method as an event handler. For the two mentioned event examples, the names of the corresponding handler methods would be on_button_clicked or on_selection_changed.

▶ The name of *methods with return value* (functional methods) describes the returned result. get_ is prefixed to describe the task of the method.[13] An example for this is the cl_abap_exceptional_values=>get_max_value method. If the method provides a truth value, is_ is prefixed instead of get_.

▶ In all other cases, the name of a method describes an activity to be performed. Accordingly, the method name is a *verb*, generally in imperative. Examples are cl_abap_regex->create_matcher and cl_abap_memory_utilities=>do_garbage_collection. Methods that are used to set attributes are described with the attribute to be set, which is prefixed with set_.

Other procedures (function modules and subroutines), which according to Rule 6.37 (No Implementations in Function Modules and Subroutines) are still necessary to wrap method calls, are named accordingly.

▶ **Exceptions**

They describe unexpected states. From the technical point of view, these are classes.[14] To differentiate them from normal classes, they are provided with a separate prefix cx_ (see Section 4.2.3, Names of Repository Objects) if they are global exception classes. The name of an exception reflects the objected state as clearly as possible, for instance, cx_sy_offset_not_allowed. If an entire hierarchy of exception classes exists, the names of the superclasses do not describe

---

13 In ABAP, such GET_ methods are generally supposed to determine the return value, for example, by calculation. Unlike in Java, for example, no own methods are supposed to be used for the mere return of attribute values. For such purposes, ABAP offers write-protected (READ-ONLY) attributes (see Section 5.1.1, Encapsulation).

14 Classical exceptions are not supposed to be used any longer (see Rule 5.9, Use Class-Based Exceptions). Except for the prefix, the same considerations apply here.

special exception situations but instead describe error categories (such as `cx_sy_data_access_error` in the mentioned example).

You should avoid abbreviations as name components if possible. Exceptions from this rule are abbreviations that typically replace the use of an entire term, for instance, GUI or XML. However, if the use of other abbreviations cannot be avoided for reasons of space, you should first of all use common abbreviations.

If no common abbreviation exits, you should proceed as follows: Vowels are omitted unless they are the first letter of the word. They are of minor significance for the recognition value. If a word starts with a double vowel it is kept completely to facilitate recognition (e.g., `outbnd` as the abbreviation for `outbound` instead of `otbnd`). If further abbreviations are required, you can additionally replace double consonants with single consonants. Even after this step, the word is generally still recognizable.

An example for a poorly selected abbreviation would be `tstmp` for *timestamp*. This abbreviation, which doesn't follow the rules mentioned, is not intuitive. Initially, the possible components `tst` or `tmp` are eye-catching, which remind of *test* or *temporary*. An association to *timestamp*, however, is difficult to recognize at first. So if you create abbreviations, you must ensure that the result is not similar to another, possibly more common abbreviation for a completely different term.

When you create abbreviations in a foreign language, you run the risk that the result accidentally represents a word or abbreviation with a completely different meaning. If in doubt, you should enter the abbreviation in a search engine to check it. If, for example, you only have four characters available and want to use the word `button`, you should select the abbreviation `bttn` (according to the abbreviation rules mentioned) instead of the first four characters.

In principle, it is useful to optically separate the name components from one another to increase legibility by using the underscore in ABAP. A separation of the name components with uppercase and lowercase, as is common in languages with C-like syntax, is not useful in ABAP for the reasons that were mentioned in Section 4.1.1. Underscores normally identify a name because ABAP words are usually not formed this way.[15]

---

[15] The only exceptions here are some format options for character string templates (e.g., `SCIENTIFIC_WITH_LEADING_ZERO`), which can only occur within character string expressions, as well as a few additions to `SELECTION-SCREEN` and `WRITE`. Character string templates are available as of Releases 7.0 EhP2 and 7.2.

You should not use digits as name components. They are often a sign of poorly selected names (because they are not very descriptive) or indicate the use of multiple individual variables for which the use of an internal table would make more sense. Exceptions include the parameters of procedures. Here, the numbering of similar parameters can definitely make sense (see Listing 4.7, for example).

The use of digits to form phonetic names is also problematic because they require some familiarization effort, and their meaning is not always obvious to everyone. A deterrent example is `trmn8r` for `terminator` (from *Code Complete*; Microsoft Press, 2004). In this context, the rather common 2 for `to` is the only justifiable exception here, which can often be found as a name component in conversion procedures and can be interpreted easily as in `convert_itf_2_html`, for example.

Tip

You must always keep in mind that the information that a name includes must remain valid. This applies to semantic, but particularly to technical information. If, for example, technical information that is included in a name changes due to a refactoring measure, all relevant names and their users must be adapted. However, this is not an easy task within released interfaces. If in doubt, names that provide incorrect information are worse than names that don't provide any information at all.[16]

Note

Less is often more. The suggestions made indicate how to compose names to include the information that is necessary in a context. They should only be used when the meaning of the name is not completely obvious from the context. For example:

```
METHOD do_something.
  CONSTANTS lcv_maximum_do_loop_count TYPE i VALUE 100.
  DO lcv_maximum_do_loop_count TIMES.
    ...
  ENDDO.
ENDMETHOD.
```

---

16 Programming guidelines are supposed to exist that only propose nondescript names for this reason. Because semantic properties are less likely than technical properties to change in the course of the (further) development, our mainly semantic specifications for naming are also in this sense sufficiently robust toward program changes.

Here, the long name `lcv_maximum_do_loop_count` prejudices the legibility. Because according to Rule 4.23 a method may only include a manageable number of statements, you can select a very simple name in simple cases:

```
METHOD do_something.
  CONSTANTS nmax TYPE i VALUE 100.
  DO nmax TIMES.
    ...
  ENDDO.
ENDMETHOD.
```

Bad Example

Listing 4.6 shows the declaration of a class that executes arithmetic calculations.[17] The names of the class and its methods are unnecessarily short, and the names of the method parameters have no semantic meaning at all.

```
CLASS calcltr DEFINITION.
  PUBLIC SECTION.
    METHODS: add IMPORTING a         TYPE i
                           b         TYPE i
                 RETURNING VALUE(c) TYPE i,
             sub IMPORTING a         TYPE i
                           b         TYPE i
                 RETURNING VALUE(c) TYPE i,
             mul IMPORTING a         TYPE i
                           b         TYPE i
                 RETURNING VALUE(c) TYPE i,
             div IMPORTING a         TYPE i
                           b         TYPE i
                 RETURNING VALUE(c) TYPE f.
ENDCLASS.
```

Listing 4.6 Nondescriptive Names

Good Example

Listing 4.7 shows the same class as Listing 4.6, but the names of the class and its methods are now spelled in full, and the names of the method parameters indicate their semantic meaning.

---

17 You should perceive this as a synthetic example for naming. Of course, in ABAP, it makes absolutely no sense to wrap the arithmetic operations on elementary numeric data types via a class (see Section 5.1.2, Modularization).

```
CLASS calculator DEFINITION.
  PUBLIC SECTION.
    METHODS: add       IMPORTING addend1          TYPE i
                                 addend2          TYPE i
                       RETURNING VALUE(sum)       TYPE i,
             subtract  IMPORTING minuend          TYPE i
                                 subtrahend       TYPE i
                       RETURNING VALUE(difference) TYPE i,
             multiply  IMPORTING factor1          TYPE i
                                 factor2          TYPE i
                       RETURNING VALUE(product)   TYPE i,
             divide    IMPORTING dividend         TYPE i
                                 divisor          TYPE i
                       RETURNING VALUE(quotient)  TYPE f.
ENDCLASS.
```

Listing 4.7 Descriptive Names

Because the operands of addition and multiplication are commutative, you can use digits here to differentiate them.

4.2.3 Names of Repository Objects

Background

Repository objects are development objects that you process using the tools of the ABAP Workbench. Each repository object is assigned to a package. Packages encapsulate the repository objects contained and provide those objects that are supposed to be usable from the outside of the package via package interfaces (see Rule 2.1, Adhere to the SoC Principle).

From the semantic point of view, packages thus represent a context for declarations, which is one level above the contexts of an ABAP program (see Section 4.2.4, Program-Internal Names). Different from the contexts of an ABAP program (programs, classes, procedures), a package doesn't generate a separate namespace.

The namespace for repository objects is defined as follows:

▶ **Prefix namespace**
 Development organizations (SAP departments, SAP partners, and SAP customers) can request a prefix namespace for their own development systems.

- A prefix namespace has a name with at least 5 and a maximum of 10 digits, and the first and the last digit must be a slash, respectively (/ . . . /).

- After the namespace has been assigned, repository objects can be created by prefixing the namespace name / . . . /, but only in systems for which the namespace is enabled. If a package is created in such a prefix namespace, it can only contain repository objects belonging to the same namespace. However, you can create multiple packages within a prefix namespace. The available length of the actual name is reduced by the length of the namespace prefix, including the slashes.

- **Customer namespace**
  If no prefix namespace is available, the names of repository objects that are created in customer systems or non-SAP development systems must have Y or Z as the first character. Then they are within the customer namespace. Repository objects whose names start with a Z can also be located within packages whose names start with Y and vice versa.

- **SAP namespace**
  If no prefix namespace is available, there are no essential restrictions for the names of repository objects that are created in SAP's own development systems. The SAP namespace therefore comprises the entire SAP NetWeaver AS ABAP.

Irrespective of the namespace in which a repository object resides, the name of the repository object is unique in the current SAP NetWeaver AS ABAP, so when you address it, you don't have to make any further specifications. The namespaces (particularly the prefix namespace) were implemented to avoid namespace conflicts during transports between systems and upgrades. For SAP's own development systems, there is a cross-system table that ensures the uniqueness of names within the SAP namespace.

Rule

Rule 4.7: Clarify the Type and Affiliation of Repository Objects in Names
Use the common naming conventions for repository objects. The defined name prefixes, CL_, IF_, and CX_, apply to objects of the class library. If possible, create all repository objects in the prefix namespaces only. Additionally, use a naming convention to clarify a package or component to which the objects belong.

Details

Classes and interfaces are the most critical entities for programming using ABAP Objects (see Rule 3.1, Use ABAP Objects). For typing an object reference, you can use either a class type or an interface type. It has proven useful to uniquely identify each of these two types in the class library by means of a prefix. Global exception classes should also be uniquely identified by a prefix. Therefore, the following naming conventions apply:[18]

- ▶ `CL_` for global classes
- ▶ `IF_` for global interfaces
- ▶ `CX_` for global exception classes
- ▶ `CL_BADI_`, `IF_BADI_`, `CX_BADI_` for classes, interfaces, and exception classes of Business Add-Ins (BAdIs)

Moreover, the names of all repository objects should clarify the package or component they belong to. Because, technically speaking, a package doesn't generate its own namespace, the naming requires strict discipline. The use of prefix namespaces is very helpful already; however, they are not intended for the package level but for bigger development projects, which usually comprise numerous packages.

For this reason, the names of the repository objects contained in a package should be labeled with a common name component that indicates the affiliation to a package or at least to an application component. Because the length of names is restricted to 30 characters or less, and the namespace prefix is contained there, you should usually use an abbreviation for this name component and not the complete package name.

In no case should you assign a generally valid name for a package-specific or component-specific repository object. This would render the name useless for a possible more general use. For example, general names of the SAP namespace such as `CHAR60` for a data element or `CL_ABAP_MATH` for a class should only be declared in absolutely fundamental Basis packages delivered by SAP and exposed by these in a generally available interface.

---

18 Some of these naming conventions are enforced by the Class Builder, while others are only evaluated.

If a developer finds a repository object with a generally valid name, he naturally assumes that he can use it freely pursuant to its name. Prior to the implementation of an operational package concept in Release 7.2, no strict checks existed to observe package boundaries. As a result, repository objects that were wrongly provided with too general names particularly in the SAP namespace but also in the customer namespace are now used across all SAP NetWeaver AS ABAP packages. This can lead to considerable difficulties if you want to implement a real package encapsulation.

Note

Rule 4.7 supplements the general Rule 4.6. With regard to technical information in the names of repository objects, the same applies as stated in Section 4.2.2, Descriptive Names (also refer to the discussion on prefixes and suffixes in Section 4.2.4, Program-Internal Names).

All development organizations are free to create own naming conventions on the basis of Rules 4.6 and 4.7. However, it must be noted that the use of a namespace prefix only leaves little space for the remaining name components. For example, the names of database tables are restricted to 16 characters. Therefore, the namespace prefix should not be too long but should essentially describe a product line using an abbreviation.

Exception

Not all repository objects can be created in prefix namespaces. Examples are authorization objects and type groups.[19] In such cases, you should create an additional package that includes all of these objects. The names of these objects as well as of the package should, if possible, contain a corresponding, normal prefix instead of the real namespace prefix / . . . /.

This similarly applies if areas are further developed that are within the SAP namespace or the customer namespace by tradition. Instead of a real namespace prefix, it can be simulated by uniform prefixes when you create new packages and their development objects.

If the ABAP Workbench itself allocates names, for instance, for Include programs (see Section 4.5, Source Code Organization), which are thus assigned to specific

---

19 You should no longer create new type groups in any case. Also refer to Rule 3.2, Select the Appropriate Program Type.

main programs, such as function groups or class pools, this name allocation always has priority over all rules to ensure the proper functioning of the Workbench and the Compiler.

Example

Figure 4.4 shows some repository objects of the sample application, which was already mentioned in Section 2.1, Separation of Concerns, in the Repository Browser of the Object Navigator of the ABAP Workbench.

As recommended in Section 4.2.2, Descriptive Names, the subpackages of the SABAP_DEMOS_CAR_RENTAL package start with the same name as the superior package and indicate their specialization via a suffix. The same applies to the package interfaces. Instead of a real namespace prefix, the repository objects of the packages have the DEMO_ prefix, which identifies them as a part of a demo package. The affiliation to the car rental application is indicated with the abbreviation CR (car rental).

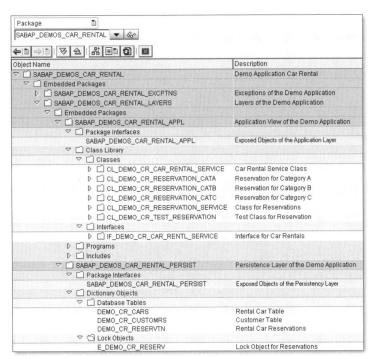

Figure 4.4 Repository Objects of a Package in the SAP Namespace

4.2.4   Program-Internal Names

Background

Program-internal names describe entities that are declared in a program and can be addressed within the program or from other programs. Examples include the names of data types and data objects as well as methods and their parameters.

Program-internal declarations can be implemented in different contexts, which all generate a separate namespace. These contexts are (in the sequence from local to global):

1. Local declarations in a procedure (method, see Rule 6.37, No Implementations in Function Modules and Subroutines)

2. Declarations of instance components and static components in a class

3. Global declarations in the declaration part of a program

Here, local declarations always mask the more global declarations of superordinate contexts. Different declarations generate a separate namespace in their context, with the exception that all components of a class are within one single namespace irrespective of their type.

According to Rule 3.1, Use ABAP Objects, and Rule 3.3, Accept the Standard Settings for Program Attributes, the names that can be used in ABAP programs are always subject to the stricter syntax rules of classes in Unicode programs; that is, they must start with a character followed by further characters and digits that can be separated by underscores.

Rule

Rule 4.8: Prevent Confusion and Unintentional Hidings in Program-Internal Declarations

Select program-internal names in such a way that they do not result in confusion with ABAP words, other declarations, or unintentional hiding of a more global name by a local name. For this purpose, you should identify global entities and the parameters of procedures with a prefix.

Details

In addition to the generally accepted Rule 4.6, Assign Descriptive Names, you must also observe Rule 4.8 for program-internal declarations to avoid confusion by the human reader.[20] Using the following prefixes, you can avoid the risk of both unintentional hiding and confusion:

▶ `g_` for global data objects

▶ `i_` for `IMPORTING` parameters

▶ `e_` for `EXPORTING` parameters

▶ `c_` for `CHANGING` parameters

▶ `r_` for `RETURNING` parameters

Further measures include the use of combined names and of component selectors.

The following sections discuss the different aspects of program-internal naming in detail and with a systematic approach.

Confusion with ABAP Words

One basic rule in almost all naming specifications is that the statements of the language must not be used as names in the source code, provided that this is actually permitted syntactically. The aim of this measure is to increase the legibility by preventing confusion between statements and names. In ABAP, however, it is difficult to adhere to such a rule consistently because the vocabulary of the programming language is very extensive and continuously grows. Normally, a developer doesn't know all ABAP words that occur in all statements and statement additions by heart, and he cannot possibly know which words will be added in future.

For this reason, it is neither useful nor feasible to completely prohibit ABAP words (ABAP keywords or additions) as names. Thanks to the color highlighting in the ABAP Editor and the case difference between operands and ABAP words, which is requested in Rule 4.3, Use the Pretty Printer Consistently and Universally, there is no risk of confusion. If in doubt, you can always use the escape character (!) in front of a name to differentiate it from a identically named ABAP word in the statement.[21]

A single ABAP word, however, usually doesn't represent a descriptive name. So a good programming style is to use ABAP words only within combined names with

---

20 Unlike the human reader, the Compiler usually knows exactly what's behind a name.

21 In some very rare cases, the Compiler cannot differentiate an ABAP word from a identically named name. In these cases, the specification of the escape character (!) is even required.

underscores (_), for instance, `account_class` instead of `class`. Because the underscore is not used in most ABAP words, it is usually a good feature to distinguish between ABAP words and names (see Section 4.2.2, Descriptive Names).

Confusion Between Different Declarations

In classes, all components are within the same namespace. Therefore, there can be no identically named data types and attributes within a class so that no confusions can occur here. In the other contexts, that is, within procedures (methods, see Rule 6.37, No Implementations in Function Modules and Subroutines) or for the global declarations of an ABAP program, different declarations generate different namespaces. There can be identically named data objects and data types, for example. Object types, that is, local classes and interfaces, have the same namespace as data types.

To prevent confusion of the viewer, it is recommended to use different names for different entities, and particularly to not use the name of data types also for data objects. Exceptions from this rule can be cases in which the meaning of a name is absolutely clear, for instance, for the declaration of a helper variable:

```
DATA i TYPE i.
```

Conversely, however, it should never occur that a data object has the name of a data type that is not the type of the object:

```
DATA i     TYPE f.
DATA tadir TYPE trdir.
```

Such declarations are confusing and therefore dangerous!

Hiding of More Global Declarations

The names in local contexts hide identically named declarations in more global contexts. In a method, for example, a data type declared with TYPES hides an identically named data type of the class, this data type then hides the identically named data type of the program, which in turn hides an identically named data type from the ABAP Dictionary.

Developers must ensure that a more global object is not hidden that is supposed to be used in the current context. Conversely, a global object must be prevented from accidentally being used instead of a local object. The reader of a source code section should always know what a name refers to. According to this, when you assign names, you should make sure that the local names do not hide more global names if possible.

In the sense of the KISS principle (see Rule 2.2, Adhere to the KISS Principle), it is recommended that the local names differ from the global names simply because they do not follow their conventions. This mainly refers to the names in global declarations of the current program or in the repository (see Section 4.2.3, Names of Repository Objects). That is, a local class should never start with the `cl_` prefix, a local interface never with `if_` prefix, and a local data object never with the `g_` prefix, for example.

▶ **Within methods**

In a method (in new function modules and subroutines, there should be no local declarations according to Rule 6.37, No Implementations in Function Modules and Subroutines), there is the danger of confusion between local names, including method parameters, and more global names as well as between declarations within the implementation and the method parameters.

A confusion of local data objects in a method with components of their own class can always be excluded by explicitly addressing class components using the name of the class and the class component selector (`=>`) or using the object reference variable `me` and the instance component selector (`->`) .

In particular, in the case of potential confusion with possibly identically named built-in functions, you should address the functional methods of its own class only using one of the selectors if the methods are used in an operand position.[22] This potential confusion only exists for short method names, however. For methods whose names consist of multiple words or that start with the prefixes `set_`, `get_`, or `is_`, there is usually no risk of confusion. Because, according to Rule 4.23, Restrict the Number of Statements in Procedures, methods should always have a manageable size, and all declarations are therefore always visible for the reader, this simple rule should be sufficient for the legibility of a method.

If the declaration of the method's parameter interface is not visible in the method implementation (as in local classes), it makes sense to additionally differentiate between the local data and the method parameters. For this purpose, the prefixes mentioned earlier have established themselves. Another prefix

---

22 If you use selectors too excessively, this can impair the legibility of the source code, which is why you have to make individual assessments here.

component 1 for the local data could also be considered, but it ultimately represents redundant information (also refer to the discussion on prefixes and suffixes in the following Notes section).

▶ **Within classes**
If you use class components, you can always exclude confusion by addressing them using the name of the class and the class component selector (=>) or an object reference variable and the instance component selector (->). The implementation of a corresponding naming convention would lead to redundant information, which would not subserve to the legibility and would be contradictory to the basic KISS principle (see Rule 2.2, Adhere to the KISS Principle). This particularly applies to the functional methods. Although they hide identically named built-in functions, an implementation of a prefix that characterizes a functional method as a method of a class would be very unusual.

▶ **Generally in programs**
You can create local classes and interfaces as well as global data types and data objects in the global declaration part of a program.

▸ For local classes and interfaces, the rule applies that their names do not follow the naming conventions for global classes and interfaces; that is, they must not start with cl_ or if_ in order to not hide any global declarations. As for local data, you can consider a naming convention of lcl_ or lif_, but this would be redundant and not necessarily required because a class or an interface without a prefix is always recognizable as a local class or local interface. The use of lif_ can possibly make sense to distinguish a local interface from a local class.

▸ According to Rule 6.3, Do Not Declare Global Variables, data types should no longer occur in the global declaration part of a program. Global data objects are only required for communication between ABAP and dynpro if classical dynpros are used (see Rule 5.19, Encapsulate Classical Dynpros and Selection Screens). Because they cannot be labeled with a preceding program name like attributes of classes,[23] you must use the already mentioned g_ prefix for global data objects to prevent confusion with local data objects and the attributes of the class in the method implementations. Global data objects can only exist in executable programs, module pools, and function groups. Global classes and interfaces cannot contain any global data objects. So a g_ prefix

---

23 Absolute names are only possible for data types and only in dynamic specifications.

for class components or interface components is the wrong choice in any case (see Appendix B, Automatic Check of Naming Conventions).

Note

For names within the source code, naming conventions are frequently established that set up specifications for the naming, including potential prefixes and suffixes. Such specifications often get bogged down in excessive formalistic strictness, and names created this way include redundant information, are hardly maintainable, and often do not fulfill the top priority of legibility and self-documenting sources. We therefore limited our discussion to the aspects in naming that we consider as essential and universal. Further specifications are only useful at the level of development groups or organizations as stated in Section 4.2.2, Descriptive Names.

Particularly if prefixes and/or suffixes are used, it is common practice to express the technical properties of the described object there. Apart from the fact that we don't consider the specification of technical information in names as necessary anyway (see Section 4.2.2), there are so many technical properties of an object in ABAP that they cannot be mapped through simple rules for short prefixes/suffixes, or combinations of different technical additions often cannot be interpreted uniquely. Here are just a few examples:

▶ With regard to the *data type* of a data object, there are naming conventions (see Appendix B, Automatic Check of Naming Conventions) in which the characters v and c as prefixes stand for variable or constant elementary data objects, respectively, and s and t as prefixes stand for structures and internal tables, respectively. Here, the type property "elementary" is wrongly equated with "variable" or "constant." If the properties "static variable" and "sorted table" are also supposed to be expressed using s, this will very likely result in errors in the name assignment, which will take you further from the goal of legible and self-documenting source codes.

▶ With regard to the *scope* or the *context* of a data object, the naming conventions often stipulate the prefixes g_ and l_ for the names of global and local data objects. We identified g_ for global data objects as the only convention that is actually required for program-internal names. The simultaneous labeling of all nonglobal objects with a prefix l_ for the local validity area, however, is completely redundant and doesn't result in any perceivable benefits. It would be even misleading to label static attributes of classes as global using the prefix g_. They are only valid within the class and therefore have completely different semantics than global data objects. Particularly, their use doesn't indicate a design weakness as it is generally the case for global data objects from today's perspective.

▶ With regard to the *method parameters*, we identified the prefixes i_, e_, c_, and r_ for importing, exporting, changing, and returning parameters as possible distinguishing features from data objects that are declared in the method. Beyond that, no further technical information needs to be expressed through additional prefixes. Particularly for method parameters, technical information in prefixes rather results in confusion than in better legibility. For example, a prefix is_ for *importing structure* would collide with the prefix is_ for truth values (see Section 4.2.2, Descriptive Names), and a prefix it_ for *importing table* can easily be understood as a general abbreviation of *internal table*. If the role the parameter plays cannot be determined from the descriptive name of a parameter and the procedure name, the naming is a complete failure or the procedure doesn't fulfill any clearly defined task. Such a conceptual weakness cannot be fixed even with technical prefixes.

In summary, it is recommended to use name additions rather cautiously, particular those with technical information. Of course, every organization is free to still opt for such conventions, which can supplement our basic rules. Particularly in the ABAP environment with its high versatility of types, many contexts, the differentiation of pass by reference and pass by value, it is probably not an easy task to create a complete, self-contained, consistent, technically correct, and — above all — plain set of rules for prefixes and suffixes. The results that we know are just mere convention, usually incomplete, and partly don't make sense.

Appendix B, Automatic Check of Naming Conventions, describes a Code Inspector check for the naming whose default setting requires technical prefixes. The underlying naming convention is afflicted with all mentioned problems. The fact that the semantic significance of a name cannot be checked automatically doesn't justify the implementation of a technical naming convention that is nontargeted but can be checked easily.

Bad Example

The example shown in Listing 4.8 demonstrates the hiding of names in different contexts. The fact that no descriptive names were selected for the data objects for the sake of simplicity can be disregarded here.

```
DATA a1 TYPE string VALUE `a1 global`.
DATA a2 TYPE string VALUE `a2 global`.
DATA a3 TYPE string VALUE `a3 global`.
DATA a4 TYPE string VALUE `a4 global`.
DATA a5 TYPE string VALUE `a5 global`.

CLASS demo DEFINITION.
  PUBLIC SECTION.
    METHODS main
      IMPORTING a1 TYPE string DEFAULT 'a1 imported'
      RETURNING value(a6) TYPE string.
    CLASS-DATA a1 TYPE string VALUE `a1 class`.
    CLASS-DATA a2 TYPE string VALUE `a2 class`.
    DATA       a3 TYPE string VALUE `a3 class`.
    DATA       a4 TYPE string VALUE `a4 class`.
ENDCLASS.

CLASS demo IMPLEMENTATION.
  METHOD main.
    DATA a3 TYPE string VALUE `a3 local`.
    DATA a4 TYPE string VALUE `a4 local`.
    CONCATENATE a1 demo=>a2 me->a3 a4 a5
      INTO a6 SEPARATED BY `, `.
  ENDMETHOD.
ENDCLASS.
```

Listing 4.8 No Prefixes for Global Data and Method Parameters

If you just consider the implementation of the `main` method in the CONCATENATE statement, it is clearly evident only for the `demo=>a2` and `me->a3` operands that they are attributes of the class and that `a4` is a local data object of the method. Only in the general overview can you see that `a1` describes an importing parameter, `a5` a global data object of the program, and `a6` a returning parameter. The global data objects `a1` to `a4` cannot be addressed in the method at all because they are hidden by local data objects or attributes of the class.

Good Example

In comparison to Listing 4.8, Listing 4.9 now includes the previously discussed prefixes to prevent hidings and to differentiate method parameters from local data objects. Again, descriptive names were not used here to focus on aspects that are essential for this example.

```
DATA g_a1 TYPE string VALUE `g_a1 global`.
DATA g_a2 TYPE string VALUE `g_a2 global`.
DATA g_a3 TYPE string VALUE `g_a3 global`.
DATA g_a4 TYPE string VALUE `g_a4 global`.
DATA g_a5 TYPE string VALUE `g_a5 global`.

CLASS demo DEFINITION.
  PUBLIC SECTION.
    METHODS main
      IMPORTING i_a1 TYPE string DEFAULT 'i_a1 imported'
      RETURNING value(r_a6) TYPE string.
    CLASS-DATA a1 TYPE string VALUE `a1 class`.
    CLASS-DATA a2 TYPE string VALUE `a2 class`.
    DATA       a3 TYPE string VALUE `a3 class`.
    DATA       a4 TYPE string VALUE `a4 class`.
ENDCLASS.

CLASS demo IMPLEMENTATION.
  METHOD main.
    DATA a3 TYPE string VALUE `a3 local`.
    DATA a4 TYPE string VALUE `a4 local`.
    CONCATENATE i_a1 demo=>a2 me->a3 a4 g_a5
      INTO r_a6 SEPARATED BY `, `.
  ENDMETHOD.
ENDCLASS.
```

Listing 4.9 Prefixes for Global Data and Method Parameters

All operands are now clearly recognizable in the CONCATENATE statement. It would be possible to implement a prefix l_ for the local names, but this is unnecessary for two reasons:

▶ The declaration is defined near the usage and is always visible to the reader.

▶ If you consistently use the selectors -> and => to address the attributes of a class, all names without a prefix and without specification of a class or a reference variable can be identified as local data objects.

By means of the minimal naming convention used here, you can address all data objects that are declared in the shown source code section in the method. Of course, the declaration of the global data objects is only implemented to demonstrate the hiding and its prevention. In programs that do not work with classical dynpros, they should no longer be used in accordance with Rule 6.3, Do Not Declare Global Variables.

4.3   Comments

Comments have no influence on the program execution and are dispensable for the computer. For the user who has to work with the source code, however, comments are of paramount importance if they make it easier to understand the code.

There are two types of comments in ABAP:

▶ **Comment lines**
A comment line that contains nothing but a comment can be defined either with the * character in the first position of the program line or with the " character at any position of a program line that is empty on the left.

▶ **Line end comments**
A line end comment is a comment that starts with the " character, which is positioned on the right of an ABAP statement or parts thereof.

Comment lines or line end comments can contain any content and are ignored by the ABAP Compiler when the program is generated.

4.3.1   Selecting the Language

Background

Here, the same applies as was said in Section 4.2.1 on selecting the language for names.

Rule

Rule 4.9: Comment Programs in English

Write all comments in ABAP programs in English only so that as many readers as possible can understand them and benefit from them.

Details

English comments are basic prerequisites for a distributed development at an international level. In addition, there are other good reasons for using English as the comment language:

▶ When Rule 4.5, Use English Names, is adhered to, the statements of an ABAP program can be considered English sentences with a little bit of goodwill. For the reader, English comments are best suited for the source code. If comments were used in another language, this would result in a continuous switching between the languages, which would be exhausting even for readers who can speak the languages used.

▶ Frequently, the unwanted, retelling comments (see Rule 4.10, Comment Meaningfully) are very similar to the described ABAP statements if they are written in English. This way, the author quickly realizes that his comment is superfluous.

Exception

Technical terms that originate from country-specific legislation (such as *Abgeltungssteuer* in German) or specific abbreviations (such as DÜVO) cannot be translated reasonably or can no longer be recognized afterwards. Such terms should be placed in quotation marks and not be translated into English. In this case, you must take into account Rule 6.56, Use 7-Bit ASCII Characters in the Source Code Only, so that country-specific characters must be replaced with 7-bit ASCII characters. The goal of Rule 4.9, Comment Programs in English, is that as many users a possible can follow the program flow. This is still possible if non-IT terms are worded in another language.

Note

This rule is independent of the selection of the original language (see Rule 3.4, Determine Original Language at Project Level).

Bad Example

Listing 4.10 shows a typical example for German comments blended with English terms, which usually don't even follow the required notation or terminology.

```
"Horizontales Splittercontrol im Hilfecontainer
CREATE OBJECT splitter_h
  EXPORTING
    parent  = help_container
    rows    = 1
    columns = 2.

"Vertikales Splittercontrol im linken Container
CREATE OBJECT splitter_v
  EXPORTING
    parent  = container_left
    rows    = 2
    columns = 1.
```

Listing 4.10 German Comments

Good Example

Listing 4.11 shows Listing 4.10, including the English comments as specified in Rule 4.9, Comment Programs in English.

```
"Horizontal splitter control in help container
CREATE OBJECT splitter_h
  EXPORTING
    parent  = help_container
    rows    = 1
    columns = 2.

"Vertical splitter control in left container
CREATE OBJECT splitter_v
  EXPORTING
    parent  = container_left
    rows    = 2
    columns = 1.
```

Listing 4.11 English Comments

The goal of this example is to show the difference between German and English comments. If according to Rule 4.6, Assign Descriptive Names, the name was selected with a higher degree of description, that is, `splitter_horizontal` instead of `splitter_h`, and so on, you could completely do without the comments according to the following Rule 4.10, Comment Meaningfully.

4.3.2 Content

Background

It is usually enough to study the ABAP statements to find out what happens in an implementation. But why something is done is more difficult to find out and frequently tediously reveals only in a much bigger context.

Rule

Rule 4.10: Comment Meaningfully
Comment your implementations in such a way that the comments describe *why* something is done and not *how*.

Details

Ideally, the source code largely documents itself if appropriate names are selected (see Section 4.2, Naming). This is the best way to document the aspect of "what happens in this program section." If this is the case, additional comments that only describe obvious behavior are superfluous and don't contribute to the comprehensibility. There is also the risk that if changes are made to the program logic, the associated comments are not adapted and thus become incorrect. As a result, such comments are not just useless but even misleading and should be avoided from the start.

Conversely, developers often tend to consider their source code as sufficiently self-documenting and leave out the descriptive comments. However, this evaluation is often deceiving, which becomes apparent when an outsider tries to understand the source code (either when he tries to enhance the source code or to identify a problem). Often, even the author of the code faces this problem if he is confronted with source code that he wrote after a longer break.

Even if the names are selected in such a way that a reader can easily retrace what happens, the why is often missing. Therefore, this information must be provided as comments in the source code. This also includes a description of the algorithms used or at least a list of these algorithms.

Tip

This section mainly discusses the commentation of the implementation of functionality. *Header comments* play another role. Such comments, which usually occur as line comments that start with an asterisk (*), subdivide large source codes into meaningful sections and can contain administrative entries. Also for these comments, the rule applies that they should not repeat what is already clearly described in the source code or otherwise. For example, the person who last changed the program or the change date is indicated in the *program attributes*. A header comment with the name of a class or method directly above the class or method is also redundant information. The differentiation of logical program parts, which cannot be indicated in the code, however, makes more sense. For example, you can subdivide the program into a global declaration part and an implementation part.[24]

---

24 Usually, this is only required if the subdivision is not done by include programs; see Section 4.5.1, Source Code Modularization.

Bad Example

Listing 4.12 shows comments whose meaning is obvious due to the commented statements.

```
"Select udat, stime from trdir
"into change_date, change_time
SELECT SINGLE udat stime
       FROM    trdir
       INTO    (change_date, change_time)
       WHERE   name = prog_name.

"Set version_date, version_time to change_date, change_time
IF sy-subrc = 0.
   IF change_date > version_date.
      version_date = change_date.
      version_time = change_time.
   ELSEIF change_date = version_date AND
         change_time > version_time.
    version_time = change_time.
  ENDIF.
ENDIF.
```

Listing 4.12 Superfluous Comments

Good Example

Listing 4.13 replaces the comments of Listing 4.12 with a description of why something happens.

```
"If a newer program exists, version timestamp must
"be adjusted to program timestamp

SELECT SINGLE udat stime
       FROM    trdir
       INTO    (change_date, change_time)
       WHERE   name = prog_name.

IF sy-subrc = 0.
   IF change_date > version_date.
      version_date = change_date.
      version_time = change_time.
   ELSEIF change_date = version_date AND
         change_time > version_time.
    version_time = change_time.
  ENDIF.
ENDIF.
```

Listing 4.13 Descriptive Comment of Why Something Happens

4.3.3   Arrangement in the Source Code

Background

In addition to the comment language and the comment content, the arrangement of the comments also plays an important role for the legibility of a program.

Rule

Rule 4.11: Arrange Comments Correctly

Place comments in front of the statements they describe. The horizontal arrangement of comments should follow the indentations of the source code. Line end comments must only be placed behind declarative or concluding statements.

Details

Vertical Positioning

In general, when users read source code they prefer to first view the comment and then the described statements. With this arrangement, the context of the comment and the associated source code passage becomes clear by intuition.

For control structures, this has the result that comment lines directly in front of a control statement (e.g., IF or WHILE) refer to the associated condition and comment lines after the control statement refer to the associated statement block. Comment lines directly in front of an ELSE or WHEN OTHERS statement are obviously put in the wrong place.

Line End Comments

Line end comments are problematic in conjunction with executable statements. Individual executable program lines are usually not so complex that they would justify a separate comment. But if you still add line end comments, these often are unwanted repetitions of what the statements clearly indicate already (see Rule 4.10, Comment Meaningfully). Moreover, they tend toward cryptic content because the line end does not provide enough space for meaningful comments in most cases. A uniform alignment of such line end comments can only be achieved with a high amount of effort.

For these reasons, you should comment entire blocks of statements. For this purpose, you use self-contained comment lines because it is difficult to express the reference to more than one statement line using line end comments.

Line end comments are suited for the following situations:

▶ To comment declarative statements

▶ To indicate block ends in larger control structures in addition to the indentation

▶ To justify pseudo comments for hiding messages of the extended program check or the Code Inspector directly in the appropriate position (see Figure 3.8).

The pseudo comments for hiding warnings of the extended program check and the Code Inspector (see Section 3.4, Checks for Correctness) play a special role.[25] They are not comments in the traditional sense but program directives that must be in the same lines as the commented statements to take full effect. These pseudo comments are to be replaced by pragmas in the longer term, which is already possible for the extended program check as of Releases 7.0 EhP2 and 7.2.

Indentations

The formatting of source code using indentations is essential for the traceability of its logical structure by a human reader and is required by Rule 4.3, Use the Pretty Printer Consistently and Universally. However, if comments are added in the source code that don't follow this formatting, they hide the logical structure and impair the legibility. Therefore, comment lines must have the same indentation as the statement lines to which they relate.

These indentations can be achieved only using the comments that start with a quotation mark (") because this character can be in any position. For a comment line that starts with an asterisk (*), it must always be in the first position. It is therefore strongly recommended to start all comments within procedures (methods, see Rule 6.37, No Implementations in Function Modules and Subroutines) with a quotation mark and the correct indentation. Comment lines that start with a quotation mark must not be confused with line end comments, which are behind the code.

Comment lines that start with an asterisk should only be used for head comments of classes and procedures, where they help to subdivide a source code into logical sections (see Section 4.3.2, Content). Moreover, they are suitable to temporarily disable statements by commenting them out because the commented-out code clearly distinguishes from real indented comments.

---

25 Before Release 7.0 EhP2, further pseudo comments were required to determine test properties of test classes. As of EhP2, real additions are available for this purpose.

Bad Example

Listing 4.14 shows the implementation part of a class with comments whose positioning doesn't follow the previous rule.

```abap
CLASS application IMPLEMENTATION. "Application class
  METHOD main.                    "Main Method

*    Item data
    DATA items    TYPE STANDARD TABLE
                  OF REF TO item.
    DATA item_ref LIKE LINE OF items.

*    Amount data
    DATA amount       TYPE i.
    DATA total_amount TYPE i.

    ...

* Loop over all items to compute total amount
    LOOP AT items INTO item_ref. "Loop over all items
      IF item_ref IS BOUND AND
         item_ref->is_valid( ) = abap_true. "Check validity
         amount = item_ref->get_amount( ).  "Get amount
        ADD amount TO total_amount. "Add amount to totals
        ...                                 "...
      ELSE.
        ...
      ENDIF.
    ENDLOOP.

    ...

  ENDMETHOD.
ENDCLASS.
```

Listing 4.14 Comments Positioned Disadvantageously

Good Example

Listing 4.15 shows the same implementation part as Listing 4.14, whereas the comments are positioned as recommended. Comment lines that start with an asterisk (*) are used as header comments of the program's structuring. Line end comments only occur behind the declaration and block ends. All other comments are in the comment lines before the described statement and are indented accordingly.

```
*--------------------------------------------------------------*
* Class implementations
*
*--------------------------------------------------------------*

CLASS application IMPLEMENTATION.

*--------------------------------------------------------------*

  METHOD main.

    DATA: items     TYPE STANDARD TABLE
                    OF REF TO item,      "Item table
          item_ref LIKE LINE OF items. "Item reference

    DATA: amount       TYPE i, "Amount per item
          total_amount TYPE i. "Total amount of items

    ...

    "Loop over all items to compute total amount
    LOOP AT items INTO item_ref.
      IF item_ref IS BOUND AND
         item_ref->is_valid( ) = abap_true.
         "Compute total amount for valid items
         amount = item_ref->get_amount( ).
         ADD amount TO total_amount.
         ...
      ELSE.
         ...
      ENDIF. "item_ref IS BOUND AND...
    ENDLOOP.

    ...

  ENDMETHOD. "main
*--------------------------------------------------------------*

ENDCLASS. "application
```

Listing 4.15 Comments Positioned Advantageously

4.4 Program and Procedure Structure

ABAP provides a lot of design freedom with regard to the program and procedure structure. However, you should not fully exploit this freedom to ensure a maintainable product.

4.4.1 Global Declarations of a Program

Background

Each ABAP program has a global declaration part in which you can declare data types, interfaces, classes, and data objects that are visible throughout the program.

From the technical perspective, the global declaration part consists of all declarations that cannot be assigned to a more local context (class, procedure). In particular, all declarations implemented in processing blocks without their own context (in event blocks and dialog modules) and those declared between completed processing blocks are assigned to the global context.[26]

In an ABAP statement, you can only refer to the preceding declarations of the currently visible contexts.

Rule

[⚙] **Rule 4.12: Implement Global Declarations Centrally**

Place the global declaration part of a program coherently and centrally at the beginning of the program.

Details

You should only use the area between the introductory statement of an ABAP program and the first implementation as the global declaration part. Only there should you implement global declarations in a meaningful sequence. This ensures that the declarations intended for the global use can really be used in all subsequent implementations.

In particular, there shouldn't be any declarative statements in contexts that do not support local data (provided that they are still used; see Rule 3.1, Use ABAP Objects). Otherwise, they wrongly give the impression of a local scope when you read the program, which may lead to a wrong understanding of the program.

You only need to deal with this rule explicitly if you work with program types other than class or interface pools. For these, the Class Builder implicitly specifies which declarations occur and where. These are the declarations of the global

---

26 Event blocks of the GET and AT SELECTION-SCREEN events are an exception here. Variables declared here are only valid within the event block.

classes or the global interface itself as well as optional local data types, classes, and interfaces in class pools (in Chapter 5, see Section 5.1.6, Local Types for Global Classes). Developers have no direct access to the main program of a class or interface pool.[27]

For other program types, that is, subroutine pools, function groups, and executable programs (see Rule 3.2, Select the Appropriate Program Type), the developer can access the entire main program. If you work with such program types, you must ensure the adherence to the rule yourself. For this purpose, the *top include* is especially suited for all programs that have an include program organization (see Section 4.5, Source Code Organization). The top include is particularly provided for the global declaration part and is therefore supported by the ABAP Workbench and ABAP Compiler. The ABAP Workbench offers the automatic creation and integration of the top include. The Compiler incorporates the corresponding top include for the syntax check of an individual include program. This way, you can syntactically check individual include programs reasonably.

The top include, if available, should always be the first include program that is incorporated by a main program, and it can contain further INCLUDE statements in turn. The top include and any include programs incorporated there may only contain declarations and no implementations.

If according to Rule 3.1, Use ABAP Objects, you mainly work with ABAP Objects, the global declaration part or the top include essentially only contains declarations of local classes and interfaces provided that Rule 4.12, Implement Global Declarations Centrally, is strictly adhered to. According to Rule 6.2, Declare Data Types and Constants in the Appropriate Context, data types should only be declared within the framework of classes and interfaces or in the ABAP Dictionary. Global data objects are only required for communication with classical dynpros and should therefore only occur in the top include of function groups that encapsulate classical dynpros (see Rule 5.19, Encapsulate Classical Dynpros and Selection Screens).

Exception

Rule 4.12 is mainly justified with the program-internal visibility and validity of declarations. It thus only fully applies to program types other than class pools. In class pools, the visibility from the outside of the class pool and the consequential

---

27 This fact is still valid even after the implementation of the source code-based Class Builder for Release 7.0 EhP2 because it only shows the declaration and implementation of the global class.

dependencies are also important; this is discussed in more detail in Chapter 5, Section 5.1.6, Local Types for Global Classes.

A further exception from Rule 4.12 unfolds if the local classes of a program are relatively independent units and if their implementations don't refer to the declarations of other local classes. In this case, you can list your declaration and implementation parts directly one after the other for legibility purposes.

Bad Example

Listing 4.16 shows a function group for encapsulating a classical dynpro after the expansion of their include programs. The two dialog modules contain data declarations that look like local declarations but have a global scope. Statically, you can only access such a data object below the declaration so that the function module has no access to g_input_field, and the PBO module has no access to g_ok_code.

```
FUNCTION-POOL z_screen.

DATA g_start_value TYPE c LENGTH 20.

FUNCTION z_handle_screen.
*"----------------------------------------------------------
*"*"Local Interface:
*"  IMPORTING
*"     REFERENCE(i_start_value) TYPE csequence OPTIONAL
*"----------------------------------------------------------
  g_start_value = i_start_value.
  CALL SCREEN 100.
ENDFUNCTION.

MODULE status_0100 OUTPUT.
  DATA g_input_field TYPE c LENGTH 20.
  g_input_field = g_start_value.
ENDMODULE.

MODULE user_command_0100 INPUT.
  DATA g_ok_code TYPE sy-ucomm.
  CASE g_ok_code.
    WHEN '...'.
      ...
  ENDCASE.
ENDMODULE.
```

Listing 4.16 Distributed Global Declarations

Good Example

Listing 4.17 shows the function group of Listing 4.16 after the global declarations have been moved to a coherent global declaration part behind the introductory statement.

The additional global data object, g_start_value, is no longer required, and you can access g_ok_code in the PBO module.

```
FUNCTION-POOL z_screen.

DATA: g_input_field TYPE c LENGTH 20,
      g_ok_code     TYPE sy-ucomm.

FUNCTION z_handle_screen.
*"----------------------------------------------------------
*"*"Local Interface:
*"  IMPORTING
*"     REFERENCE(i_start_value) TYPE csequence OPTIONAL
*"----------------------------------------------------------
  g_input_field = i_start_value.
  CALL SCREEN 100.
ENDFUNCTION.

MODULE status_0100 OUTPUT.
  CLEAR g_ok_code.
ENDMODULE.

MODULE user_command_0100 INPUT.
  CASE g_ok_code.
    WHEN '...'.
      ...
  ENDCASE.
ENDMODULE.
```

Listing 4.17 Global Declaration Part at the Beginning of the Program

4.4.2   Local Declarations

Background

You can place local declarations in a procedure (method, see Rule 6.37, No Implementations in Function Modules and Subroutines). These are data types, data objects, and field symbols that are valid in the context of the procedure only. Therefore, they can only be addressed in the code of the procedure and are only available during the execution of the procedure (the data objects declared with STATICS form an exception here).

Procedure-local declarations can be listed at any position of a procedure. However, the position of the declaration doesn't influence the scope of the declared object (which always comprises the entire procedure) but only the static visibility.

Rule

[⚙]

Position the local declarations of a procedure (method, see Rule 6.37, No Implementations in Function Modules and Subroutines) coherently and at the beginning of a procedure. The local declarations must not be distributed across the implementation of the procedure.

Details

Local declarations within a procedure (method, see Rule 6.37, No Implementations in Function Modules and Subroutines) are statically visible starting from the point of the program where they are positioned to the end of the procedure. But because they are valid in the entire procedure, you can dynamically access the declared entities within the entire procedure. The following program example illustrates the different behavior:

```
METHOD demo_method.
  FIELD-SYMBOLS <field_symbol> TYPE any.
  ...
* ASSIGN dobj TO <field_symbol>.      "Syntax error ...
  ASSIGN ('DOBJ') TO <field_symbol>. "No error
  ASSERT <field_symbol> IS ASSIGNED.
  ...
  DATA dobj TYPE i.
ENDMETHOD.
```

Because the different behavior of the dynamic and the static variant of the ASSIGN statement is rather unexpected (refer to Chapter 6, Section 6.6, Dynamic Programming Techniques, for details on dynamic programming), all declarations are supposed to be carried out at the beginning of the procedure, that is, between the introductory and the first executable statement. Then, the static and the dynamic visibility sections match.

This rule contradicts the common recommendations for other programming languages. They recommend declaring local variables as close to their use as possible to restrict their scope tightly. In ABAP, however, there is no block-local validity of local variables. By positioning a declaration within the statement block of a loop, you cannot restrict the scope of this declaration to this statement block. Rather, the variable is valid within the entire procedure. So a declaration at the position where it is used represents a real pitfall for developers or readers of a program who don't know this.

Because according to Rule 4.23, Restrict the Number of Statements in Procedures, the size of a procedure is supposed to be selected in such a way that the procedure remains clear for the reader, there is no good reason why you shouldn't declare all variables as a whole at the beginning of a procedure.

Note

Within processing blocks that do not support any local data (dialog modules and event blocks), you must omit declarative statements completely as specified in Rule 4.12, Implement Global Declarations Centrally.

In function modules and subroutines, there shouldn't be any local data but only a method call according to Rule 6.37, No Implementations in Function Modules and Subroutines.

Bad Example

Listing 4.18 shows a local data declaration in a loop. Readers who are familiar with another programming language or even the developer of the program himself would probably expect that the number variable is set to the value 10 for each loop pass. Effectively, number is set to 10 exactly once when the method starts because the variable is generated only once for the context of the method and provided with a start value.

```
METHOD main.
  ...
  DO 10 TIMES.
    DATA number TYPE i VALUE 10.
    ...
    "number = 11, 13, 16, 20, ...
    number = number + sy-index.
    ...
  ENDDO.
  ...
ENDMETHOD.
```

Listing 4.18 Local Data Declaration in a Loop

Good Example

Listing 4.19 shows the corrected version of Listing 4.18, which behaves as could be expected of Listing 4.18 without any deeper ABAP knowledge. Because there is no block-local scope of data in ABAP, you must proceed as shown in Listing 4.19.

```
METHOD main.
  DATA number TYPE i.
  ...
  DO 10 TIMES.
    number = 10.
    ...
    "number = 11, 12, 13, 14, ...
    number = number + sy-index.
    ...
  ENDDO.
  ...
ENDMETHOD.
```

Listing 4.19 Local Data Declaration at the Beginning of a Procedure

4.5 Source Code Organization

ABAP source code is stored in the ABAP Repository in the central database of SAP NetWeaver as ABAP and not in the source code files like in most other programming environments. Source codes can be subdivided into individual units using include programs. Additionally, there are *macros,* which will be discussed in the section on callable modularization units (see Chapter 6, Section 6.5.9, Macros).

4.5.1 Source Code Modularization

Background

The *include program* is the unit within the ABAP environment that corresponds to a source code file of other environments that can be integrated in another program. Include programs are used for the source code modularization and are incorporated in main programs for this purpose. Include programs are not compilation units; that is, they cannot be compiled independently. However, they can be activated and transported separately. The main programs of include programs (class pools, interface pools, function groups, subroutine pools, and executable programs; see Rule 3.2, Select the Appropriate Program Type) are compilation units for which the content of the specified include program is integrated at the position of an `INCLUDE` statement when they are compiled.

Rule

Rule 4.14: Modularize Source Code Using Include Programs	[⚙]

Distribute the source code of large ABAP programs across multiple include programs, in which you should select the level of detail of the modularization reasonably appropriate to the program structure.

Details

A suitable source code modularization using include programs facilitates the development and maintenance of large programs in different ways:

▸ The ABAP Editor's lock management works at the level of include programs. This way, multiple developers can make changes to a larger program at the same time if the relevant source code passages are located in different include programs.

▸ Include programs are activated separately. Consequently, you can activate individual modifications of a main program independently provided they are in different include programs.

▸ Include programs can be transported separately. This way, you can distribute corrections within a system landscape in a targeted manner without having to transport the entire main program. This minimizes potential conflicts between maintenance levels.

The development environment already prescribes a modularization in different include programs for many main programs. For example, the visibility sections and methods of global classes[28] or the function modules of a function group are each stored in separate include programs. The top include for global declarations, which was already mentioned for Rule 4.12 (Implement Global Declarations Centrally), is also supported by the ABAP Workbench and the ABAP Compiler.

---

28 The source code-based Class Builder that was implemented in Releases 7.0 EhP2 and 7.2 shows the expanded include programs as one single program but continues to store the individual parts separately.

Moreover, you can also implement a manual modularization using include programs if required. In this process, you can partly perform further modularizations of the include programs specified by the Workbench, or you can create include programs for main programs that are not modularized automatically (subroutine pools and executable programs).

For manually created include programs, you must ensure that they contain a logically related part of the source code, which represents a unit that can be maintained and transported independently. However, you should not distribute logically related units, such as individual procedures (methods, see Rule 6.37, No Implementations in Function Modules and Subroutines) or the declaration parts of local classes,[29] across multiple include programs.

The names of manually created include programs should be based on the naming conventions of the ABAP Workbench for automatically generated include programs. They establish a relationship between the include program and the main program and support Rule 4.15, Do Not Use Include Programs Multiple Times.

4.5.2 Multiple Use of Include Programs

Background

From the technical point of view, it is possible to use an include program multiple times by integrating it several times with a main program or different main programs.

Rule

[✿]

> **Rule 4.15: Do Not Use Include Programs Multiple Times**
>
> Use an include program for the modularization of exactly one main program. It must not be integrated with multiple different main programs. Also an include program should only be integrated once within a main program.

---

29 The declaration parts of global classes are automatically distributed across multiple include programs, which is specified by the ABAP Compiler. Such a distribution by the ABAP developer is neither useful nor desirable for local classes.

Details

The multiple use of include programs is highly problematic conceptually. This particularly concerns the use of include programs for the reuse of

▶ Type definitions

▶ Data declarations

▶ Local classes

▶ Procedure implementations

It is strongly recommended to only use suitable means for reuse, such as global classes or interfaces, for the reasons specified in the following sections.

Restricted Maintainability

The integration of an include program with several main programs dramatically restricts the maintainability both of the include program itself and of the main programs using it. Changes to such an include program can be unproblematic in the context of selected main programs but can make other main programs syntactically incorrect at the same time. To that effect, main programs that integrate include programs that were developed in other systems are particularly critical.

Increased Resource Consumption

If main programs that use shared include programs are executed at the same time, these include programs must be loaded multiple times by the ABAP runtime environment, which increases memory consumption. In the past, include programs were used multiple times for the central definition of constants, for example. Today, you should use a global interface or global class for this purpose. Because it is loaded only once, the memory consumption does not increase with every new use as it does for include programs with any multiple use.

The memory consumption also increases if an include program is used multiple times within one main program (e.g., through integration in the source code of multiple function modules of a function group or in the source code of multiple methods of a class) because this bloats the main program unnecessarily. When using centrally defined, standalone types (see Rule 6.1, Use Standalone Data Types) and storing required constants in suitable classes or interfaces, there remains no suitable scenario in which include programs used multiple times within a main program make any sense.

Missing Semantic Context

Like source code files in other programming environments, include programs are integrated with a main program as pure text and without any semantics. The semantics only unfolds in the context of the main program and the position where the include program is integrated. Consequently, especially class definitions that are integrated into different main programs via an include program result in technically different classes whose objects have different reference types and cannot be exchanged between the main programs.

Bad Example

Listing 4.20 shows an include program that contains declarations of constants intended for use in multiple programs. According to Rule 4.15, Do Not Use Include Programs Multiple Times, such an approach is no longer permitted.

```
*&---------------------------------------------*
*&   Include Z_ORDERS_OF_MAGNITUDE
*&---------------------------------------------*

CONSTANTS:
  mega  TYPE p DECIMALS 6 VALUE '1000000.0',
  kilo  TYPE p DECIMALS 6 VALUE    '1000.0',
  milli TYPE p DECIMALS 6 VALUE       '0.001',
  micro TYPE p DECIMALS 6 VALUE '0.000001'.
```

Listing 4.20 Include Program with Reusable Constants

Good Example

Listing 4.21 shows the same declarations of constants as Listing 4.20, but this time, in a global class suitable for reuse. Here, a corresponding ABAP Unit test method would even be possible that checks the consistency of the constants.

```
CLASS zcl_orders_of_magnitude DEFINITION PUBLIC .
  PUBLIC SECTION.
    CONSTANTS:
      mega  TYPE p DECIMALS 6 VALUE '1000000.0',
      kilo  TYPE p DECIMALS 6 VALUE    '1000.0',
      milli TYPE p DECIMALS 6 VALUE       '0.001',
      micro TYPE p DECIMALS 6 VALUE '0.000001'.
ENDCLASS.
```

Listing 4.21 Global Class with Reusable Constants

4.6   Alternative Notations

In ABAP, it is possible to a certain extent to express statements in different notations that the Compiler ultimately interprets identically. For the sake of legibility, you should attach importance to a uniform notation in which some alternatives are used only in specific situations and others not at all.

4.6.1   Alternative Language Constructs in Statements

Background

Alternative language constructs refer to parts of statements that can have different notations. One reason is the continuous further development of the language, which often involves the implementation of new notations, whereas previous notations cannot be prohibited due to downward compatibility.

Rule

Rule 4.16: Use a Clear Notation
If there are different notations for a statement, you must decide on a persistent notation and use it consistently within a development. Here, it is recommended to use the notation that reflects the semantic of the statement most clearly.

Details

To support the legibility and if multiple alternative notations are possible, you should always select the notation that is clearest, can be read most easily, and, if possible, corresponds to the notation of other statements. Examples include the following:

▶ With regard to selecting the relational operators (= or `EQ`, > or `GT`, < or `LT`, >= or `GE`, <= or `LE`), it is recommended to use only one or the other type of operators in the context of a program. The variant with the characters =, <, and > can be considered more up-to-date but also contributes to the overloading of these characters. The logical operators that consist of two characters, by contrast, are a better match for other logical operators, such as `CO`, `CN`, and so on, for which no alternatives exist.

▶ Within logical expressions, you should prefer the `NOT` addition of the `BETWEEN`, `IN`, `IS ASSIGNED`, `IS BOUND`, `IS INITIAL`, and `IS SUPPLIED` predicates to the identically-named logical operator, `NOT` because this increases the legibility. For example, an expression of the `a IS NOT INITIAL` form is easier to understand than the expression, `NOT a IS INITIAL`, which is logically identical. This corresponds to the approach for relational expressions, which are intuitively expressed as `a <> b` and not as `NOT a = b`.

▶ You should prefer the `LENGTH len` addition to the declarative statements, `DATA` and `TYPES`, to the length specification in parentheses (`len`). Then, the notation corresponds to the notation of `CREATE DATA ... LENGTH`. Moreover, the form in parentheses can easily be confused with the dynamic token specifications (in Chapter 6, see Section 6.6, Dynamic Programming Techniques) and should be reserved for these specifications wherever possible.

▶ Within the parameter list of the statements, `EXPORT` and `IMPORT`, you should prefer the equals sign (=) to the additions, `FROM` or `TO`. Then, the notation corresponds to the notation of parameter lists for other calls, such as methods, function modules, and transformations.

▶ You can use the optional addition, `SUBSTRING`, of the statements, `FIND` and `REPLACE`, to obtain a clearer differentiation from the alternative addition, `REGEX`.

▶ Instead of the `LENGTH` addition to the `READ DATASET` statement, you should always use the equivalent addition, `ACTUAL LENGTH`. In doing so, you can differentiate it more clearly from the similar `MAXIMUM LENGTH` addition.[30]

Bad Example

Listing 4.22 shows a nonuniform use of the `FIND` statement within a program. The first and the third `FIND` statement are alternative notations with the same meaning.

```
DATA text TYPE string.
...
FIND '...' IN text.
...
FIND REGEX '...' IN text.
...
FIND SUBSTRING '...' IN text.
...
```

Listing 4.22 Nonuniform Notation in a Program

---

30 The last two examples are typical for extensions of the language by new additions, where the old spelling must be retained as an abbreviation for downward compatibility reasons.

Good Example

Listing 4.23 shows the same statements as Listing 4.22 in a uniform notation whereas the semantic difference between the search for a substring and for a regular expression are expressed syntactically clear.

```
DATA text TYPE string.
...
FIND SUBSTRING '...' IN text.
...
FIND REGEX '...' IN text.
...
FIND SUBSTRING '...' IN text.
...
```

Listing 4.23 Uniform Notation in a Program

4.6.2 Chained Statements

Background

Successive ABAP statements that have the same starting part can be expressed in a *chained statement*. A chained statement consists of the identical starting part that is specified once and that is concluded by a colon (:). Behind this colon, the remaining parts are separated by commas (,). Only the last part is concluded with a period (.). During the syntax check and the compilation, a chained statement is treated like the respective sequence of individual ABAP statements, where the common starting part is put in front of each remaining part. The identical starting parts are not limited to the keyword.

Rule

> **Rule 4.17: Use Chained Statements Only in Appropriate Positions** [✓]
>
> Use chained statements mainly for declarations. They should be used by all means for related declarations of the TYPES BEGIN OF ... TYPES END OF ... type.

Details

The main motivation for the use of chained statements is to increase the legibility of programs. This goal is fulfilled with the correct use in declarations. In other statements, chained statements can decrease the legibility or result in incorrect program behavior in the worst case.

Rule 4.2, One Statement at Most per Program Line, must be adhered to if you use chained statements.

Declarations

For extensive declarations,[31] you can use chained statements to improve the legibility. In particular, you can use multiple chained statements to achieve a grouping of related declarations:

```
DATA:
  airplane             TYPE REF TO cl_airplane,
  airplane_attributes  TYPE cl_airplane->airplane_attributes.

DATA:
  airport              TYPE REF TO cl_airport,
  airport_attributes   TYPE cl_airport=>airport_attributes.
...
```

The grouping of declarative statements that semantically represent a composite statement is even more important. For example, the declaration of structured types and data objects in ABAP is done using individual statements whose close relationship should be expressed by a chained statement:

```
TYPES:
  BEGIN OF file,
    name          TYPE string,
    owner         TYPE sy-uname,
    creation_date TYPE timestamp,
  END OF file.
```

For structures that take in components of another structure using the statements, INCLUDE TYPE or INCLUDE STRUCTURE, this approach cannot be used consistently because the beginning of the statement is different and therefore the chained statement must be interrupted. According to Rule 6.4, Do Not Include Components of Structures, the use of the INCLUDE statement is no longer recommended anyway.

Operational Statements

For operational statements, however, chained statements are not recommended because they usually don't ensure a better legibility (see Rule 4.19, Use Operator Notation, for exceptions). An example is:

---

31 Local declarations that are too extensive, however, indicate a deficient separation of tasks (see Rule 4.23, Restrict the Number of Statements in Procedures) and should therefore not occur.

```
CALL METHOD meth EXPORTING para = : '1', '2', '3'.
```

Here, the exploitation of the fact that the common starting parts in front of the colon common is not limited to the keyword was a little overdone. A chained statement with a better legibility would be:

```
CALL METHOD:
  meth EXPORTING para = '1',
  meth EXPORTING para = '2',
  meth EXPORTING para = '3'.
```

But in this case, the best notation can manage without a chained statement anyway (see Rule 4.18, Formulate Static Method Calls Without CALL METHOD):

```
meth( '1' ).
meth( '2' ).
meth( '3' ).
```

Unexpected Behavior

A wrong understanding of chained statements can easily cause the creation of syntactically correct statements with unexpected behavior. Prominent examples are introductory statements within control structures. Here, the use of chained statements usually doesn't lead to the intended result.

Let's take a look at the following TRY control structure in which the CATCH statements are implemented using a chained statement:

```
TRY.
    ...
  CATCH: cx_1, cx_2, cx_3.
    "exception handling
    ...
ENDTRY.
```

A reader and presumably the developer of these lines would assume that this is a CATCH block that handles three exceptions. But, in fact, the complete syntax is as follows:

```
TRY.
    ...
  CATCH cx_1.
  CATCH cx_2.
  CATCH cx_3.
    "exception handling
```

```
   ...
ENDTRY.
```

Although the cx_1 and cx_2 exceptions are caught, the corresponding CATCH blocks are empty. Only the third exception cx_3 has a CATCH block that is not empty. The syntax that the developer presumably intended is as follows:

```
TRY.
   ...
  CATCH cx_1 cx_2 cx_3.
    "exception handling
   ...
ENDTRY.
```

For the WHEN blocks within a CASE control structure, the similar facts apply:

```
WHEN: a, b, c.
```

This is not equivalent to the more probable

```
WHEN a OR b OR c.32
```

Another example in which the use of chained statements can easily become a trap is an Open SQL statement. Let's take a look at two examples:

▶ The following chained statement expands to two SELECT statements that both supply a work area with values and of which only the second one has a WHERE condition:

```
SELECT SINGLE carrid connid
       FROM spfli
       INTO: carrid_wa, connid_wa
       WHERE carrid = '...'.
```

Certainly, the following INTO clause was meant here:

```
INTO (carrid_wa, connid_wa).
```

---

32 As of Releases 7.0 EhP2 and 7.2, the extended program check (see Rule 3.7, Use the Extended Program Check) warns against empty statement blocks after CATCH and WHEN. This way, you can detect the incorrect use of chained statements within TRY and CASE control structures using the extended program check.

▶ In the following example, the seemingly single statement does not update the discount *and* the telephone number of the customer with the customer ID 00017777. Instead, these are two statements of which the first changes the discount for *all* customers and the second changes the telephone number of the customer with the customer ID 00017777.

```
UPDATE scustom SET:  discount  = '003',
                     telephone = '0621/444444'
             WHERE id          = '00017777'.
```

Even if the previous examples of the chained statements would show the semantic that is expected by the developer, such a use is not recommended in any case because each reader would probably expect a different program behavior, and the legibility and maintainability of the source code would be impaired considerably.

4.6.3 Method Calls

Background

Static calls of methods can be formulated in two different ways. The long form

```
CALL METHOD meth EXPORTING ...
```

is based on the notation of the function module call. Alternatively, you can use a short form

```
meth( ... ).
```

which uses a parenthesis notation instead of the introductory ABAP words, CALL METHOD. You can also use a combination of CALL METHOD and parentheses.

Rule

Rule 4.18: Formulate Static Method Calls Without CALL METHOD
Use the long form of the method call using CALL METHOD only for dynamic method calls.

Details

The short form of the static method call is clearer. The redundant ABAP words, CALL METHOD, provide no additional information to the reader. Using the short form, self-contained method calls have the same appearance as functional method calls on operand positions.

For dynamic method calls,[33] the long form with CALL METHOD is syntactically necessary. If it is only used there, the different notations provide another distinguishing feature between the static and dynamic method call.

Bad Example

Listing 4.24 shows the long form of a static method call using CALL METHOD, which is no longer recommended.

```
...
CALL METHOD cl_class=>do_something
    EXPORTING
        some_input  = value1
    IMPORTING
        some_output = value2
    CHANGING
        some_change = value3.
...
```

Listing 4.24 Long Form of the Static Method Call

Listing 4.25 shows the same static method call as Listing 4.24, in which parentheses are inserted additionally. In this form, which is also syntactically correct, either CALL METHOD or the parentheses are superfluous.

```
...
CALL METHOD cl_class=>do_something(
    EXPORTING
        some_input  = value1
    IMPORTING
        some_output = value2
    CHANGING
        some_change = value3 ).
...
```

Listing 4.25 Long Form of the Static Method Call with Parentheses

Good Example

Listing 4.26 shows the same method call as Listing 4.25 but without CALL METHOD as recommended. If a method has only importing parameters, you can omit the

---

33 See the program example for the dynamic method call in Rule 6.47, Avoid Runtime Errors During Dynamic Processing.

EXPORTING addition. If it is a single importing parameter, you can also omit its name.

```
...
cl_class=>do_something(
    EXPORTING
        some_input  = value1
    IMPORTING
        some_output = value2
    CHANGING
        some_change = value3 ).
...
```

Listing 4.26 Short Form of the Static Method Call

4.6.4   Assignments and Calculations

Background

For assignments and some arithmetic calculations, in addition to the operator notation there are also own ABAP keywords available:

▶ You can implement assignments using the assignment operators =, ?=, or alternatively using the keyword MOVE in combination with TO or ?TO.

▶ You can perform the basic arithmetic operations like all other calculations using an arithmetic expression or alternatively using one of the keywords, ADD, SUBTRACT, MULTIPLY, and DIVIDE.

Chapter 6, Section 6.2, Assignments, Calculations, and Other Accesses to Data, provides further information on assignments and calculations.

Rule

> **Rule 4.19: Use Operator Notation**
>
> Use the operator notation with the equals sign (=) instead of notation with ABAP keywords for assignments and calculations.

Details

Frequently, assignments or calculations, including the MOVE, ADD, SUBTRACT, MULTIPLY, and DIVIDE statements, are more difficult to read than the corresponding expression in the operator notation. Other calculations, except for the basic arithmetic operations, cannot be expressed in own ABAP keywords anyway.

Exception

The statement notation allows for the use of chained statements (see Rule 4.17, Use Chained Statements Only in Appropriate Positions), which can be useful in these exceptional cases:

```
ADD increment TO: sum_individual,
                  sum_total.
```

For calculation operations of the form, $a = a + 1$, in which the target variable and one of the operands are identical, the use of the ADD, SUBTRACT, and so on statements enables a clearer overview, which is particularly obvious if the name of the target variable is relatively long:

```
SUBTRACT 1 FROM reference->structured_attribute-component.
```

Here, the user can directly see that the value of the specified variable is reduced by one. In the operator notation, this is possibly not the case if it is not immediately clear that the target variable and one of the operands are identical. In these cases, you can and should deviate from Rule 4.19, Use Operator Notation, and the specifications of Section 4.6.2, Chained Statements. The legibility of the source code has top priority.

Bad Example

Listing 4.27 shows the downcast of an interface reference variable to a class reference variable with the keyword MOVE.

```
DATA: cref TYPE REF TO cl_class,
      iref TYPE REF TO if_interface.
...
MOVE iref ?TO cref.
```

Listing 4.27 Downcast with ABAP Keyword

Good Example

Listing 4.28 shows the same example as Listing 4.27 in the recommended operator notation.

```
DATA: cref TYPE REF TO cl_class,
      iref TYPE REF TO if_interface.
...
cref ?= iref.
```

Listing 4.28 Downcast in Operator Notation

4.6.5 Calculation Expressions

Background

Calculation expressions are

- Arithmetic expressions
- Bit expressions
- Character string expressions (as of Releases 7.0 EhP2 and 7.2)

You can execute calculation expressions at suitable operand positions or on the right side of the equals sign of the COMPUTE statement. The specification of the COMPUTE keyword is optional.

Rule

> **Rule 4.20: Omit the COMPUTE Keyword**
>
> Omit the specification of the COMPUTE keyword whenever a calculation expression is used on the right side of the equals sign (=).

Details

To improve the legibility of a program, you should preferably use the notation of the COMPUTE statement without the COMPUTE keyword itself. In this notation, the specification of the calculation expression on the right side of the equals sign doesn't differ from the specification at any other operand position. Moreover, the literal meaning of the COMPUTE keyword, which originates from a time when there were only arithmetic expressions, isn't particularly suited for character string expressions.

If no calculation expression is specified on the right side of the equals sign (=) of the COMPUTE statement except for a single data object, this is not a complete calculation expression. No calculation with a calculation type takes place but only a simple assignment. In this case, you should not use the COMPUTE keyword by any means so that the reader doesn't expect any conversion into a calculation type.

Exception

The COMPUTE keyword must be specified if the EXACT addition, which is possible as of Releases 7.0 EhP2 und 7.2, is supposed to be specified; this addition results in an exception if a rounding occurs in a calculation with decimal floating point numbers. This has no disadvantage because the COMPUTE EXACT expression can absolutely be considered a special statement that is supposed to stand out in the source code. The same applies to the MOVE EXACT statement, which is also new.

Bad Example

Listing 4.29 shows a simple assignment and a character string expression on the right side of COMPUTE, including the specification of the COMPUTE keyword whose literal sense is not suitable here, however.

```
COMPUTE result = dobj.
COMPUTE result = text1 && condense( text2 ).
```

Listing 4.29 Character String Expression with COMPUTE

Good Example

Listing 4.30 shows the same example as Listing 4.29 without the superfluous COM-PUTE statement.

```
result = dobj.
result = text1 && condense( text2 ).
```

Listing 4.30 Character String Expression Without COMPUTE

4.7   Complexity

Similar to the previous sections of this chapter, the goal of program complexity is to keep the legibility of the source code as simple as possible for the human reader. The computer has no problem compiling or executing highly complex programs, nor does unformatted source code constitute any problem. The human reader, however, is usually overextended with the high program complexity.

High complexity in this sense expresses itself, for example, in voluminous procedures (methods, see Rule 6.37, No Implementations in Function Modules and Subroutines) and control structures with a very deep nesting or confusing classes without clearly defined tasks. The program complexity must not be confused with the complexity of the task to be mastered by the program. Even in case of a high task complexity, it is always possible to keep the program complexity within the individual procedures and classes manageable by clearly separating the tasks (see Rule 2.1, Adhere to the SoC Principle).

To understand a program, the reader must trace the flow mentally and keep an eye on the different paths through the program that result from the control structure under different external conditions. For voluminous procedures or deep nesting, this is highly difficult. In this case, the author of the program may have been equally overextended, and the program could therefore be erroneous. In any case, this increases the time required for corrections or further developments as well as the risk that errors are made here. What makes the situation even more difficult is that complex procedures can only be tested with a great deal of effort due to the high number of possible execution paths. Formulating a test case for every single execution path is often impossible due to the high number.

4.7.1 Expressions

Background

An expression is part of an ABAP statement that returns a result. An expression consists of one or more operands in combination with operators or special ABAP words. Possible expressions are logical expressions and calculation expressions. The latter, in turn, are subdivided into arithmetic expressions, bit expressions, and character string expressions (as of Releases 7.0 EhP2 and 7.2). You can use data objects, appropriate other expressions, and calls of built-in functions and functional methods as operands of expressions. In character string processing, regular expressions for searches and pattern comparisons are also used.

As of Releases 7.0 EhP2 and 7.2, you can nest the expressions mentioned and combine them in many different ways. Nested and chained calls are possible for functional methods as of these releases. The maximum nesting depth of expressions is restricted to 32 by the ABAP Compiler.

Rule

Rule 4.21: Limit the Complexity of Expressions

Use expressions at operand positions in such a way that a program remains legible and comprehendible.

Details

The possibilities for expressions, which were highly extended for Releases 7.0 EhP2 and 7.2, make the use of helper variables superfluous at many points. The use of expressions and functional calls at operand positions is useful under the following prerequisites:

▶ The result of an expression or a calculation is required only once. If an intermediate result is required multiple times, it should be calculated only once and saved in a helper variable.[34]

▶ The data type of the result matches the operand position or the conversion rules for an expression or call used at an operand position are suitable for the task to be implemented. If special type conversions must be performed, for instance, for date or time fields, you possibly require helper variables of an appropriate type.

Here, you must always keep an eye on the legibility of a program. You should never be too ambitious and combine everything that's possible into one single expression. If an expression becomes too complex, it should be split at suitable points, and the intermediate results should be saved in helper variables. This particularly applies to the character string processing with character string templates (as of Releases 7.0 EhP2 and 7.2) and to regular expressions, which are very powerful on the one hand but can also make a program illegible quickly on the other hand. Comments can also help to describe the functionality of a complex expression (see Section 4.3, Comments).

Bad Example

Listing 4.31 shows an arithmetic expression in a logical expression in a loop. The same total must be recalculated for each loop pass.

```
LOOP AT itab ASSIGNING <wa>.
  IF oref->meth( <wa> ) < sy-tabix * ( offset + length ).
    ...
  ENDIF.
ENDLOOP.
```

Listing 4.31 Repeated Execution of a Calculation in a Loop

Good Example

Listing 4.32 has the same functionality as Listing 4.31. However, the total is only calculated once before the loop.

```
limit = offset + length.
LOOP AT itab ASSIGNING <wa>.
  IF oref->meth( <wa> ) < sy-tabix * limit.
```

---

34 Currently, the ABAP Compiler does not assume this task implicitly.

```
      . . .
    ENDIF.
  ENDLOOP.
```

Listing 4.32 One-Time Execution of a Calculation Before a Loop

4.7.2 Nesting Depth

Background

The nesting depth is the number of statement blocks that are nested due to the use of control structures (branches, loops). We discuss the nesting depth at the level of a procedure (method, see Rule 6.37, No Implementations in Function Modules and Subroutines). According to Rule 6.44, No Implementations in Dialog Modules and Event Blocks, implementations may not occur at other points.

The maximum nesting depth is restricted to 256 by the ABAP Compiler.

Rule

Rule 4.22: Restrict the Nesting Depth of Control Structures

Restrict the maximum nesting depth within a procedure (method, see Rule 6.37, No Implementations in Function Modules and Subroutines) to five levels.

Details

In addition to the number of executable statements (see Section 4.7.3, Procedure Volume), the control structures of a procedure (method, see Rule 6.37, No Implementations in Function Modules and Subroutines) are also decisive for their clarity and traceability. Nested branches and loops (IF, CASE, DO, WHILE, LOOP statements, etc.) become less clear and more difficult to trace with every nesting level. For this reason, the nesting depth must be restricted within a procedure, for example, by moving functionality to other procedures.

A maximum nesting depth of five levels is considered tolerable. A deeper nesting requires a great deal of effort to trace the program flow based on the source code. This would considerably constrain the maintenance and further development.

Note

The use of modern language elements can help to restrict the maximum nesting depth. This is the case if a statement or a built-in function replaces an entire control structure, for instance, for REPLACE with the ALL OCCURRENCES addition or for the numerical extremum functions, nmax( ) and nmin( ), to determine the maximum or minimum value (as of Releases 7.0 EhP2 and 7.2). The former replaces a loop, the latter an IF control structure.

Example

The transition from Listing 3.3 to Listing 3.4 in Chapter 3, ABAP-Specific Basic Rules, shows how you can reduce the nesting depth by using modern language elements. Figure 2.3 in Chapter 2, General Basic Rules, shows a general example.

4.7.3 Procedure Volume

Background

The procedure volume is the number of executable ABAP statements in a procedure (method, see Rule 6.37, No Implementations in Function Modules and Subroutines). In theory, the upper limit of this number is indefinite and is only limited by the maximum program size that still fits into the current program memory.

Rule

> **Rule 4.23: Restrict the Number of Statements in Procedures**
>
> Restrict the number of executable ABAP statements of a procedure (method, see Rule 6.37) to a manageable size. For this purpose, the recommended reference value is a maximum of 150 executable statements per procedure.

Details

Very voluminous procedures (methods, see Rule 6.37) generally feature a complex decision structure, usually have a lot of procedure parameters, and work with a multitude of local data. Such procedures, which often don't assume a clearly defined single task, are difficult to understand and therefore particularly prone to errors. You should prefer multiple smaller procedures with narrow parameter interfaces[35] and closely defined tasks, respectively.

The number of executable statements is a simple measure for the complexity of a procedure. In this sense, all statements that aren't declarations and don't define

---

35 In this context, the ideal parameter interface has just a few input parameters and only one return value (see Section 6.5.2, Type of the Formal Parameters of Procedures).

processing blocks are considered an executable statement. Concretely, this corresponds to the statements at which the program execution can be stopped in the Debugger.[36]

Note

The recommendation to not write procedures that are too large should not lead to the other extreme, that is, to many and very small procedures. True to the motto "modularize instead of atomize," procedures should have a reasonable size that is consistent with the ABAP programming language (see Rule 5.2, Modularize Instead of Atomize).

Exception

Strictly linear code, for instance, the programmatic filling of a table with single values, cannot be subdivided reasonably into multiple procedures. In these cases, a restriction of the number of statements doesn't make sense.

Example

For a general example, see Figure 2.3 in Chapter 2, General Basic Rules.

4.7.4   Class Size

Background

The class size is the number of components (attributes, methods, events) of a class. The ABAP Compiler predefines a maximum number of 65,536 components, whereas the total memory consumption by static attributes, instance attributes, and constants is restricted to 500KB each.[37]

Rule

Rule 4.24: Maintain Reasonable Class Sizes
Ensure that classes and interfaces do not contain an excessively high number of attributes, methods, and events. The components contained must be specific for a class and must not fulfill tasks that are too versatile. The same applies to function groups.

---

36 Exceptions are procedure-closing statements, such as ENDMETHOD, at which you can stop in the Debugger; however, these are not considered as executable statements.

37 In case of deep data objects (tables, strings, and data references) only the fixed size of the reference, not the variable size of the referenced data object, counts.

Details

Complexity not only happens at the level of procedure implementations. The number of procedures to be considered and the data processed by these procedures are also essential for the traceability of source code.

A class, an interface, or, where required, a function group[38] should not be mistaken as a container for any functionality. It is rather the abstraction of a certain subject or an object from real life. Particularly, the modularization of a complex problem in objects with a manageable size facilitates the understanding of the code. For this purpose, the classes and interfaces must be designed accordingly and must each cover a manageable and easily comprehensible functionality.

If a class or an interface includes a high number of attributes and methods, this is obviously not the case. The same applies to the number of function modules of a function group (with regard to the use of function groups, see Rule 3.1, Use ABAP Objects). Voluminous classes, interfaces, and function groups either offer too heterogeneous functionality or, conversely, are highly specialized, which restricts their reusability unnecessarily.

In addition to the high complexity, which decreases the maintainability of voluminous classes and function groups, you must consider another technical aspect: Already when you use just a small part of the functionality offered, this results in the loading of the entire class or function group into the program memory, which negatively impacts the memory utilization.

Note

According to Rule 4.23, Restrict the Number of Statements in Procedures, you should preferably use multiple procedures that are not too large and have clearly defined tasks instead of a few, large procedures. Apart from that, classes should not contain too many methods (see Rule 4.24, Maintain Reasonable Class Sizes). Nevertheless, these two rules are not contradictory provided that the procedures do not become too small and are grouped sensibly into different classes with a clearly defined task field. In this process, very specialized classes can be created that don't require any global visibility.

---

38 Here, function groups play the same role as abstract final classes of which you cannot generate instances. The function modules correspond to static public methods, and the global data corresponds to private static attributes.

Functionality that is only required within a global class, function group, or any other program, should therefore be encapsulated in *local classes*. (According to Rule 3.1, Use ABAP Objects, the complete functionality of function groups, subroutine pools, and executable programs should be implemented in local classes anyway.) An example for such a self-contained functionality is the display logic for classical dynpros within a function group (see Rule 5.19, Encapsulate Classical Dynpros and Selection Screens). A sensible reuse of classes that call the dynpros of the function group is not possible outside the function group. Therefore, local classes are the preferred elements for that task.

Such an approach also makes sense for global classes. By moving highly specialized functionality to smaller, local classes, you reduce the number of methods of the global class, which improves the clarity and simplifies the maintainability of the class. When you use local classes within global classes, you must ensure a suitable positioning to avoid unnecessary dependencies (see Rule 5.6, Position Local Declarations Appropriately).

4.7.5 Dead Code

Background

Dead code involves program parts that are never executed because they are not yet or no longer required or have never been actually required. Such code can accumulate in the development (rejected prototypes) or maintenance (changeover to new code without deleting the old code) of programs.

Rule

Rule 4.25: Remove Dead Code

Remove any unused or inaccessible program parts completely from live programs.

Details

Although dead code doesn't affect the executed program parts directly, it is still damaging for the product. Program parts that cannot be accessed during program execution do not provide any benefit but result in increased costs in the course of a program's lifecycle because they must be identified as unused in the maintenance and further development. In the worst case, they are also adapted during further developments or refactoring measures with a possibly high degree of effort if they are not immediately recognized as unused without any doubt. Moreover, they unnecessarily increase the space requirement in the program buffer during the program execution.

Ultimately, dead code also interferes with the goal of a very high test coverage by module tests using ABAP Unit or scenario tests using eCATT (see Section 2.3, Correctness and Quality). Code that is not used in the live system is either tested laboriously or is not tested and thus results in poor test coverage putatively. Unused and inaccessible program parts must therefore be identified and removed in time.

Note

If recognizable, test tools (see Section 3.4, Checks for Correctness) indicate dead code. Examples include the following:

► The syntax check provides warnings about unused private methods of local classes.

► The extended program check provides warnings for unused declarations or statement blocks in control structures that can never be reached.

Such static checks, however, can never be complete because not every use of a program part has to be recognizable statically. Therefore, the Coverage Analyzer is another important tool to isolate candidates for dead code.

"I call architecture frozen music."
—Johann Wolfgang von Goethe

5   Architecture

The guidelines of this chapter specify the use of the ABAP programming language and do not represent any general guidelines on the architecture or the programming model of ABAP application programs on SAP NetWeaver Application Server ABAP. Therefore, this chapter only discusses selected architecture aspects that are closely linked with the use of certain ABAP language elements.

5.1   Object-Oriented Programming

An optimal object-oriented design is not an easy task nor is it the subject of this chapter. It is definitely worthwhile to consult the relevant literature for this purpose. Particularly the book *Design Patterns* (Addison-Wesley, 1995) provides numerous suggestions for ABAP developers. This chapter is limited to some basic recommendations that are suitable to increase the comprehensibility and maintainability of source code as well as some ABAP specifics in the work with global and local classes.

Developers who have the relevant experience in the area of object-oriented development in other programming languages should be aware of the differences between ABAP Objects and Java, for example:

▶ In Java, all superior data objects, particularly container variables such as strings, are modeled using classes. ABAP, by contrast, provides very powerful, built-in types. In addition to the built-in ABAP strings, you are also provided with internal tables (see Figure 6.4) that are used for the structured storage of data and represent the most powerful ABAP type. For this reason, the implementation of own container types via ABAP classes generally doesn't make sense.

▶ Through optimizations and JIT compilation, Java reaches a high processing speed for methods. In ABAP, however, the high processing speed is primarily attained through some very powerful and complex individual statements. This is another reason why the implementation of own container classes is usually not useful because the direct access to an appropriate internal table is always faster than custom access logic written in ABAP, for example.

Of course, you can transfer algorithms and the rough class structure from an application that was written in another object-oriented programming language to ABAP. However, the more the depth increases, the bigger the differences become. For this reason, you need to make appropriate adaptations to transfer a detailed design of another language successfully to ABAP Objects.

5.1.1 Encapsulation

Background

A program that is created based on the procedural programming model and that includes many procedures and global variables is usually difficult to understand because the numerous possible interdependencies via these publicly accessible variables and procedures are difficult to comprehend. The solution that the object-oriented approach provides particularly for this problem includes visibility sections that are not public. Here, the reader can restrict to the public interfaces of the classes involved when he tries to obtain an overview of the software's functioning. The nonpublic visibility sections only contain details of the implementation that are not important for a view from the outside.

Of course, this clear overview benefit is only implemented in places where the developer makes use of the nonpublic visibility sections. The same applies to the nonpublic object generation and final classes for which it becomes clear immediately whether objects can also be generated outside of the class or whether derived classes can exist.

For the development or the design of an application, it is useful to encapsulate as restrictive as possible initially and to undo the encapsulation only where required.

Rule

[✓] **Rule 5.1: Utilize the Encapsulation Options as Much as Possible**

Utilize the encapsulation options provided in the form of nonpublic visibility sections, nonpublic object generation, and final classes as much as possible. The use of units that are encapsulated in such a way should preferably be free of side effects.

Details

This simple rule provides practical access to object-oriented programming that results in programs that are more robust and better maintainable than if you use procedural ABAP — even without an extended object-oriented design phase. For an appropriate encapsulation you should

- Keep the number of public components of a class as small as possible (components, which may be private, protected, or package-visible — as of Release 7.2 — should therefore be created in the corresponding visibility section)

- Declare public attributes only as READ-ONLY.

- Consider the private instantiation of classes.

- Mark classes that are not intended as superclasses as FINAL (see Section 5.1.4, Inheritance).

Conversely, within an encapsulated unit, that is, within a class, you should avoid accessing more global data directly. Within methods, you should generally modify attributes of the class only. Write access to global data outside the class is not recommended. If at all, such accesses should only be done using specially marked methods. The use of methods of a class is not supposed to evoke any side effects outside the class itself.

Note

As of Release 7.2, an additional package visibility section (PACKAGE SECTION) is available that makes the components of a class visible to the members of the same package. Consequently, the public visibility section (PUBLIC SECTION) should only be used for components that are supposed to be visible outside the package in which the class resides.[1]

5.1.2 Modularization

Background

The programming model that was mainly propagated before the implementation of ABAP Objects is called *structured programming*:

---

1 Irrespective of whether access should also be from outside the package, you can integrate interfaces in the PUBLIC SECTION only. For classes that implement interfaces, the PACKAGE SECTION does not represent a replacement for the PUBLIC SECTION.

▸ Here, the programs are split into procedures expediently.

▸ Sequences, branches, and loops are the only control structures permitted.

The implementation of object-oriented programming languages, such as ABAP Objects, doesn't make structured programming obsolete. The object-oriented programming is based on the structured programming and extends and supplements it.

With regard to ABAP, you must observe that ABAP is still a programming language of the fourth generation (4GL)[2] that has been developed especially for the application programming in the SAP environment, that is, for the mass data processing in business applications. Therefore, ABAP includes more language elements than an elementary programming language in which the more complex functionality is usually implemented in libraries. This ranges from simple statements for the string processing, which are provided as methods of string classes in other object-oriented languages such as Java, to the processing of complex mass data objects, such as internal tables, to very complex statements for operating interfaces such as Open SQL or for calling data transformations (XML), for which other languages have entire class hierarchies.

As already mentioned at the beginning of Section 5.1, Object-Oriented Programming, the performance of the ABAP language is therefore optimized mainly with regard to the execution of its complex statements for mass data processing and less with regard to the individual method call.

Rule

[⚙] **Rule 5.2: Modularize Instead of Atomize**

Modularize your program in classes so that the individual methods don't cover trivial functionality. Methods that consist of only one or just a few statements should be an exception in ABAP and not the rule.

Details

According to Rule 3.1, Use ABAP Objects, you are supposed to use only methods of ABAP Objects for the implementation of functionality, for many good reasons. But ABAP remains ABAP, and the good reasons that argue for a well-structured

---

2 A programming language of the fourth generation is designed to implement applications for a specific application area as efficiently as possible.

program haven't lapsed with the introduction of ABAP Objects. Instead, the ABAP language elements, which have proven themselves in many application cases, are still valid today, and are continuously further developed, are supposed to be used in their present form also in ABAP Objects.

An already well-structured classical ABAP program, for instance, a function group that fulfills a specific task and is modularized via subroutines, should therefore be transferable to a class without any major changes to the implementation, whereby it is provided with all further benefits of ABAP Objects.

However, the modularization at the level of a few single statements is and will remain untypical for ABAP. On the one hand, this has performance reasons because the costs for the call of the method must remain low in comparison to the costs for executing the implementation. For example, instead of providing the `get_attribute` methods, which are typical for other object-oriented languages and only set their return value to the value of an `attribute` attribute, you should use public `READ-ONLY` attributes in ABAP.[3] On the other hand, virtually all nonfundamental statements[4] of ABAP already play the same role that the methods of system classes assume in other programming languages. The use of such a statement corresponds to a method call so to speak, and another wrapping is usually not necessary.

Also, for legibility and maintainability reasons, a method with a reasonable size (see Rule 4.23, Restrict the Number of Statements in Procedures) would be preferable to splitting into atomic units, that is, into methods with only one or two statements.

Exception

Procedures that encapsulate nothing but the call of another procedure form an exception here. A single procedure call represents the implementation of an entire procedure. This particularly applies to function modules and subroutines, which may only be created in exceptional cases anyway (see Rule 3.1, Use ABAP Objects). They are supposed to include exactly one method call (see Rule 6.37, No Implementations in Function Modules and Subroutines), which delegates the implemen-

---

3 If the read access to an attribute is linked with further actions, for example, authorization checks, `get_attribute` methods are appropriate, of course.

4 This includes all language elements that don't have any equivalent in an elementary language like Java.

tation to ABAP Objects. Here, the gain in security through the stricter checks in ABAP Objects outweighs the disadvantages of very short procedures.

Bad Example

Listing 5.1 shows the rudimentary implementation of a string class in ABAP Objects. The methods of this class each contain only a single statement. A user must generate objects of the class and call the methods to handle the strings.

```
CLASS cl_string DEFINITION PUBLIC.
  PUBLIC SECTION.
    METHODS:
      constructor IMPORTING value       TYPE string OPTIONAL,
      set_string  IMPORTING value       TYPE string,
      get_string  RETURNING VALUE(value) TYPE string,
      shift_left  IMPORTING places      TYPE i,
      shift_right IMPORTING places      TYPE i,
      ...
  PRIVATE SECTION.
    DATA string TYPE string.
ENDCLASS.

CLASS cl_string IMPLEMENTATION.
  METHOD constructor.
    string = value.
  ENDMETHOD.
  METHOD set_string.
    string = value.
  ENDMETHOD.
  METHOD get_string.
    value = string.
  ENDMETHOD.
  METHOD shift_left.
    SHIFT string LEFT BY places PLACES.
  ENDMETHOD.
  METHOD shift_right.
    SHIFT string RIGHT BY places PLACES.
  ENDMETHOD.
  ...
ENDCLASS.

...

CLASS application IMPLEMENTATION.
```

```
  ...
  METHOD do_something.
    DATA string TYPE REF TO cl_string.
    CREATE OBJECT string EXPORTING value = 'abcde'.
    ...
    string->shift_left( ... ).
    ...
  ENDMETHOD.
  ...
ENDCLASS.
```

Listing 5.1 Unnecessary String Class with Atomic Methods

Good Example

Listing 5.2 shows the ABAP-typical handling of strings. A method directly declares a data object of the string type and directly uses the corresponding ABAP statements for processing.

```
CLASS application IMPLEMENTATION.
  ...
  METHOD do_something.
    DATA string TYPE string.
    ...
    SHIFT string LEFT BY ... PLACES.
    ...
  ENDMETHOD.
  ...
ENDCLASS.
```

Listing 5.2 Direct Use of ABAP Statements

As of Releases 7.0 EhP2 and 7.2, there is a corresponding built-in function for almost every string processing statement. They can also be used in operand positions so that another reason for the encapsulation of statements in methods is omitted. The SHIFT LEFT statement in this example can be replaced as follows, whereas shift_left is a built-in function:

```
string = shift_left( val = string places = ... ).
```

5.1.3 Static Classes and Singletons

Background

The classes of ABAP Objects support two types of components:

- Instance components, that is, instance attributes, instance events, and instance methods. You can address the instance components of a class only via instances of the class (objects).

- Static components, that is, static attributes, static events, and static methods. The static components of a class can be addressed not only using an object but also using the name of the class, so it can be used independent of an instance of the class.

A class that only contains static components and no instance components is referred to as a static class. When used, a global static class is loaded with its class pool like any ABAP program into the current internal session once and cannot be deleted from it explicitly. The static methods (which are declared via CLASS-METHODS) of a class cannot be redefined in subclasses.

A singleton is a design pattern in which the class assumes the responsibility of object generation and ensures that only exactly one object exists per internal session, which is provided to the users. You can find a detailed description of this topic in *Design Patterns* (Addison-Wesley, 1995).

Rule

[⚡] **Rule 5.3: Do Not Use Static Classes**

Preferably use objects instead of static classes. If you don't want to have a multiple instantiation, you can use singletons.

Details

If no real object-oriented design exists that, for example, would use the multiple instantiation of classes, the adherence to Rule 3.1, Use ABAP Objects, often results in the definition of classes that only contain static methods (declared using CLASS-METHODS). These methods are then used as simple procedures.

But even if a multiple instantiation is not wanted explicitly, you should prefer object creation to the use of static classes for the reasons listed in the following. You can use the *singleton design pattern* to prevent the multiple instantiation:

- The explicit object creation is essential for object-oriented programming. Static classes, however, are implicitly loaded the first time they are used, and the corresponding static constructor — if available — is executed. They remain in the memory as long as the current internal session exists. Therefore, if you use static classes, you cannot actually control the time of initialization and have no option to release the memory occupied by the attributes again as soon as the class function is no longer required.

▸ Another important argument that speaks against the use of static classes is the limited functionality of the static constructor in comparison to an instance constructor. A static constructor has no parameter interface and cannot propagate any exceptions (see Section 5.2, Error Handling), which is why you cannot always respond appropriately to an error situation in the static constructor, and this results in a runtime error in extreme cases. However, the exceptions of an instance constructor can be handled.

▸ By using static classes, you spoil your polymorphism options, which are actually provided by object-oriented programming. On the one hand, you cannot redefine static methods; on the other hand, there is no access via reference variables, the other "pillar" of polymorphism. However, it is beneficial to keep the option of polymorphism open:

  ▸ Even if you initially don't plan to overwrite the behavior of a method later on using inheritance or redefinition, this request frequently arises in the course of the further development.

  ▸ To implement module tests with ABAP Unit, it is often unavoidable to redefine the behavior of certain methods to resolve problematic dependencies, for instance, within the framework of the technique, *Subclass and Override Method* (see *Working Effectively with Legacy Code*; Prentice Hall, 2007).

To keep the option of redefinition open, you should always use instance methods instead of static methods.

As of Releases 7.0 EhP2 and 7.2, you can express the provision of a singleton object and the subsequent call of an instance method in the very compact form of a *chained method call*:

```
cl_singleton=>get_instance( )->do_something( ).
```

Because an additional object reference variable and an additional factory call are omitted, any aesthetic disadvantages in the use of a singleton design pattern are also omitted.

Exception

Classes that only cover trivial functionality can still be implemented as static classes. Here, you must precisely assess whether one of the aspects mentioned previously has any effect. The necessity for a class constructor can be an indicator. As soon as a static class requires a nontrivial class constructor to provide the desired functionality, you should use objects instead.

Bad Example

Listing 5.3 shows a static class with solely static methods as well as the use of one of these methods. In general, it is not directly obvious from the source code whether the method call also results in the call of the static constructor or whether it has already been executed earlier, for instance, as a result of a simple attribute access.

```
CLASS static_class DEFINITION.
  PUBLIC SECTION.
    CLASS-METHODS: class_constructor,
                   meth1,
                   meth2,
                   ...
ENDCLASS.

...
static_class=>meth1( ).
...
```

Listing 5.3 Static Class and Its Use

Good Example

Listing 5.4 shows an implementation of the singleton design pattern in which a static method enables the access to the only object of the class.

```
CLASS singleton_class DEFINITION CREATE PRIVATE.
  PUBLIC SECTION.
    CLASS-METHODS get_instance
     RETURNING VALUE(r_instance) TYPE REF TO singleton_class
     RAISING cx_some_failure.
    METHODS constructor
     RAISING cx_some_failure.
    METHODS: meth1,
             meth2.
             ...
```

```
  PRIVATE SECTION.
    CLASS-DATA instance TYPE REF TO singleton_class.
ENDCLASS.

CLASS singleton_class IMPLEMENTATION.
  METHOD get_instance.
    IF instance IS NOT BOUND.
      CREATE OBJECT instance.
    ENDIF.
    r_instance = instance.
  ENDMETHOD.
  ...
ENDCLASS.

...
  TRY.
      singleton_class=>get_instance( )->meth1( ).
    CATCH cx_some_failure.
      ...
  ENDTRY.
```

Listing 5.4 Singleton and Its Use

In Listing 5.4, the `get_instance` method is used to return the object reference to the object that is created with the first call. So this example seemingly breaks Rule 5.2, Modularize Instead of Atomize, according to which no methods are supposed to be created in ABAP that only return the value of an attribute. However, this objection is not justified here because the main task of the `get_instance` method is to enable the object user to control the time of object creation. Only then can the user respond to any exceptional situation during the object creation as usual.

In special cases in which the object creation is carried out unparameterized and is always successful, you can dispense the `get_instance` method and publish the object reference using a `READ-ONLY` attribute. Because the object is then created within the static constructor,[5] this approach is still afflicted with some of the described problems of the static classes.

---

5 The singleton variant, in which the object is created in the static constructor, is also referred to as eager singleton. While in other programming languages the static attribute of the eager singleton is usually private and therefore a `get`-method exists for this static attribute, in ABAP, this is not required as a `READ-ONLY` attribute can be used. The variant, in which the object is created in the `get`-method, is referred to as lazy singleton.

5.1.4 Inheritance

Background

Inheritance is referred to as the derivation of subclasses of a superclass, whereas the subclass adopts the components of the superclass. A subclass can be specialized by the declaration of new components and the redefinition of instance methods. ABAP Objects supports the single inheritance in which a class can have multiple subclasses but only one direct superclass.[6] This results in an inheritance hierarchy in the form of an inheritance tree in which a unique path leads from each subclass to the root class. In ABAP Objects, all classes are subclasses of the built-in abstract root class, `object`. Final classes, that is, classes that are defined with the `FINAL` addition, conclude a path of the inheritance tree at the bottom.

Rule

Rule 5.4: Avoid Deep Inheritance Hierarchies
Avoid deep inheritance hierarchies because they can easily become a maintenance problem.

Details

In the positive sense, deep inheritance hierarchies express successfully implemented reuse. However, they often turn out to be a maintenance problem because they are inherently complex due to the large number of classes involved:

▶ The behavior of classes at the bottom end of the inheritance hierarchy is difficult to retrace because they potentially inherit a lot of methods.

▶ Classes with many subclasses have a major influence on the overall system, which makes it difficult to calculate the effects of changes in a superclass.

▶ A large number of subclasses can also indicate an unsuitable abstraction.

To avoid the unwanted reuse of own classes through inheritance, it is advisable to conclude paths of inheritance trees with final classes. As of Release 7.2, you can also use the new operational package concept to avoid unwanted inheritance

---

6 In connection with the corresponding orthogonal concept of interfaces, something similar to a multiple inheritance is created, at least with regard to attributes and method declarations. Method implementations, however, are not inherited by integrating an interface.

outside your own package. This way, you can keep the option of inheritance open within selected packages but disallow the derivation by outsiders.

Note

If you want to use the options of polymorphism, interfaces are the less complicated solution in comparison to inheritance. Particularly if you just want to reuse interfaces (in the original sense of the word), you should preferably use interfaces as object types instead of abstract classes. Here, you can also form compound interfaces. Due to the single inheritance, the interface concept offers the only way to create such compound interfaces for classes in ABAP.

5.1.5 Class References and Interface References

Background

Interface components in objects can be addressed both using a class reference variable and an interface reference variable. When you use a class reference variable for the access, the interface component is addressed using the name of the interface and the interface component selector (~). If a suitable interface reference variable is used for the access, the component is addressed directly using its name.

Rule

Rule 5.5: Access Interface Components Using an Interface Reference Variable
Access the interface components from outside of a class only using a corresponding interface reference variable and not using the interface component selector (~).

Details

The external access to interface components using an interface reference variable results in easier-to-understand code because it is clearer that the user of the class is interested in this particular aspect that is provided by the interface. The access using a class reference variable by contrast also suggests that such components are used that are not available via an interface.

Generally, the interface component selector is supposed to be used only within classes and interfaces to address the interfaces that are integrated there. If an interface component of an integrated interface is supposed to be available as a separate component, you can declare an alias name using ALIASES.

Bad Example

Listing 5.5 shows the call of an interface method using a class reference variable and the interface component selector (~), which is not recommended according to Rule 5.5, Access Interface Components Using an Interface Reference Variable.

```
CLASS cl_class DEFINITION PUBLIC.
  PUBLIC SECTION.
    INTERFACES if_intf.
  ...
ENDCLASS.

...

    DATA cref TYPE REF TO cl_class.
    ...
    cref->if_intf~meth( ).
    ...
```

Listing 5.5 Access from Outside Using an Interface Component Selector

Good Example

Listing 5.6 shows the method call from Listing 5.5 using an interface reference variable. In contrast to `cref->if_intf~meth`, `iref->meth` expresses that components of a class are accessed that are hierarchically on the same level as all public components but reside in a different part of the public interface.

```
CLASS cl_class DEFINITION PUBLIC.
  PUBLIC SECTION.
    INTERFACES if_intf.
  ...
ENDCLASS.

...

    DATA iref TYPE REF TO if_intf.
    ...
    iref->meth( ).
    ...
```

Listing 5.6 Access from Outside Using an Interface Reference Variable

5.1.6 Local Types for Global Classes

Background

Within class pools, like in virtually any other ABAP program, you can define data types, local interfaces, and local classes to ensure a better structure of the implementation of the global class. From a technical point of view, these optional declaration parts together with the declaration part of the global class form the global declaration part of the class pool (in Chapter 4, see Section 4.4.1, Global Declarations of a Program).

These local declarations of a class pool are invisible outside the class pool and can therefore only be used in the private visibility section (PRIVATE SECTION) of the declarations of the global class or within their method implementations. These two usage types have different technical visibility requirements because friends of a global class have access to its private visibility section. Local type declarations that are used in the PRIVATE SECTION must therefore be accessible for any possible friends of the class, whereas those type declarations that are only used within the method implementations are completely meaningless for other classes.

In general, local classes consist of the declaration part and the associated method implementations. The latter are invisible to the friends of the global class and have thus technically the same visibility requirements as local type declarations that are only used within the implementation.

You create local data types, interfaces, and classes within a class pool using the LOCAL DEFINITIONS/IMPLEMENTATIONS function of the Class Builder, which stores such declaration and implementation parts in the include programs provided for this purpose. Here, it is distinguished between the two areas, LOCAL DEFINITIONS/ IMPLEMENTATIONS and CLASS RELEVANT LOCAL DEFINITIONS, to meet the different technical visibility requirements mentioned previously.

Rule

Rule 5.6: Position Local Declarations Appropriately [⚙]

Position the local declarations of a class pool at appropriate positions depending on the requirements. Types that are only used within the implementation of the global class need to be in a different position than types that are also addressed in the PRIVATE SECTION of the global class.

Details

From the perspective of a class pool, you can store all local type definitions and the associated implementations of the local classes in the CLASS RELEVANT LOCAL DEFINITIONS area. However, such an approach is disadvantageous from the dependency management perspective. Only for changes to the local type declarations of a class pool, which are used in the PRIVATE SECTION of the global class, dependent classes (subclasses and friends of the global class) have to be invalidated and regenerated. But in reality, this invalidation occurs for all changes in the CLASS RELEVANT LOCAL DEFINITIONS area. For this reason, you are provided with the additional area, LOCAL DEFINITIONS/IMPLEMENTATIONS, which is intended for local type declarations, which are only used within the class implementation of the global class, and for the implementation part of local classes. If this area is changed, dependent classes are not invalidated.

To prevent unnecessary new generations of other classes, which are based on unwanted technical dependencies, after changes have been made to the global class, you must therefore define the *class-local types* in the Class Builder at the appropriate positions:

▶ Select GOTO • LOCAL DEFINITIONS/IMPLEMENTATIONS • LOCAL DEFINITIONS/ IMPLEMENTATIONS to declare such types that are only used within the method implementations of the global class.[7] The local classes should be implemented here as well.

▶ If you select GOTO • LOCAL DEFINITIONS/IMPLEMENTATIONS • CLASS RELEVANT LOCAL DEFINITIONS, the system takes you to the types, which you can also refer to in the PRIVATE SECTION.

Declaration and implementation of a local class are only supposed to be distributed across the areas, LOCAL DEFINITIONS/IMPLEMENTATIONS and CLASS RELEVANT LOCAL DEFINITIONS, if they are to be referred to in the PRIVATE SECTION. However, if the local class is only used within the implementation of the global class, both the declaration and the implementation are to be carried out in the CLASS RELEVANT LOCAL DEFINITIONS/IMPLEMENTATIONS area.

---

7 This particularly applies to local test classes that are defined for production classes. These can never be referenced from a production code per se and should therefore never be defined in the CLASS RELEVANT LOCAL DEFINITIONS area. As of Release 7.0, there is a separate area, LOCAL TEST CLASSES, available for this purpose. In older releases, LOCAL IMPLEMENTATIONS is the appropriate location both for the declaration and for the implementation of local test classes.

Note

The rule specified here specializes the general Rule 4.12, Implement Global Declarations Centrally, with regard to class pools. They are especially oriented toward the external call of methods of their respective global class and are therefore particularly integrated within a dependency network. For this reason, Rule 4.12 cannot apply to its full extent.

5.1.7   Instance Constructor

Background

When you define an ABAP class, you specify who may create an instance of this class or who may access the instance constructor of the class. For this purpose, the CREATE addition is provided for the CLASS ... DEFINITION statement. The CREATE PUBLIC addition is the default setting and allows for the instancing by any user of the class. By specifying CREATE PROTECTED, you can restrict the object creation to the class itself and its subclasses. With the CREATE PRIVATE addition, objects can only be created via the class itself.[8] The CREATE PACKAGE addition restricts the object creation to the users within the same package (as of Release 7.2).[9]

From a technical point of view, the instance constructor can be declared (using the METHODS constructor statement) in all visibility sections, which are more general or equal to the instantiation specified in the CREATE addition of the CLASS ... DEFINITION statement. But the actual visibility is controlled by the CREATE addition.

Rule

Rule 5.7: Declare the Instance Constructor in the Public Visibility Section
Always declare the instance constructor of a global class in its public visibility section and independent of the instantiation that was specified by the CREATE addition in the class definition.

[✿]

---

8 The restriction of the object creation to the class itself is useful in connection with the singleton design pattern, for example, where the class itself performs the object creation (see Section 5.1.3, Static Classes and Singletons).

9 This is only possible for classes that simultaneously open their protected visibility section for objects of the same package using the OPEN FOR PACKAGE addition.

Details

The components of global ABAP classes are stored separately according to the visibility section they belong to. Depending on the usage type of the class, only parts of the class are considered by the ABAP Compiler during compilation. This procedure requires that the constructor of a global class is always declared in the public visibility section of the class. For these technical reasons, the instance constructor of a global class is always supposed to be declared in the public visibility section (`PUBLIC SECTION`). If it is declared in another visibility section, in individual cases, this may result in unjustified syntax errors when global classes are used.

Exception

The technical restrictions mentioned only apply to the processing of global classes. Within local classes, the instance constructor can also be defined in other visibility sections. But this positioning should correspond with the visibility section specified using the `CREATE` addition. Such a strategy enables you to use types for the parameter interface of the instance constructor of a local class that are only accessible in a restricted visibility section.

5.2   Error Handling

During the program execution, you must always expect the occurrence of error situations. They can occur in the form of

▸ Internal errors due to erroneous implementations or improper use of the underlying services

▸ External errors due to wrong inputs by the user or unexpected resource bottlenecks

In ABAP, several options are available to react to such error situations.

5.2.1   Reaction to Error Situations

Background

ABAP provides the following concepts that a program can use to properly react to different error situations:

▶ **Exceptions**

Exceptions are events during the execution of an ABAP program in which the program flow is stopped because a logical continuation of the program is not possible. Exceptions are raised either by the ABAP runtime environment or with ABAP statements (`RAISE EXCEPTION`) in the program. The exception handling enables a reaction to such events. An exception that is not handled results in a runtime error; that is, the program terminates and outputs a short dump that describes the exception.

▶ **Assertions**

Assertions formulate conditions in a program that must be met to ensure a proper continuation of the program. Assertions are defined using the `ASSERT` statement.

▶ **Messages**

Messages are texts that can contain up to four placeholders for value replacements and that can be displayed using the `MESSAGE` statement or sent otherwise.

These three concepts either involve the handling of the error situations by the program or the user (exceptions or error messages) or result in a controlled program termination (assertions or exit messages).

Rule

Rule 5.8: Select a Proper Reaction to Error Situations	[✓]
Select the appropriate concept of error handling (exception, assertion, or message) for the respective error situation so that the error can either be handled adequately in the further course of the program or that the program is terminated in a controlled manner.

Details

For each error situation, you should deliberately decide on one of the three concepts for error handling:

▶ Exceptions are used in all unexpected situations that the programmer doesn't have under control. These include, for example, invalid parameter values during the procedure call or unavailable external resources, such as files (see Section 5.2.2, Classical and Class-Based Exceptions).

▶ Assertions are used to detect inconsistent program states that necessitate an immediate program termination (see Section 5.2.9, Assertions).

▶ Messages are used only as dialog messages for error dialogs within the scope of classical dynpro processing (if still in use). A program termination in situations in which a logical program execution is no longer possible should be implemented using assertions instead of termination or exit messages (see Section 5.2.10, Messages).

The MESSAGE statement is not only used to display dialog messages in a classical dynpro but can also be deployed to terminate a program in a controlled manner or raise classical exceptions in the MESSAGE ... RAISING variant if the appropriate message type is selected. This invites you to combine the different concepts, which may lead to problems. This can be traced to the old programming model that was only driven by classical dynpros in which an error situation directly required the output of a message to the user.

For contemporary programming that takes the separation of concerns (SoC) into account (see Rule 2.1, Adhere to the SoC Principle), the question whether a message must be sent to the user due to an error situation can usually only be answered in a higher software layer. The layer in which such an error situation occurs must therefore react with an exception initially, which in turn represents a new situation for a higher layer to which it can react with a dialog message or any other error message.

The following sections describe the options for error handling and their corresponding rules in more detail.

5.2.2 Classical and Class-Based Exceptions

Background

For reasons of downward compatibility, there are two options to define treatable exceptions yourself in ABAP:

▶ **Classical exceptions**
These exceptions can only be declared in the interfaces of methods or function modules using EXCEPTIONS and can be raised within such a procedure using the RAISE or MESSAGE RAISING statements. The calling program of the procedure can use the EXCEPTIONS addition of the CALL METHOD[10] or CALL FUNCTION state-

---

[10] The use of the EXCEPTIONS addition does not require the long form of the method call and therefore is not opposed to the adherence of Rule 4.18, Formulate Static Method Calls Without CALL METHOD.

ments to assign return values for the `sy-subrc` system field to the exceptions that it wants to handle and evaluate this field after the call.

▶ **Class-based exceptions**
These exceptions are defined by exception classes of which the system may[11] generate an exception object when an exception is raised. A class-based exception can either cancel the current context or allow for a resume (since Releases 7.0 EhP2 and 7.2). Raising is carried out using the RAISE EXCEPTION statement, and handling occurs using CATCH in a TRY control structure. Class-based exceptions can be raised in any procedures and can be further propagated by any procedures.

The coexistence of the two exception concepts is specified as follows:

▶ You cannot declare classical and class-based exceptions together in the interface of a procedure. Within a processing block, you can raise either classical or class-based exceptions only.

▶ For reasons of interoperability, within a processing block, you can both handle class-based exceptions and evaluate the return values of function modules and methods using classical exceptions.

Rule

Rule 5.9: Use Class-Based Exceptions
Only raise class-based exceptions in new procedures provided that you can dispense classical exceptions from the technical point of view.

Details

Self-defined classical exceptions are little more than return values. If you raise a classical exception in a procedure using the RAISE statement, the `sy-subrc` system field is set according to the raised exception after the return to the calling program. By querying `sy-subrc`, the calling program must always check itself whether an exception occurred and react to it if required, for example, by appropriate handling or explicit forwarding to the own calling program (by raising a separate equivalent exception). This doesn't add to the clarity of the program.

---

11 If a handler uses the INTO addition for CATCH.

The occurrence of class-based exceptions, however, results in a change of the program flow. They can be handled either directly or be propagated upwards along the call hierarchy. This way, not every procedure (method, see Rule 6.37, No Implementations in Function Modules and Subroutines) must consider every possible exception situation. This supports the SoC within an application (see Rule 2.1, Adhere to the SoC Principle). Because the exception can be represented by an object of an exception class, this exception object can gather additional information on the exception situation and transport it to the handler. In contrast to classical exceptions, this can also include specific exception texts (see Section 5.2.4, Exception Texts).

By default, raising an exception stops the entire current context even if the exception is handled. But there can be situations, for instance, a mass data processing, in which a single error doesn't justify the cancellation of an entire service. For these cases, you can raise and propagate class-based exceptions as RESUMABLE as of Releases 7.0 EhP2 and 7.2. A handler can decide whether a service is canceled completely or — for example, after a corresponding log entry has been written — is resumed using the RESUME statement.

Class-based exceptions completely replace the classical exceptions for new code (of course, there are exceptions from this rule) and extend it by the resumability. Although classical exceptions on the raiser side are completely obsolete from a technical point of view, you must still consider the following for older code: Even if you have the raiser side under control, you cannot simply change older procedures over to class-based exceptions because then you would have to adapt all usage locations.[12]

When you call existing procedures that use classical exceptions, you must certainly handle them in the new code. In this case, it is recommended to map the classical exceptions to equivalent class-based exceptions using RAISE EXCEPTION. This way, you achieve a class-based error handling that is holistic to the outside. The exception situation can then be forwarded to higher call layers without each layer having to react to this situation explicitly.

---

12 In fact, such a changeover is only possible if the use of an interface is restricted to the repository objects of one or a few packages. However, the effective use of such an encapsulation is only possible in the operational package concept as of Release 7.2.

Exception

Prior to Release 7.2, class-based exceptions are not supported in Remote-enabled Function Modules (RFM). In releases prior to 7.2, you must continue to use and handle classical exceptions in the Remote Function Call (RFC). As of Release 7.2, RFMs can raise class-based exceptions, and these can be handled in the TRY control structures when the RFC interface is called (the EXCEPTIONS addition then controls which handling is implemented). Release 7.2 is therefore the first release that no longer imposes any technical restrictions preventing a consistent use of class-based exceptions in new ABAP code.

Bad Example

Listing 5.7 shows the declaration and the raising of a classical exception in a method as well as their handling via the evaluation of sy-subrc after a call of the method. This procedure infringes Rule 5.9, Use Class-Based Exceptions.

```
CLASS application DEFINITION.
  PUBLIC SECTION.
    METHODS do_something
      EXCEPTIONS application_error.
ENDCLASS.

CLASS application IMPLEMENTATION.
  METHOD do_something.
    ...
    RAISE application_error.
    ...
  ENDMETHOD.
ENDCLASS.

DATA oref TYPE REF TO application.
oref->do_something(
  EXCEPTIONS application_error = 4 ).
IF sy-subrc <> 0.
  ...
ENDIF.
```

Listing 5.7 Classical Exception

Good Example

Listing 5.8 shows the definition of an exception class, its declaration in a method interface, and the raising inside of a method as well as its handling using CATCH after the call of the method in a TRY block.

```
CLASS cx_application_error DEFINITION
  INHERITING FROM cx_static_check.
ENDCLASS.

CLASS application DEFINITION.
  PUBLIC SECTION.
    METHODS do_something
      RAISING cx_application_error.
ENDCLASS.

CLASS application IMPLEMENTATION.
  METHOD do_something.

    ...

    RAISE EXCEPTION TYPE cx_application_error.

    ...

  ENDMETHOD.
ENDCLASS.

DATA oref TYPE REF TO application.
TRY.
    oref->do_something( ).
  CATCH cx_application_error.

    ...

ENDTRY.
```

Listing 5.8 Class-Based Exception

This plain example doesn't necessarily indicate the big advantage of class-based exceptions over classical exceptions. But it clearly shows in nested procedure calls and the handling of exceptions that were raised in more distant call levels.

5.2.3 Exception Categories

Background

Each class-based exception belongs to one of the three different exception categories that each specify whether the exceptions must be declared in procedure interfaces. From a technical point of view, an inheritance relationship determines to which exception category an exception belongs. All exception classes are subclasses of the following abstract global classes, which in turn inherit from CX_ROOT:

▶ CX_STATIC_CHECK

Exceptions of this category must be declared explicitly in the parameter interface of a procedure if they are supposed to be propagated from it. The syntax check statically checks whether all of the exceptions that may be raised in the procedure using RAISE EXCEPTION or that are declared in the interfaces of called procedures are either handled with CATCH or declared explicitly in the parameter interface.

▶ CX_DYNAMIC_CHECK

Exceptions of this category must also be declared explicitly in the parameter interface of a procedure so that they can be propagated. This is not checked statically by the syntax check but dynamically at runtime.

▶ CX_NO_CHECK

Exceptions of this category must not be declared explicitly in the parameter interface of the procedure. The CX_NO_CHECK class and thus its subclasses are always declared implicitly, and the corresponding exceptions are always propagated.

Rule

Rule 5.10: Use the Appropriate Exception Category	[✓]

When you create and raise class-based exceptions you must use an exception category that is appropriate to the error situation:

▶ CX_STATIC_CHECK for the static safeguarding of the exception handling

▶ CX_DYNAMIC_CHECK for error situations that can be prevented by preconditions

▶ CX_NO_CHECK for situations that cannot be handled directly

Details

The individual exception categories are intended for the following error situations:

▶ As a general rule, exceptions that occur in a procedure must either be handled there or be declared in the procedure interface to tell the calling program which exceptions are to be expected. Exceptions of the CX_STATIC_CHECK category are syntactically checked with this regard. Therefore, this category is justified whenever a procedure (method, see Rule 6.37, No Implementations in Function Modules and Subroutines) is to be forced to handle an exception or at least forward it explicitly. But if an exception can be prevented reliably using previous checks, exceptions of the CX_DYNAMIC_CHECK category should be preferred.

▸ If the program logic can exclude potential error situations, the related exceptions do not have to be handled or declared in the parameter interface. This is the case, for example, if it is explicitly checked before a division that the denominator does not equal zero. For this case, you can and should use exceptions of the CX_DYNAMIC_CHECK category. These exceptions only need to be handled or declared if their occurrence cannot be excluded otherwise. In a well-modeled application, the exceptions are usually prevented in the program using corresponding conditions, and the CX_DYNAMIC_CHECK category should be the most frequent exception category.

▸ The CX_NO_CHECK category is designed for exception situations that can occur virtually at any time and cannot or are not supposed to be handled directly. Otherwise, you would have to catch or declare all exceptions that can occur with resource bottlenecks. This would have the result that these exceptions must be specified in almost every parameter interface, which would make programs confusing rather quickly.

Note

The resumability of a class-based exception is not a property of the exception class but is specified with the RESUMABLE addition of the RAISE EXCEPTION statement (as of Releases 7.0 EhP2 and 7.2) when the exception is raised. The property can get lost for exceptions of the categories, CX_STATIC_CHECK and CX_DYNAMIC_CHECK, during propagating if they are not declared with RESUMABLE there. For CX_NO_CHECK, the resumability is always retained implicitly.

5.2.4 Exception Texts

Background

Every global exception class has a predefined exception text with the same name as the exception class. In the Class Builder in the Texts tab, you can edit the predefined text and define further exception texts. The exception texts of an exception class can be created either with reference to messages (see Section 5.2.10, Messages) or as texts in the Online Text Repository (OTR).

For each exception text, the Class Builder creates a static constant in the exception class, which has the same name as the exception text. This can be transferred to the TEXTID parameter of the instance constructor to determine the exception text when the exception is raised. If the parameter is not transferred, the predefined exception text is used. This has the same name as the exception class.

From a technical point of view, you can also pass arbitrary messages or texts of the OTR as exception texts using the TEXTID parameter of the instance constructor.

Rule

> **Rule 5.11: Provide Appropriate Exception Texts in the Exception Class and Only Use Those** [✓]
>
> When you create an exception class, you must deliberately decide on an appropriate text type (messages for user dialogs or OTR text for internal texts) in which you create the exception texts. When you raise the exception, you may only use these corresponding texts.

Details

The following guideline applies to the use of the text type:

▸ Message texts should only be used if the text is supposed to be sent to the program user. This can be the case in application programs but should not occur in system programs. The restriction to 73 characters is also a disadvantage of short texts of messages.

▸ Texts from the OTR should mainly be used in the system programs in which the text is not supposed to be sent to the program user.

Technically, any data object can be transferred to the TEXTID input parameter of the instance constructor when the exception is raised, if this data object specifies either any message or any OTR text depending on the text type. However, it is strongly recommended to not choose this option. An exception must only be raised with its specific texts. Therefore you should transfer only the corresponding constants of the exception class to the TEXTID input parameter of the instance constructor.

Exception

In cases in which a class-based exception is used to wrap a classical exception (see Section 5.2.2, Classical and Class-Based Exceptions), and this classical exception is linked with a message text via MESSAGE ... RAISING, the class-based exception can use the same message text irrespective of whether it is a system or an application program.

181

Note

Classical exceptions don't have any exception texts assigned. If, for reasons of downward compatibility, you still need to work with classical exceptions, the MES-SAGE ... RAISING statement provides the option to emulate exception texts there. Therefore, when you cannot work with class-based exceptions, you should prefer MESSAGE ... RAISING over RAISE because you can provide additional text information to an exception.

Bad Example

Listing 5.9 shows the transfer of a UUID (Universal Unique Identifier) for an arbitrary OTR text to the TEXTID input parameter of the instance constructor when raising an exception. According to Rule 5.11, Provide Appropriate Exception Texts in the Exception Class and Only Use Those, you may only transfer an exception text of the exception class for which each exception class contains corresponding constants.

```
...

DATA otr_id TYPE sotr_conc.

otr_id = '9753EBD0102AD0418D902B8D972083C4'.

RAISE EXCEPTION TYPE zcx_exception_text
  EXPORTING
    textid = otr_id.

...
```

Listing 5.9 Using a Freely Selected Exception Text

Good Example

Listing 5.10 shows the transfer of the constant for the associated OTR text to the TEXTID input parameter of the instance constructor when raising an exception, as it is prescribe in Rule 5.11,.

```
...

RAISE EXCEPTION TYPE zcx_exception_text
  EXPORTING
    textid = zcx_exception_text=>zcx_exception_text.

...
```

Listing 5.10 Using the Associated Exception Text

5.2.5 Using Exception Classes

Background

The concept of freely definable exception classes is that you can create an exception class that aptly describes the exception situation to be mapped. The description includes both the name of the exception class and the associated exception texts as well as their documentation. By creating multiple exception texts, you can already subdivide an exception class into multiple subexceptions. Subclasses of exception classes can further specialize them.

Rule

> **Rule 5.12: Use Appropriate Exception Classes Only**   [✓]
>
> To describe a given error situation, only use an exception class that includes the correct name and the appropriate attributes and texts as well as the correct documentation. It is strongly recommended to not reuse inappropriate exception classes.

Details

The reuse of existing exception classes with wrong meaning ruins the benefits of freely definable exception classes. The exception situation is no longer described appropriately by the generated exception object. The maintainability and understanding of the code are left behind. In particular, you also run the risk that the exception is handled incorrectly because a hierarchically higher calling program layer can never anticipate that an exception that was handled in this layer is raised in a semantically incorrect context.

To raise a suitable exception, the following procedure can be used in which you must always pay attention to the correct exception category (see Rule 5.10, Use the Appropriate Exception Category):

1. Search for an existing exception class that is released for use in the current context within the scope of the package concept and corresponds to the error situation.

2. Search for an existing and almost exactly matching exception class and specialize it through inheritance and/or the addition of new exception texts.

3. Create a new, exactly matching exception class, possibly within the framework of a predefined inheritance hierarchy.

Bad Example

Listing 5.11 shows the wrong use of the cx_sy_arithmetic_overflow system class that exists in every system for an application-specific exception situation. This system exception should usually only be raised by the ABAP runtime environment when an arithmetic calculation is executed.

```
CLASS warehouse DEFINITION.
  PUBLIC SECTION.
    METHODS calculate_storage_capacity
      RAISING cx_sy_arithmetic_error.
ENDCLASS.

CLASS warehouse IMPLEMENTATION.
  METHOD calculate_storage_capacity.
    ...

    RAISE EXCEPTION TYPE cx_sy_arithmetic_overflow.

    ...
  ENDMETHOD.
ENDCLASS.
```

Listing 5.11 Using an Inappropriate Exception Class

Good Example

Listing 5.12 shows the use of an application-specific exception class that was created especially for this purpose and whose name expresses the situation correctly.

```
CLASS cx_warehouse_out_of_capacity DEFINITION
  INHERITING FROM cx_static_check.
ENDCLASS.

CLASS warehouse DEFINITION.
  PUBLIC SECTION.
    METHODS calculate_storage_capacity
      RAISING cx_warehouse_out_of_capacity.
ENDCLASS.

CLASS warehouse IMPLEMENTATION.
  METHOD calculate_storage_capacity.
    ...

    RAISE EXCEPTION TYPE cx_warehouse_out_of_capacity.

    ...
  ENDMETHOD.
ENDCLASS.
```

Listing 5.12 Using an Appropriate Exception Class

5.2.6 Handling and Propagating Exceptions

Background

If a class-based exception occurs, it is propagated along the call layers until the exception is handled or an interface is violated:

▶ If the exception occurs in a TRY block, the system searches for a suitable CATCH block that handles it.

▶ If the context of a procedure is exited when searching for a handler, its parameter interface is checked. Only exceptions that were declared there can be propagated from the procedure. Exceptions of the categories, CX_STATIC_CHECK and CX_DYNAMIC_CHECK, must be declared explicitly with RAISING; exceptions of the CX_NO_CHECK category are always declared implicitly. If the interface is violated, the predefined exception, CX_SY_NO_HANDLER, is raised at the calling position of the procedure, whereas a reference to the original exception is stored in its PREVIOUS attribute.

If no handler is found in any of the TRY control structures involved, or if the exception occurs outside a TRY control structure, this results in a runtime error at the raise position of the exception. The short dump of the runtime error contains the name of the exception class and the exception text.

Rule

[✓]

Rule 5.13: Catch Exceptions or Forward Them Appropriately
Only catch those exceptions that you can handle reasonably in the current context. When you forward exceptions from the underlying software layers, they are supposed to be mapped to corresponding exceptions of the current software layer.

Details

When you call a procedure whose interface includes class-based exceptions, you must decide for each of these exceptions whether they can be handled at this position or must be forwarded to your own calling program. Exceptions that cannot be handled reasonably at the current call level must be forwarded to the superordinate call level. For class-based exceptions, this is done implicitly by avoiding a handling within the current call level. Only in cases in which you are absolutely sure that neither catching nor propagating are of any use, should a runtime error occur.

When you forward exceptions along the call sequence across multiple layers, they usually move from lower technical layers to higher more abstract layers that are closer to the application. The calling program in these higher layers doesn't necessarily know the implementation details of the lower layers and therefore cannot interpret exceptions appropriately. For this reason, exceptions are not supposed to exceed the boundaries between software layers but are supposed to be mapped on suitable exceptions with a higher degree of abstraction.

For the forwarding between software layers, it is therefore recommended to not rely on the automatic propagation but catch the original exception and carry out a mapping of an exception of the current context by raising a new exception.[13] This way, you ensure that the calling program of a procedure only receives exceptions that it can understand. For reasons of package encapsulation (operational as of Release 7.2), such a procedure will be required anyway if exceptions are supposed to be forwarded between software layers.

Note

By forwarding to higher software layers, this usually results in a generalization of formerly very special exceptions. The more general an exception is, the higher the software layer usually is in which it is handled. In particular, the most general of all possible exceptions, that is, the exceptions of the `CX_STATIC_CHECK`, `CX_DYNAMIC_CHECK`, `CX_NO_CHECK`, or `CX_ROOT` type, should only be caught at the top software layers at most and only if a runtime error must be avoided by all means.

5.2.7 Cleanup After Exceptions

Background

Each `TRY` control structure can contain a `CLEANUP` block. If a class-based exception occurs in the `TRY` block of the same `TRY` control structure but is handled in a `CATCH` block of an external `TRY` control structure, the `CLEANUP` block is executed before the exception's context is deleted. When you execute a handler, the `CLEANUP` blocks of the `TRY` control structures that have been browsed unsuccessfully for a handler are executed from the inside to the outside.

---

13 Here, the relationship between the originally raised and the final exception should be preserved using the `previous` attribute.

Whether the execution is carried out before or after the handling depends on the BEFORE UNWIND addition of the CATCH statement. However, the CLEANUP blocks are not executed if the system resumes in the context of the exception during the exception handling using RESUME (both as of Releases 7.0 EhP2 and 7.2).

Rule

Rule 5.14: Cleanup Before Forwarding	[✓]

Carry out the necessary cleanup in the CLEANUP block before you forward an exception to the superordinate call layers.

Details

Each exception changes the program flow and can therefore represent a serious threat to the consistency of an application. If you decide to forward an exception instead of handling it (see Rule 5.13, Catch Exceptions or Forward Them Appropriately), you must make sure that the current software layer is left in a consistent state. For this purpose, you can implement the CLEANUP block appropriately to carry out the cleanup before the exception is forwarded to the superordinate software layers.

Bad Example

Listing 5.13 shows the forwarding of an exception without the previously opened resource — a database cursor in this case — being closed explicitly, which implicitly delegates the closing of the database cursor to possible exception handlers.

```
TRY.
  OPEN CURSOR db_cursor
    FOR SELECT ...
    ...
  CATCH cx_sy_sql_error INTO exc.
    RAISE EXCEPTION TYPE cx_persistency_error
      EXPORTING previous = exc.
ENDTRY.
```

Listing 5.13 Forwarding of an Exception Without Cleanup

Good Example

Listing 5.14 shows the same example as Listing 5.13; here, however, the database cursor is closed in the CLEANUP block.

```
TRY.
  OPEN CURSOR db_cursor
    FOR SELECT ...
    ...
  CATCH cx_sy_sql_error INTO exc.
    RAISE EXCEPTION TYPE cx_persistency_error
      EXPORTING previous = exc.
  CLEANUP.
    CLOSE CURSOR db_cursor.
ENDTRY.
```

Listing 5.14 Forwarding of an Exception with Cleanup

5.2.8 Catchable Runtime Errors

Background

Already prior to the implementation of class-based exceptions, it was possible to handle selected error situations as *catchable runtime errors* during the execution of ABAP statements. These catchable runtime errors are predefined and assigned to the ABAP statements that can trigger them. Several catchable runtime errors can be grouped together in exception groups and handled jointly under the group name. The handling is implemented using the CATCH SYSTEM-EXCEPTIONS statement and is similar to the handling of classical exceptions of procedures (see Section 5.2.2, Classical and Class-Based Exceptions) by setting the sy-subrc system field and its subsequent evaluation.

For reasons of downward compatibility, these catchable runtime errors still exist. Since the implementation of class-based exceptions, an exception class with the CX_SY_ prefix is assigned to each catchable runtime error, whereas the exception groups have been replaced with superclasses. A corresponding error situation can be handled either as a catchable runtime error or a class-based exception. Conversely, however, not all predefined class-based exceptions have been assigned to a catchable runtime error. No new catchable runtime errors are created any longer, and existing runtime errors that are to be made treatable are no longer converted into catchable runtime errors but are assigned to exception classes instead.

Therefore, exception classes play a more general role in ABAP than classical exceptions and catchable runtime errors: They can be defined separately to be raised in error situations of the application, or they are raised as system exceptions during the execution of the ABAP statements.

Rule

[✿]

Do not use the CATCH SYSTEM-EXCEPTIONS statement to handle catchable runtime errors. Instead, you should handle the corresponding class-based exceptions.

Details

The CATCH SYSTEM-EXCEPTIONS statement is obsolete (in Appendix A, see Section A.4.5, Exception Handling) and is only available for compatibility reasons. There is no reason to use this statement any longer because today, the error handling is carried out uniformly using class-based exceptions.[14]

Note

Within a processing block in which class-based exceptions are handled in TRY control structures or raised using RAISE EXCEPTION, this rule is enforced by the syntax check.

Bad Example

Listing 5.15 shows the obsolete handling of catchable runtime errors.

```
CATCH SYSTEM-EXCEPTIONS arithmetic_errors = 4
                        OTHERS            = 8.
   result = 1 / number.
ENDCATCH.
IF sy-subrc <> 0.
   ...
ENDIF.
```

Listing 5.15 Handling of Catchable Runtime Errors

Good Example

Listing 5.16 has the same functionality as Listing 5.15 but replaces the obsolete handling of catchable runtime errors with the handling of the associated class-based system exceptions.

```
TRY.
      result = 1 / number.
```

---

14 Although this statement belongs to language constructs that are declared obsolete in Appendix A, this rule is included here because of its subject proximity.

```
    CATCH cx_sy_arithmetic_error.
        . . .
    CATCH ...
        . . .
ENDTRY.
```

Listing 5.16 Handling of System Exceptions

5.2.9   Assertions

Background

Using the ASSERT statement, you can express an assertion in an ABAP program. Such an assertion either is always active, or you can activate it from the outside by assigning it to a *checkpoint group*. When an active assertion is reached, the system evaluates the corresponding condition. When this condition is violated and depending on the type of activation, the following may occur:

▶ The program is terminated with the ASSERTION_FAILED runtime error.

▶ The system jumps to the ABAP Debugger.

▶ A log entry is created.

Assertions together with breakpoints and log points form the *checkpoints* of a program, which aren't a component of the application logic but are used to support the development and maintenance.

Rule

[✓] | Rule 5.16: Use Assertions

Use assertions to check the state of a program with regard to its consistency at all appropriate points.

Details

Each program logic is based on certain assumptions. If these assumptions are not met, the program is obviously erroneous, and a further, useful program execution is not possible. In this case, the program execution should be terminated immediately to avert larger damage, for instance, in the form of persisted incorrect data. This way, you can even detect those errors at an early stage that would otherwise remain undetected.

To guarantee such consistency, the ASSERT statement is best because it is directly linked with a condition and results in a program termination if this condition is violated.

Furthermore, assertions add to the maintainability of the program by enabling the developer to express his assumptions explicitly. The reader of the source code immediately knows about these assumptions and can better retrace the program logic.

If the check of an assertion condition is too time-consuming, you can use *activatable assertions* that are linked with checkpoint groups. They can be activated in a targeted way during the development, the tests, or troubleshooting and are not executed otherwise. If it is suspected that a live system doesn't work properly, you can switch on the activatable assertions.

Exception

States that are beyond the control of the developer, for instance, invalid call parameter values or the availability of external resources, must not be checked using assertions. Here, you must use exceptions so that the calling program can respond to such unexpected states.

Example

Listing 5.17 shows a program section in which a line is read from an internal table. The program logic assumes that this access is always successful. This expectation is both checked by the subsequent assertion at runtime and documented for the reader.

```
. . .
READ TABLE items INTO current_item INDEX current_index.
ASSERT sy-subrc = 0.
. . .
```

Listing 5.17 Using an Assertion

5.2.10 Messages

Background

Messages are texts that are created using the message maintenance (Transaction SE91) and are stored in the T100 system table. You use messages in ABAP programs mainly by the MESSAGE statement. This statement sends a message whereas you can determine the type of display and the subsequent program behavior by specifying a message type. For this purpose, the following message types are distinguished:

- Status message (S)
- Information message (I)
- Warning (W)
- Error message (E)
- Termination message (A)

In addition, there is a special message type, exit message (X), which terminates a program with a runtime error in a targeted way.

The actual system behavior after sending a message strongly depends on the context. The current version of the ABAP keyword documentation contains a detailed list of the effects the different message types have in contexts, such as dialog processing, background processing, during an RFC, during the processing of HTTP requests, and so on.

In their original purpose, messages serve as dialog messages to display short information (I and S types) during classical dynpro processing and to handle incorrect inputs of the user (W and E types). Additionally, messages also have points of contact with exceptions:

- The MESSGAGE ... RAISING statement is a combination of the statements, MESSAGE and RAISE, which enables you to link classical exceptions with messages.

- With the special, predefined classical exception, error_message, you can handle error and termination messages, which occur during the execution of function modules, in the same way as exceptions.[15]

- In exception classes, you can define exception texts with a reference to messages (see Section 5.2.4, Exception Texts).

Ultimately, the message types, A and X, can also be used for a direct program termination.

---

15 This also concerns messages that are sent by the ABAP runtime environment, for example, during the automatic input check of classical dynpros.

Rule

> **Rule 5.17: Use Messages Only for Error Handling in Classical Dynpros and as Exception Texts**   **[✿]**
>
> Send dialog messages only during the PAI processing of classical dynpros. Apart from the use as exception texts, messages are not supposed to be used otherwise. In particular, messages are not supposed to be used any longer to force a program termination.

Details

The wide use of messages for different purposes is linked with the old programming model, which was only driven by classical dynpros in which an exception situation directly required the output of a message to the user. This concept was adopted for other situations such as targeted program terminations. Triggering a dialog message within procedures of the application logic contradicts the principle of SoC (see Rule 2.1, Adhere to the SoC Principle) and limits the reusability of the relevant procedure (method, see Rule 6.37, No Implementations in Function Modules and Subroutines) to the context of the classical dynpro processing. The predefined exception, `error_message`, can clearly be considered a makeshift that enables you to execute procedures that send messages in the application layer or in the background.

In new programs, the use of messages should be limited as described in the following sections.

Dialog Messages

In cases in which you still work with classical dynpros (see Section 5.3, User Interfaces), messages of the `E`, `I`, `S`, and `W` types are still suitable to send information to the user or to hold an error dialog at the time of PAI in accordance with their original purpose. The latter is particularly supported by the `FIELD` and `CHAIN` statements of the dynpro flow logic.

Exception Texts

As specified in Rule 5.11, Provide Appropriate Exception Texts in the Exception Class and Only Use Those, you can use messages as exception texts to be sent to the program user. This primarily involves exceptions of the presentation layer. The `MESSAGE` statement supports the direct sending of such exception texts as dialog messages by specifying a reference to a corresponding exception object directly there.[16]

Moreover, messages in procedures in which you still have to work with classical exceptions can serve as a replacement for real exception texts by using the MESSAGE ... RAISING statement instead of RAISE. In this process, information on the exception text is transferred to the handler in the system fields sy-msgid and sy-msgv1 to sy-msgv4, which are supplied via the MESSAGE statement. This particularly works for the handling of exceptions during an RFC for which no class-based exception handling is possible before Release 7.2.

Program Terminations

The A and X message types that lead to program terminations should not be used any longer:

▶ If you send a termination message of type A, the ROLLBACK WORK statement is executed implicitly. This can lead to unexpected results if the message does not result in a termination but is handled with error_message as a classical exception. To be on the safe side, you should explicitly use the statements, ROLLBACK WORK and LEAVE PROGRAM, to exit the program.

▶ If you send a message of the X type, the program is terminated with the MESSAGE_TYPE_X runtime error. For forced program terminations due to internal inconsistencies, you should use assertions now (see Rule 5.16, Use Assertions). The values that are transferred via the FIELDS addition to the ASSERT statement are usually better suited for problem analysis than a message.

Exception

Exit messages can still be used if it is absolutely necessary that the text of the message is to be displayed in the short dump of the runtime error. However, this should not be misunderstood as communication with the user because a runtime error is not an adequate means here.[17]

---

16 From the technical point of view, you must specify a reference to an object whose class includes the IF_T100_MESSAGE interface.

17 For a simple, unconditional program termination, however, you are no longer supposed to use exit messages. Instead, in cases in which this is necessary, you can specify a logical condition in ASSERT, which is always false.

5.3   User Interfaces

The UI is the interface between the human user and the machine, in our case between the user and the executed ABAP program. The UIs that are used in the ABAP environment are Graphical User Interfaces (GUIs) that are operated with the keyboard, mouse, and other input devices. They are based on different UI technologies and use either the SAP-specific SAP GUI or — as web-based technologies — generate HTML pages to be displayed via web browsers.

5.3.1   Selecting the User Interface Technology

Background

Various UI technologies can be used in the ABAP environment. We distinguish between classical technologies, which are based on the SAP GUI and are almost completely integrated with the ABAP language, and new web-based technologies, which display the UI via web browsers and are accessed by an ABAP program through object-oriented interfaces (APIs).

The classical SAP GUI technologies include the following:

- **Classical dynpros**
  A classical dynpro is a component of an ABAP program. You create it using the Screen Painter of the ABAP Workbench and call it either via a transaction code or via the `CALL SCREEN` statement. Calling a dynpro always starts a dynpro sequence.

- **Selection screen**
  A selection screen is a specific classical dynpro that isn't manually created in the Screen Painter. Instead, you define it using the `PARAMETERS`, `SELECT-OPTIONS`, and `SELECTION-SCREEN` ABAP statements. A selection screen is called either implicitly when executable programs are started or explicitly via the `CALL SELECTION-SCREEN` statement.

- **Classical lists**
  A classical list is used for the structured and formatted output of data. Specific ABAP statements (`WRITE`, `FORMAT`, etc.) enable you to store formatted data in a list buffer and display it in a specific system dynpro. A classical list is called either automatically when an executable program is executed or with the `LEAVE TO LIST-PROCESSING` statement.

The new web-based technologies include the following:

▶ **Business Server Pages**
Business Server Pages (BSP) are the counterpart of JavaServer Pages (JSP). BSPs are HTML pages with partly dynamic content. The dynamic content is generated by server-side scripts that are written in ABAP. On the application server, such a script occurs as a generated class of ABAP Objects. You create BSPs using the Web Application Builder of the ABAP Workbench.

▶ **Web Dynpro ABAP**
Web Dynpro ABAP is a technology for creating platform-independent web-based interfaces. The architecture of Web Dynpro is based on the MVC approach (Model View Controller)[18] with regard to the SoC (in Chapter 2, see Section 2.1, Adhere to the SoC Principle). Web Dynpro applications are created with the Web Dynpro Explorer of the ABAP Workbench and appear as classes of ABAP Objects on the application server.

Rule

[▪] | **Rule 5.18: Use Web Dynpro ABAP**

If possible, use Web Dynpro ABAP to create the UIs of new application programs.

Details

Officially, Web Dynpro ABAP is the SAP standard UI technology for the development of modern web applications in the ABAP environment. The MVC approach automatically ensures a separation of presentation and application logic according to Rule 2.1, Adhere to the SoC Principle.

Compared to Web Dynpro, the BSP technology is much more fundamental. It supports an MVC approach for the SoC, but the developers are still responsible for its relization. BSPs can be considered the predecessor technology of Web Dynpro ABAP whose use is nowadays restricted to cases where a web application is based on a single HTML page for which scripting is required and whose function cannot be implemented with Web Dynpro ABAP.

---

18 The three components of the model view controller are the data model, which describes the application, the view for presentation, and the program controller for responding to user actions.

The classical SAP UI technology — that is, classical dynpros that are based on the SAP GUI, including selection screens and lists — is no longer sufficient for modern and flexible business applications for which the UI must be made available in a portal, for example. The MVC approach is supported neither by frameworks nor by the appropriate tools.

Exception

The various UI technologies aren't interoperable; that is, an application that is based on classical dynpros (including selection screens and classical lists) can usually not be partly changed to Web Dynpro ABAP. Moreover, in the past, the generally followed dynpro programming model was not really oriented toward SoC, which makes it difficult or even impossible to implement a changeover in the context of further development. Consequently, in exceptional cases, classical dynpros and/or selection screens may be required if a new development needs to be included in an existing framework. For these exceptional cases, the following rules are formulated to ensure modern handling of these generally obsolete UI technologies.

Tip

Usually, you can readily change the UI technology of an application that is modeled in strict adherence to Rule 2.1, Adhere to the SoC Principle, on the SoC (see the next example).

Note

Web Dynpro ABAP itself is not part of the ABAP language, and specific guidelines regarding its use are not part of this book, which mainly focus on the use of the ABAP language for the implementation of services.

Bad Example

Figure 5.1 shows a UI for the already mentioned car rental example (see Figure 4.4 in Chapter 4, Structure and Style). This UI is based on classical dynpros and selection screens. According to Rule 5.18, Use Web Dynpro ABAP, however, using this UI technology in application programs is no longer recommended.

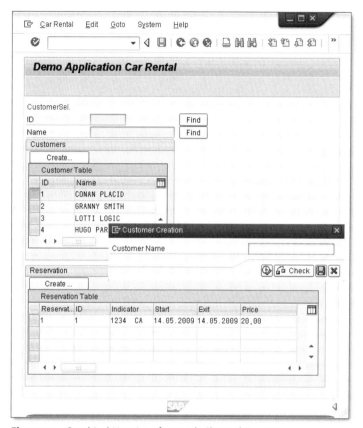

Figure 5.1 Graphical User Interface with Classical Dynpros

Good Example

Figure 5.2 shows a modern UI that is based on Web Dynpro ABAP for the same example as in Figure 5.1.

Tip

Because the sample application strictly separates all concerns, you can use it with different UIs without having to interfere in the application and persistency logic. The SoC is therefore a critical prerequisite for potential changeovers from classical dynpros to Web Dynpro ABAP.

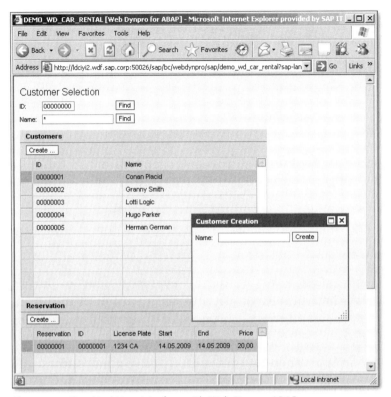

Figure 5.2 Graphical User Interface with Web Dynpro ABAP

5.3.2 Encapsulating Classical User Interfaces

Background

According to Rule 2.1, Adhere to the SoC Principle, the SoC is one of the basic rules of these ABAP programming guidelines. This separation, which refers to a strict division of ABAP code into parts for presentation services, application services, and persistency services, is technically also feasible for classical UI technologies that are based on dynpros. The MVC approach is not directly supported, but SoC can also be achieved by consequently using the available encapsulation technologies.

This SoC, however, was rarely implemented in classical dialog programming in which the presentation logic, application logic, and persistency logic were often combined in a monolithic module pool.

Rule

[⚙] | **Rule 5.19: Encapsulate Classical Dynpros and Selection Screens**

Create classical dynpros and selection screens in programs of the presentation layer that are specifically provided for this purpose. You can use function groups as the program type here.

Details

The separation of the display logic from the application logic is also necessary when using classical UI technologies for the following reasons:

- ▸ To reuse individual components
- ▸ For automated tests of the program logic, irrespective of the UI
- ▸ For being able to change the UI technology

In addition, the communication between classical dynpros or selection screens and ABAP programs is implemented via global variables. This poses conceptual problems and cannot be reconciled with a modern, object-oriented approach for application programs.

Because class pools do not support classical dynpros and selection screens, you can only use function groups for their encapsulation. In this role, a function group must be considered a global class. Here, the data of its global declaration part assume the role of the private attributes, and the function modules assume the role of the public methods. The corresponding procedure is described in detail in *ABAP Objects* (SAP PRESS, 2007) and is illustrated in Figure 5.3 (which was taken from *ABAP Objects*) for general dynpros. It applies respectively to selection screens.

In addition to the UI elements, these function groups may only contain display logic as local classes. The communication of the application logic with the display logic takes place via the function modules of this function group. You can still call the first dynpro of a dynpro sequence using a transaction code. This method is used when the user is supposed to start the application.

The guidelines described in this book are also valid in such a function group. Particularly the dialog modules (PBO and PAI) , which are called by the dynpro, or the event blocks of selection screen processing must not contain any program logic but directly delegate the processing to the respective methods of local classes (see Rule 6.44, No Implementations in Dialog Modules and Event Blocks). The same applies to the function modules that play the role of the external interface (see Rule 6.37,

No Implementations in Function Modules and Subroutines). Furthermore, you must restrict the scope of the global data of the function group to a minimum that is required for the communication with dynpros (see Rules 5.1, Utilize the Encapsulation Options as Much as Possible, and 6.3, Do Not Declare Global Variables).

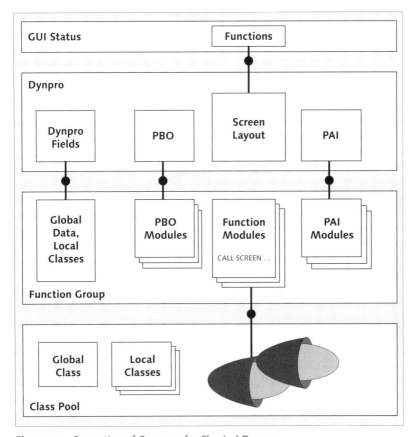

Figure 5.3 Separation of Concerns for Classical Dynpros

Exception

Adhering to Rule 5.19, Encapsulate Classical Dynpros and Selection Screens, doesn't allow you to use standard selection screens. Consequently, an exception must be made to this rule for executable programs that are supposed to be executed during background processing. The reason for this is that their parameter interface must be a standard selection screen that is defined in the program. Here, an encapsulation in a function group is not possible. However, in this case also, the selection screen processing events are supposed to call the respective method of a local class within the executable program only.

Bad Example

Take a look at the right-hand side of Figure 2.1 in Chapter 2. A dialog program — usually a single module pool — processes all facets of an application.

Good Example

Listing 5.18 shows a part of a function group with expanded include programs. This function group encapsulates the dynpro that is displayed in Figure 5.1 (shown earlier) and the selection screen according to Rule 5.19, Encapsulate Classical Dynpros and Selection Screens. The connection to the application layer is solely established via the `if_demo_cr_car_rentl_service` interface, which is also used in the Web Dynpro application shown earlier in Figure 5.2.

```
FUNCTION-POOL demo_cr_car_rental_screens.

* Top Include

SELECTION-SCREEN BEGIN OF SCREEN 200 TITLE text-ccr.
PARAMETERS g_name TYPE demo_cr_customer_name.
SELECTION-SCREEN END OF SCREEN 200.

TABLES demo_cr_scustomer_cntrl.

CONTROLS: customers    TYPE TABLEVIEW USING SCREEN 0100,
          reservations TYPE TABLEVIEW USING SCREEN 0100.

DATA g_ok_code TYPE sy-ucomm.

DATA: g_customers TYPE TABLE OF demo_cr_scustomer_cntrl,
      g_customer  LIKE LINE OF  g_customers.

DATA: g_reservations TYPE TABLE OF demo_cr_sreservation_cntrl,
      g_reservation  LIKE LINE OF  g_reservations.

* Local Class Declarations

CLASS screen_handler DEFINITION.
  PUBLIC SECTION.
    CLASS-DATA car_rental_service
      TYPE REF TO if_demo_cr_car_rentl_service.
    CLASS-METHODS: class_constructor,
```

```
                         status_0100,
                         user_command_0100,
                         cancel.
  PRIVATE SECTION.
    CLASS-METHODS: customer_search_by_id,
                   ...
ENDCLASS.

CLASS customer_table DEFINITION.
  PUBLIC SECTION.
    CLASS-METHODS: change_tc_attr,
                   mark.
ENDCLASS.

...

* Function Module

FUNCTION demo_cr_call_car_rental_screen.
  CALL SCREEN 100.
ENDFUNCTION.

* PBO Modules

MODULE status_0100 OUTPUT.
  screen_handler=>status_0100( ).
ENDMODULE.

MODULE customers_change_tc_attr OUTPUT.
  customer_table=>change_tc_attr( ).
ENDMODULE.

...

* PAI Modules

MODULE cancel INPUT.
  screen_handler=>cancel( ).
ENDMODULE.

MODULE user_command_0100 INPUT.
  screen_handler=>user_command_0100( ).
ENDMODULE.

MODULE customers_mark INPUT.
  customer_table=>mark( ).
ENDMODULE.
```

```
. . .

* Local Class Implementations

. . .
```

Listing 5.18 Function Group for Encapsulating a Dynpro

The dynpro with number `100` is called in a function module but can also be linked with a transaction code. In the classical PBO and PAI modules, methods of local classes are called whose implementation is not illustrated here. There is a class for general screen handling and a class for each table control. In the implementations of the class, the application layer is accessed via the mentioned interface.

5.3.3 Lists

Background

A list is a medium for outputting structured and formatted data. The following lists are available in ABAP:

▶ Classical lists, which are written to a list buffer using ABAP statements and displayed on a special list dynpro

▶ Output of the SAP List Viewer (ALV), which is displayed in GUI controls[19] during the processing of classical dynpros. You access ALV lists via classes, such as `CL_SALV_TABLE` (nonhierarchically tabular lists), `CL_SALV_HIERSEQ_TABLE` (hierarchically sequential lists), or `CL_SALV_TREE` (hierarchically tabular lists).

Classical lists are the only option to send ABAP data from ABAP programs directly to the SAP spool system as so-called print lists. If you use the SAP List Viewer, the lists that are displayed in the viewer are automatically converted to classical print lists during printing.

Rule

[⚙] **Rule 5.20: Use the SAP List Viewer**

Do not use classical lists. If you still deploy dynpro-based, classical UI technologies, you should use the SAP List Viewer (ALV) or other GUI control-based technologies instead of classical lists in live programs.

---

19 GUI controls are components of the SAP GUI that are displayed during the dynpro processing and addressed via the ABAP classes of the *Control Framework*.

Details

Using classical lists is no longer recommended for the following reasons:

▶ The processing of lists is based on global data and events of the ABAP runtime environment.

▶ The list buffer that is used for classical lists is bound to an executable program or a dynpro sequence and not to classes and objects.

▶ It is almost impossible to separate presentation logic and application logic when writing to lists.

▶ The UI of a classical list is not standardized and thus usually not accessible.

The concept of classical lists is therefore mostly incompatible with the ABAP Objects concept, and you cannot encapsulate classical lists in function groups as easily as classical dynpros and selection screens.

While the application developer must ensure accessibility (see Rule 5.21, Ensure Accessibility) in classical lists with a great deal of effort, the ALV lists automatically correspond to the accessibility requirements because the ALV already provides the required services, such as user-specific settings.

Exception

Small helper programs that are not provided for live use in application systems can continue to use classical lists for system-related console output. The WRITE statement here assumes the same role as System.out.println(...) in Java or printf in C.

In cases in which an ALV output seems to be overdimensioned, you can also deploy other means, such as Textedit Control or Browser Control (or its wrapping in dynamic documents) for the formatted output of nontabular content. As before, you have to ensure accessibility yourself here.

Bad Example

Figure 5.4 shows a classical list output whose programming is described in *ABAP Objects* (SAP PRESS, 2007). According to Rule 5.20, Use the SAP List Viewer, however, using classical lists in application programs is no longer recommended.

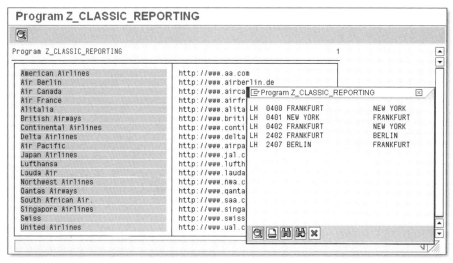

Figure 5.4 Classical Lists

Good Example

Figure 5.5 displays the same list content as Figure 5.4 but in ALV lists this time (the programming is also described in *ABAP Objects*). ALV lists replace classical lists in those cases in which classical dynpros are still used.

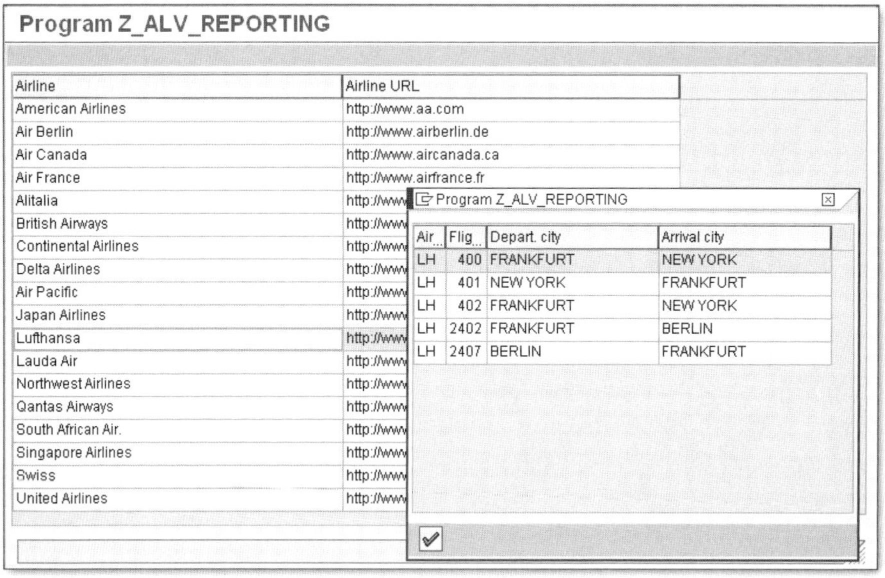

Figure 5.5 ALV Lists

5.3.4   Accessibility

Background

Accessibility is one of the product standards listed in Chapter 2, Section 2.3, Correctness and Quality, and ensures that IT products can also be used by handicapped persons. For UIs, this particularly means that you have to consider concerns of visually impaired or blind persons, who usually have to rely on screen reader programs that read the screen content out loud.

Rule

> **Rule 5.21: Ensure Accessibility**
>
> Ensure that your UIs are accessible, irrespective of the UI technology used, so that handicapped persons can also use them.

Details

In general, you must design UIs in such a way that utilities, such as *screen readers* or *magnifiers*, can process them without problems. For this purpose, you must meet the following requirements:

- All input and output fields must have meaningful names.
- All table columns must have a heading.
- All icons must have a tooltip.
- Information mustn't be expressed by colors only.
- Input and output fields are supposed to be logically grouped in frames, each with a meaningful title.

This is another reason for using most recent UI technologies, such as Web Dynpro ABAP or ALV. They automatically provide accessible UIs. If obsolete technologies, such as classical dynpros or classical lists, are used, application developers themselves have to ensure that the accessibility requirements are met. For classical dynpros and selection screens, the test tools that are introduced in Chapter 3, Section 3.4, Checks for Correctness, also provide some checks that indicate statically determinable violations of these rules. For classical lists, however, such checks can only be performed when the lists are displayed.

Tip

Regarding the use of the Browser Control in classical dynpros, the `CL_HTMLTIDY` class should be mentioned. This class enables you to check HTML files for formal correctness and accessibility. You should only display such HTML files in a Browser Control that have been checked with `CL_HTMLTIDY`. The `CL_ABAP_BROWSER` class, which is available as of Releases 7.0 EhP2 and 7.2 and wraps the Browser Control for simple displays of HTML files, carries out a check with `CL_HTMLTIDY` by default.

5.4 Data Storage

ABAP programs generally work with data that are imported from persistent storage media to the internal session of the current program execution and are available to the program as transient data there. For performance reasons, you can also store data in the shared memory of the current application server, which can be used by all programs of an application server. Accessing data in the shared memory is considerably faster than accessing data in persistent storage media.

5.4.1 Persistent Data Storage

Background

ABAP programs can have both read and write access to data in the following persistent storage media:

- Relational database tables in databases
- Data clusters in special database tables
- Binary files or text files on the application server
- Binary files or text files on the workstation if SAP GUI is used

According to Rule 2.1, Adhere to the SoC Principle, such accesses are wrapped in service classes of the persistency layer of an application.

Rule

[⚙] **Rule 5.22: Plan Persistent Data Storage Carefully**

Select the persistent storage media that are used by the application as well as the possible data transport routes between these media with care. The following rule of thumb applies:

- ▶ Database tables for the general storage of raw data
- ▶ Data clusters for the storage of formatted data
- ▶ Files for the data exchange with external systems

Details

When you plan persistent data storage, you should follow these steps:

1. On an SAP NetWeaver AS ABAP, storing in relational database tables is always the first choice. ABAP supports this with Open SQL that is integrated into the language. An object-oriented access is possible via Object Services. The majority of the data is stored in the central standard database of the application server. You can access additional databases via secondary database connections (managed via the DBA Cockpit).

2. The following data can be stored in data clusters when using the EXPORT and IMPORT statements:

   - ▶ Formatted data as the result of comprehensive analyses

   - ▶ Data that are not suitable for relational databases because the data do not exist in the first normal form (such as nested internal tables)

   - ▶ Object graphs after a serialization to XML

3. The persistent storage of data in files of the application or presentation server is usually the least suitable for SAP NetWeaver AS ABAP application programs because it is generally platform-dependent (codepages, byte order). In addition, such data is then only available on a particular application server, which can be problematic in a load distribution scenario with automated server selection. Such files may be required for the data exchange with external systems, however.

In no case can you use existing database tables (or files) to store data that are not provided for this purpose. As of Release 7.2, the operational package concept enables you to restrict read and write access to database tables for specific packages. Prior to this release, this has to be done via convention. A database table must always be considered a semantic entity that is only allowed to contain the corresponding data. This even applies if a table with the required structure already exists. If in doubt, you should create a specific database table.

You must also be careful when using seemingly system-wide resources, such as the predefined INDX database table for data clusters. If at all, such a resource may only be used to store temporary data for the short term. You should create specific database tables, for example, INDX-type tables, for application-specific and longer-lasting data.

Note

These guidelines do not include more detailed performance notes for a persistent storage of data. Adhere to the respective notes in the ABAP Keyword Documentation and additional relevant publications on this critical product standard (in Chapter 2, see Section 2.3, Correctness and Quality), such as the books *SAP Performance Optimization Guide* (SAP PRESS, 2008) and *ABAP Performance Tuning* (SAP PRESS, 2009).

5.4.2 Database Accesses

Background

ABAP provides the following options for accessing data in database tables:

▶ **Open SQL**
A subset of SQL (Structured Query Language) implemented as ABAP statements that comprises the DML portion (Data Manipulation Language). The Open SQL statements access the database tables of an SAP NetWeaver AS ABAP database, which are defined in the ABAP Dictionary, through the Open SQL interface, irrespective of the platform.

▶ **Native SQL**
Database-specific SQL statements and some SAP-specific statements that can be executed in ABAP programs between the EXEC SQL and ENDEXEC statements. Native SQL statements are not checked in full by the syntax check and are transferred nearly unchanged to the SAP NetWeaver AS ABAP database by the Native SQL interface. Besides DML statements, you can also use DDL statements (Data Definition Language).

▶ **ADBC**
ADBC (ABAP Database Connectivity), a class-based API, which allows for object-oriented access to the Native SQL interface. The ADBC methods enable you to trigger dynamic SQL commands to a database system and process the result.

In addition to accessing the central database of an SAP NetWeaver AS ABAP via the default connection, all three access types also allow for accessing other databases via additional connections.

Rule

Rule 5.23: Use Open SQL [⚙]

Use Open SQL wherever possible for general persistency services. Use Native SQL and ADBC only for tasks that are not suited for Open SQL.

Details

Only Open SQL is completely independent of the database platform used. Consequently, Open SQL doesn't comprise all SQL statements that are possible on a specific database but only the intersection of the DML scope of all database systems that SAP NetWeaver AS ABAP supports. Database tables that can be processed by Open SQL can be directly used as structured types to declare appropriate work areas in ABAP. Only Open SQL supports SAP buffering of table content in shared memory (see Section 5.4.4, Using the Shared Memory).

You should use Native SQL if the task cannot be solved with Open SQL. Services that use Native SQL usually depend on the used database system and cannot be executed on all SAP NetWeaver AS ABAP. In the case of platform-independent services, you must then provide implementations for all supported databases. In contrast to Open SQL, Native SQL doesn't support dynamic token specifications in which all clauses of a statement can be expressed using variables (in Chapter 6, see Section 6.6, Dynamic Programming Techniques).

ADBC supplements Native SQL with object-oriented and dynamic accesses. The instances of classes, such as CL_SQL_STATEMENT, represent SQL statements, and their methods allow for their execution. You can always use ADBC if a database needs to be accessed via the Native SQL interface instead of the Open SQL interface and if static access is not sufficient.

5.4.3 Client Handling

Background

A client indicates a data area on the database of an SAP NetWeaver AS ABAP that contains independent application data. Application data of different clients share the same database tables but are identified by their three-digit client ID in those.

When logging on to an SAP NetWeaver AS ABAP, you must specify the client ID to select the client whose data is supposed to be used for the user session. By default, Open SQL statements support automatic client handling in which the data of the current client are accessed. This is because WHERE conditions contain an implicit condition for the current client and because clients that are specified in the work areas of statements that write to the database are ignored.

The current client is defined in the sy-mandt system field (in Chapter 6, see Section 6.3, System Fields). You can override the automatic client handling of Open SQL using the CLIENT SPECIFIED addition. Native SQL and ADBC (see Section 5.4.2, Database Accesses) do not implement automatic client handling.

Rule

[✓] **Rule 5.24: Do Not Access Data of Other Clients**

In the persistency services of business applications, access the data of the current client only.

Details

Each client within the application server should be considered a self-contained unit. You shouldn't use the CLIENT SPECIFIED addition in Open SQL statements of business applications. This also applies to the access to the current client because it bypasses SAP buffering (see Section 5.4.4, Using the Shared Memory).

Usually, you don't need to evaluate the sy-mandt system field unless you have to access the database tables via Native SQL or ADBC for urgent reasons (see Rule 5.23, Use Open SQL). In this case, the client ID is required to explicitly select the data of the current client.

Tip

Client-independent database tables, that is, tables without client ID, are usually system tables. Cross-client access to such tables is therefore reserved for system programs.

Bad Example

Listing 5.19 shows an Open SQL access to a database table where the current client is specified explicitly. This leads to performance loss for buffered tables and requires an additional explicit WHERE condition.

```
SELECT SINGLE ...
      FROM dbtab CLIENT SPECIFIED
      INTO ...
      WHERE mandt = sy-mandt AND
            ...
```

Listing 5.19 Specifying the Client Explicitly

Good Example

Listing 5.20 shows the common usage of Open SQL, which implicitly implements automatic client handling and usually doesn't bypass SAP buffering.

```
SELECT SINGLE ...
      FROM dbtab
      INTO ...
      WHERE ...
```

Listing 5.20 Automatic Client Handling

5.4.4 Using the Shared Memory

Background

The shared memory of an application server is a very important medium for buffering data with the goal of high-performance access. For this purpose, you can use the shared memory as follows:

▶ To implicitly store data from database tables temporarily using SAP buffering, which can be determined when defining the tables in the ABAP Dictionary

▶ To explicitly store data clusters in the cross-transaction application buffer using the EXPORT TO SHARED MEMORY or EXPORT TO SHARED BUFFER statements

▶ To explicitly handle (data) objects stored there using Shared Objects, which are generated using the AREA HANDLE addition of the CREATE OBJECT or CREATE DATA statements

Rule

Rule 5.25: Implement the Explicit Buffering in the Shared Memory Using Shared Objects [⚙]

Work with Shared Objects to explicitly use the shared memory for cross-program data buffering. The appropriate application scenarios are shared buffer and exclusive buffer. The access to Shared Objects should be wrapped in loader and broker classes.

Details

For explicit access to the shared memory, Shared Objects (`CREATE AREA HANDLE`) provide the following advantages compared to the cross-transaction application buffer (`SHARED MEMORY, SHARED BUFFER`):

▸ You can store any kind of (data) objects, including their mutual inter-dependencies.

▸ You can use (data) objects in the Shared Objects memory just like objects in the internal session.[20]

▸ Multiple programs can simultaneously access the same memory area without having to copy data to their own internal session.

Scenarios in which you can use Shared Objects efficiently include the following:

▸ **Usage as a shared buffer**
A shared buffer contains a large data set to which many users have read access but which is changed rarely and is usually provided by a single program.

▸ **Usage as an exclusive buffer**
An exclusive buffer contains data that are accessed by only one program at a time but that is maintained for various programs across transaction boundaries.

You shouldn't use the shared memory for different purposes, for example, if this results in many modifying accesses of parallel users, because the current locking concept doesn't support this.

You should encapsulate the access to the shared memory in specific classes, and application programs should only access the shared memory via these classes. Normally, there are two classes, which you can also combine into one class:

▸ A *loader* for creating and changing area instances

▸ A *broker* for read access to area instances

---

20 Technically, the Shared Objects memory can be considered an extension of the internal session during the time, the memory is bound to it.

Such wrapping ensures the following:

▸ A central management of the internal session's connection to the shared objects memory and the corresponding locks

▸ Central exception handling and the respective fallback strategies[21]

▸ Potential authorization checks

This makes the application program more legible, more robust, and easier to maintain.

Bad Example

Listing 5.21 shows how an internal table, `index_table`, which has been prepared elsewhere and buffered in the cross-transaction application buffer, is imported to a program. To store it locally, a local data object is required. You can carry out such tasks more efficiently if you use Shared Objects.

```
"Get index page from data cluster
IMPORT index_html = index_html
       FROM SHARED MEMORY docutables(...) ID ...
ASSERT sy-subrc = 0.
```

Listing 5.21 Buffering a Table in a Data Cluster

Good Example

Listing 5.22 shows how you can access an internal table, `index_table`, that has been prepared elsewhere and buffered in the Shared Objects memory. By calling a `get` method, the corresponding broker ensures that its `root` attribute refers to a Shared Object that contains the table. You then don't require a local data object to access the internal table.

```
"Get index page from shared memory
cl_docu_tables_broker=>get_index_table( ).
ASSERT cl_docu_tables_broker=>root->index_html
       IS NOT INITIAL.
```

Listing 5.22 Buffering a Table as a Shared Object

---

21 For example, if the Shared Object's memory overflows, you can ensure that objects in the internal session are used without the using program needs to be notified about this.

"There's no freedom without security."
– Wilhelm von Humboldt

6 Secure and Robust ABAP

The recommendations and rules in this chapter will enable you to develop secure and robust ABAP programs whose behavior doesn't hold any surprises (neither on the developer nor on maintainer side).

6.1 Data Types and Data Objects

Besides classes and objects, data types and data objects are absolutely essential for any kind of ABAP programming.

▶ **Data type**
A data type describes a data object as a class describes an object.[1] ABAP interprets the content of a data object in accordance with its data type. Data types are either bound as a property of data objects or are standalone data types. Standalone data types can be defined globally in the ABAP Dictionary or locally using TYPES in an ABAP program.

▶ **Data object**
A data object is an instance of a data type, just as an object is an instance of a class. It exists in the internal session of an ABAP program or as a Shared Object in the shared memory and uses memory for the contained data. Data objects are created either implicitly when a program or a procedure is loaded (*named data object*) or using the CREATE DATA statement (*anonymous data object*). Named data objects are variables (DATA statement, CLASS-DATA statement, etc.) or constants (CONSTANTS statement).

---

1 In this sense, a data type is comparable to a class without methods.

A data type describes both the technical properties of a data object (e.g., of which elementary types it consists and how long it is) and the semantic properties (which entity is represented by such a data object). There are additional properties for types that are defined in the ABAP Dictionary, for instance, for the input/output in a classical dynpro or in Web Dynpro.

From the ABAP runtime environment perspective, only the technical properties of a data object are interesting. For the legibility of the source code, however, the semantic information that is linked to the appropriate use of types is essential. Consequently, some of the rules that are discussed in this section could also be introduced in Chapter 4, Structure and Style, because in addition to the robustness, the style — which doesn't affect the program execution but is critical for the legibility and maintainability — also plays a role here.

6.1.1 Bound and Standalone Data Types

Background

A bound data type only exists as a property of a data object. It is created if a data object is not declared with reference to a standalone data type that defines all technical properties but if technical properties are defined in the DATA statement.[2] The resulting type is a property of the declared variable and bound to it. If it is required at various places, it has to be redefined for each use, respectively.

A standalone data type is declared in the ABAP Dictionary or using the TYPES statement and defines all technical properties of a data object with one exception: In their definition, table types can be generic with regard to the key specification (see the example in Section 6.5.5, Typing of Formal Parameters). A standalone generic type can only be used for typing but not for data declarations.[3]

Rule

> **Rule 6.1: Use Standalone Data Types**
>
> Use standalone data types instead of constructing bound data types during the declaration of data objects.

---

2 In this chapter, DATA is used as a synonym for all statements that declare data objects.
3 Again, there is one exception: In a DATA statement, the standard key is added to a generic standard table type.

Details

The following reasons support the declaration of standalone types:

▸ The declaration of a standalone data type allows multiple data objects (or interface parameters or field symbols) to use a type without always having to redefine this type.

▸ Even if only one data object of this type is required at first, it is highly possible that further data objects are added during the course of the development. If the type needs to be adapted at a later stage, you can do this centrally.

▸ After all, the declaration of a standalone type and its use for the declaration of data objects is nothing more than following Rule 2.1, Adhere to the SoC Principle.

The data type should always have a specific meaning. Its name has to be selected accordingly (see Chapter 4, Section 4.2). This way the name is provided with specific semantics, which increases the legibility of the program. Therefore, you should declare different data types for technically identical but semantically different data objects. This also increases the probability that a type can be adapted without major program changes at a later stage.

You should thus avoid the declaration of merely technical data types that cannot be associated with specific semantics because it doesn't increase the legibility or extensibility of a program.

Tip

Rule 6.2 defines where the standalone data types should be declared.

Bad Example

Listing 6.1 shows the declaration of two data objects that are supposed to have the same data type. The technical properties, length, and number of decimal places, however, are defined as independent, bound data types in the respective DATA statements.

```
. . .
DATA number_1 TYPE p LENGTH 6 DECIMALS 2.
DATA number_2 TYPE p LENGTH 6 DECIMALS 2.
. . .
```

Listing 6.1 Bound Data Types

Good Example

Listing 6.2 outsources the definition of the technical properties of the data objects from Listing 6.1 to a separate TYPES statement. The standalone data type is declared only once and can then be used multiple times.

```
TYPES number_type TYPE p LENGTH 6 DECIMALS 2.
...
DATA: number_1 TYPE number_type,
      number_2 TYPE number_type.
...
```

Listing 6.2 Standalone Data Type

6.1.2   Declaration of Data Types and Constants

Background

Data types and constants can be declared in the following contexts:

▶ **Cross-program**

  ▶ In the ABAP Dictionary

  ▶ In global classes and interfaces

  ▶ In type groups

▶ **Program-local**

  ▶ In the global declaration part of a program

  ▶ In local classes and interfaces

  ▶ In procedures (methods, see Rule 6.37)

Technically, type groups as well as classes and interfaces are also ABAP programs in which data types and constants are created using the TYPES and CONSTANTS statements. In contrast to other ABAP programs, the declarations are also statically visible in other programs depending on the visibility section.[4]

Rule

[▪]   **Rule 6.2: Declare Data Types and Constants in the Appropriate Context**

Declare data types and constants in the context that provides the best possible encapsulation.

---

4 Absolute type names even enable you to dynamically access types of all programs.

Details

Data types and constants are supposed to be declared in the context in which they are visible for all potential users according to Rule 5.1, Utilize the Encapsulation Options as Much as Possible, but not beyond:

▶ **Program-local data types and constants**

  ▶ Data types that are only required by local data objects (usually helper variables) or constants that are only required in a procedure (method, see Rule 6.37) are supposed to be declared as local data types or constants.

  ▶ Data types and constants that are only required within local classes are supposed to be declared in the corresponding visibility section of the classes or integrated via an interface.

  ▶ If data types are required in multiple local classes and interfaces of a program, they are supposed to be created in the appropriate visibility section of a local class or an interface. These can also be local classes or interfaces that contain nothing else than such types or constants. In the global declaration part of programs, declarations of data types or constants are required neither for technical nor for semantic reasons.

▶ **Cross-program data types and constants**

  ▶ Date types and constants that are required by the user of a global class or interface to use the class or the interface are supposed to be declared in the public (or package-public) visibility section of the global class or in the global interface.[5] Examples include data types that are used for the typing of interface parameters of methods as well as constants that are expected as actual parameters by methods, such as the IDs of the exception texts of exception classes (see Listing 5.10 in Chapter 5).

  ▶ Data types that are required by different programs, classes, or interfaces are declared as real types of the ABAP Dictionary (not in type groups). These are usually semantically independent types for which the ABAP Dictionary provides additional services, such as descriptive texts and documentation options. In this context, you must consider the SoC according to Rule 2.1.

---

5 Prior to Releases 7.0 EhP2 and 7.2, the ABAP Compiler had problems in specific situations (crossing references) with using types that had been defined in interfaces or the public visibility section of classes. In these cases, you must declare more global types in the ABAP Dictionary.

For example, a structure of the ABAP Dictionary should never be used simultaneously for the typing of (Web) Dynpro fields and the definition of a database table. Ideally, the declaration of data types takes place in encapsulated packages, which manage the mutual use of their repository objects and whose package interfaces only provide the types that are actually required outside the package.

You should generally avoid declaring or even providing merely technical types without semantic meaning within application development packages in the ABAP Dictionary. The declaration of such types, such as `INT2` or `CHAR10`, should be restricted to fundamental basis packages (in Chapter 4, see Section 4.2.3, Names of Repository Objects).

▶ You should not create any new type groups. Data types are supposed to be declared in global classes or interfaces or as real types of the ABAP Dictionary. You should create constants in global classes or interfaces only. However, you can still use existing type groups (see Rule 6.11, Use the `abap_bool` Data Type for Truth Values).[6]

However, you need to declare new types or constants in a context only if *semantically appropriate* and more global types or constants don't already exist (see Rule 6.5). For example, if there is an appropriate data type of the ABAP Dictionary, you don't have to create a local data type in the class for the typing of an interface parameter of a method of a global class. In this case, the data type in the ABAP Dictionary may have to be published in the same package interface as the class.[7]

Note

The misuse of include programs for the declaration of data types and data objects that can be reused across various programs is not allowed according to Rule 4.15, Do Not Use Include Programs Multiple Times.

---

6 As of Releases 7.0 EhP2 and 7.2, you no longer have to load type groups explicitly using the `TYPE-POOLS` statement (see Appendix A, Section A.2.1, Declaring Type Groups).

7 This would also be the case, however, if an interface parameter is typed with a data type of the class that refers to a data type of the ABAP Dictionary.

Bad Example

Listing 6.3 shows the declaration of constants in a type group that are required across different programs. The name of the type group must precede the names of the constants as a prefix. According to Rule 3.2, you should not create any new type groups. For constants that are required across various programs, Rule 6.2 recommends a declaration in global classes or interfaces.

```
TYPE-POOL zicon.

  TYPES zicon_icon TYPE ...

  CONSTANTS:
    zicon_cancel       TYPE zicon_icon VALUE icon_cancel,
    zicon_check        TYPE zicon_icon VALUE icon_check,
    zicon_check_words  TYPE zicon_icon VALUE icon_intensify,
    zicon_document     TYPE zicon_icon VALUE icon_hlp,
    zicon_download     TYPE zicon_icon VALUE icon_export,
    ...
```

Listing 6.3 Declaration of Constants in a Type Group

Good Example

Figure 6.1 illustrates the declaration of the constants from Listing 6.3 in a global class. Here, their visibility is restricted to the actual Package, which is possible as of Release 7.2. In other programs, the constants are addressed via cl_..._icons=>.

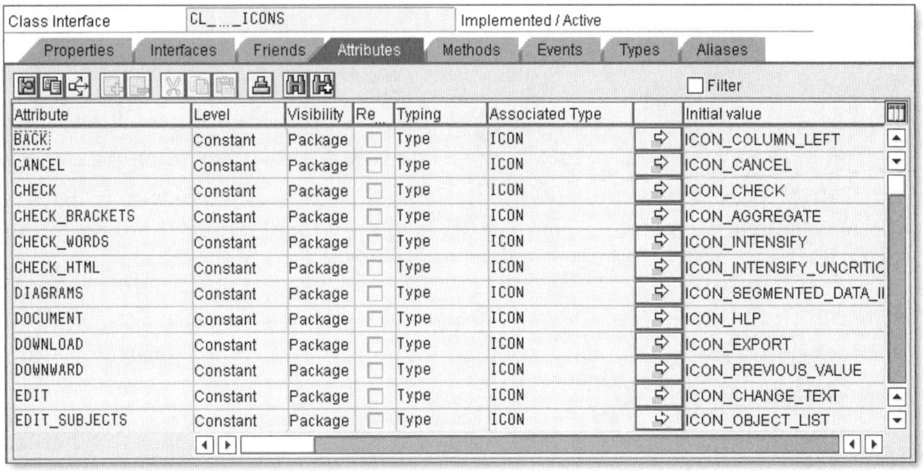

Attribute	Level	Visibility	Re	Typing	Associated Type		Initial value	
BACK	Constant	Package	☐	Type	ICON	⇨	ICON_COLUMN_LEFT	
CANCEL	Constant	Package	☐	Type	ICON	⇨	ICON_CANCEL	
CHECK	Constant	Package	☐	Type	ICON	⇨	ICON_CHECK	
CHECK_BRACKETS	Constant	Package	☐	Type	ICON	⇨	ICON_AGGREGATE	
CHECK_WORDS	Constant	Package	☐	Type	ICON	⇨	ICON_INTENSIFY	
CHECK_HTML	Constant	Package	☐	Type	ICON	⇨	ICON_INTENSIFY_UNCRITIC	
DIAGRAMS	Constant	Package	☐	Type	ICON	⇨	ICON_SEGMENTED_DATA_II	
DOCUMENT	Constant	Package	☐	Type	ICON	⇨	ICON_HLP	
DOWNLOAD	Constant	Package	☐	Type	ICON	⇨	ICON_EXPORT	
DOWNWARD	Constant	Package	☐	Type	ICON	⇨	ICON_PREVIOUS_VALUE	
EDIT	Constant	Package	☐	Type	ICON	⇨	ICON_CHANGE_TEXT	
EDIT_SUBJECTS	Constant	Package	☐	Type	ICON	⇨	ICON_OBJECT_LIST	

Class Interface: CL_..._ICONS — Implemented / Active

Tabs: Properties | Interfaces | Friends | Attributes | Methods | Events | Types | Aliases

☐ Filter

Figure 6.1 Declaration of Constants in a Class

6.1.3   Declaration of Variables

Background

Variables can be declared in the following contexts:

▶ Cross-program: as attributes of global classes and interfaces

▶ Program-local

  ▸ In the global declaration part of a program

  ▸ As attributes of local classes and interfaces

  ▸ In procedures (methods, see Rule 6.37)

Variables that are declared within most of the event blocks or dialog modules as well as between completed processing blocks also belong to the global declaration part of a program but violate Rule 4.12, Implement Global Declarations Centrally.

Program-local variables that are declared in the global declaration part of a program are generally referred to as *global variables.*

Rule

[▪]   **Rule 6.3: Do Not Declare Global Variables**

Do not declare variables in the global declaration part of a program. Variables may only be declared as attributes of classes and interfaces or locally in methods.

Details

This rule is derived from Rule 3.1, Use ABAP Objects. If you disregard helper variables in procedures (methods, see Rule 6.37), the content of the variable of a program indicates the state of the program and consequently the state of an application. In object-oriented programming, the class replaces the program, and the state of an application is no longer the state of the programs but the state of the classes or objects.

Furthermore, Rule 5.1, Utilize the Encapsulation Options as Much as Possible, also assumes a critical role. The data of an application is sufficiently protected from misuse only in the visibility sections of classes.

Except for the following exception, you should not declare any global variables in a new ABAP program. They indicate a poor programming style, which doesn't consider proven concepts, such as task separation or encapsulation. If you need to access the same data of a program from multiple local classes and interfaces, you must create them in an appropriate visibility section of a local class or an interface. This can also be local classes or interfaces that contain nothing else than such attributes.

Tip

Rule 6.3 also applies to the declaration of field symbols with the `FIELD-SYMBOLS` statement (see Section 6.6.6, Accessing Data Objects Dynamically).

Exception

If you still use classical dynpros and selections screens (contrary to Rule 5.18, Use Web Dynpro ABAP), global variables are required as interfaces for the communication between ABAP and classical dynpros. Only for this purpose, global variables can be declared using the following statements:

▸ `DATA`, `TABLES`, and `CONTROLS` for general dynpros (see also Rule 6.7, No Table Work Areas Except for Classical Dynpros)

▸ `PARAMETERS` and `SELECT-OPTIONS` for selection screens

In these cases, you have to ensure the maximum possible encapsulation of those global variables (see Rule 5.19).

Bad Example

Listing 6.4 shows the top include of a function group for document display. In addition to the required interface work area, which is declared with `TABLES`, further global variables exist that indicate the state of the display. However, according to Rule 6.3, you're not allowed to use global variables for other purposes than for the communication with a classical dynpro.

```
FUNCTION-POOL show_documents.

TABLES document_structure.

DATA: g_language      TYPE sy-langu,
      g_display_mode TYPE ...
      ...

CLASS screen_handler DEFINITION.
  PUBLIC SECTION.
    ...
```

Listing 6.4 Global Variables

Good Example

Compared to Listing 6.4, Listing 6.5 shows an enhanced example. The previously global variables are encapsulated in a class that is specifically provided for the state of the display and can be addressed via `display_status=>` in the other classes of the program.

```
FUNCTION-POOL show_documents.

TABLES document_structure.

CLASS display_status DEFINITION.
  PUBLIC SECTION.
    CLASS-DATA: language     TYPE sy-langu,
                display_mode TYPE ...
                ...
ENDCLASS.

CLASS screen_handler DEFINITION.
  PUBLIC SECTION.
    ...
```

Listing 6.5 Static Attributes of a Local Class

6.1.4   Including Structures

Background

For the program-internal composition of structures with the `BEGIN OF` and `END OF` additions of the `TYPES` and `DATA` statements, you can use the `INCLUDE TYPE` or `INCLUDE STRUCTURE` statement to integrate all components of another structure with the current structure at this place without creating a specific substructure. You can specify a name for shared addressing and a suffix to avoid name conflicts. The ABAP Dictionary provides the same functionality.

Substructures, in contrast, are formed if the components of a structure themselves are structured. A structure with substructures is called a nested structure.

Rule

[⚙]   **Rule 6.4: Do Not Include Components of Structures**

Do not integrate the components of other structures via `INCLUDE` when declaring a structure. If required, you can include the components in a real substructure.

Details

The reasons for this rule are the following:

- The integration of components can lead to name conflicts. This is particularly problematic if structures of other contexts are integrated and changed retroactively.

- Despite the potential assignment of a name, the integrated structures cannot be addressed as such without restrictions.

- The necessary internal type information is individually stored for each integrated component. For the components of a substructure, however, this information is stored only once for the substructure.

- In contrast to real substructures, structures that are integrated with `INCLUDE` cannot be declared as boxed components.[8]

- The `INCLUDE` statement interrupts a chained statement that has been created with `BEGIN OF` and `END OF` (in Chapter 4, see Section 4.6.2, Chained Statement).

If no real substructures can be formed, you must avoid name conflicts as much as possible by using suffixes (`RENAMING WITH SUFFIX` addition). This recommendation also applies to the integration of structures in the ABAP Dictionary where you cannot always create real substructures (e.g., for database tables).

Bad Example

Listing 6.6 shows the integration of the components of a structure with another structure, which is not recommended according to Rule 6.4.

```
TYPES:
  BEGIN OF structure_1,
  ...
  END OF structure_1.

TYPES:
  BEGIN OF structure_2,
  ...
  INCLUDE TYPE structure_1 AS sub_structure.
TYPES:
```

---

8 A boxed component is a structured component, which is managed through an internal reference and thus supports initial value sharing. This can considerably reduce the memory requirements for rarely filled components (as of Release 7.0 EhP2 and 7.2).

```
    . . .
  END OF structure_2.
```
Listing 6.6 Including Structure Components

Good Example

Listing 6.7 shows the declaration of a component of a structure as a substructure as recommended in Rule 6.4.

```
TYPES:
  BEGIN OF structure_1,
  . . .
  END OF structure_1.

TYPES:
  BEGIN OF structure_2,
  . . .
    sub_structure TYPE structure_1.
  . . .
  END OF structure_2.
```
Listing 6.7 Declaration of a Substructure

6.1.5   Using Types

Background

You can use the data types that are declared according to Rules 6.1 and 6.2 to declare and create data objects as well as to type field symbols or interface parameters. For this purpose, they are specified after the TYPE addition of the corresponding statements.

Rule

 Rule 6.5: Use Semantically Appropriate Data Types Only

Only use existing types if they correspond to the semantics of the typed object. You mustn't select an existing type only according to the technical properties.

Details

If the type of a data object or an interface parameter is not just an elementary ABAP type, it provides the reader of the source code with information on the semantics of this variable. This makes it easier to understand the meaning of individual variables.

You should therefore only use data types whose semantics also correspond to the usage. The technical properties of a type alone do not justify its use in a specific context because this affects the legibility of the program.

This applies particularly to the reuse or multiple use of existing types. If an application requires a data type with specific technical properties, you shouldn't just use the next best type with these properties from the ABAP Dictionary. Unfortunately, this has been frequently done in the past. In this case, strictly encapsulating the packages can help you avoid the unwanted use of specific data types.

Tip

This rule particularly applies to the use of ABAP Dictionary structures. You should, for instance, never use the same structure that defines a database table as a template for input/output fields of classical dynpros or in Web Dynpro. Rule 2.1, Adhere to the SoC Principle, would be violated then as well.

Bad Example

In Listing 6.8, a variable that is clearly provided for a truth value according to its name and usage is declared with a technically correct but semantically wrong data type. `syst-batch` is actually the data type for the `sy-batch` system field (see Section 6.3, System Fields), which indicates whether a program is executed in the background.

```
DATA is_empty TYPE syst-batch.
...
IF is_empty IS INITIAL.
  ...
ENDIF.
```

Listing 6.8 Using a Semantically Wrong Type

Good Example

Compared to Listing 6.8, Listing 6.9 shows an enhanced example that uses the provided type for truth values, `abap_bool`, of the `abap` type group (see Section 6.1.11, Data Objects for Truth Values). The truth value is compared against a constant from the same type group provided for this purpose.

```
DATA is_empty TYPE abap_bool.
...
IF is_empty EQ abap_false.
  ...
ENDIF.
```

Listing 6.9 Using a Semantically Correct Type

6.1.6   Referring to Data Types or Data Objects

Background

In addition to using data types for declarations and typing with the TYPE addition (see Section 6.1.5, Using Types), you can also directly refer to the data type of a data object that is visible here using the alternative addition, LIKE. This includes the reference to data objects of the same program, interface parameters of the current procedure, attributes of global classes and interfaces as well as constants in type groups.

Rule

[✓]   **Rule 6.6: Declare Dependent Data Objects with Reference to Other Data Objects**

If a data object directly depends on another data object, directly refer to it using LIKE for the declaration. In all other cases, use TYPE to refer to a standalone data type.

Details

For example, if a helper variable of the type of an input parameter is required within a procedure (method, see Rule 6.37), you shouldn't declare it with reference to the type of the parameter using TYPE but with reference to the parameter itself using LIKE. You can also declare work areas using LIKE LINE OF if the parameter is an internal table. In the case of typing with LIKE, you can retroactively change the type of the parameter without always having to adapt the procedure implementation.

However, if no close reference to another data object is given, it is usually more useful to declare data objects with reference to a standalone data type (see Rule 6.1) using TYPE.

Tip

You should never implement an obsolete reference to flat structures or database tables or views of the ABAP Dictionary with `LIKE` (see Appendix A, Section A.2.4, Referring to Data Types).

Bad Example

Listing 6.10 shows the declaration of a helper variable in a method that is supposed to be of the same data type as an interface parameter. The `TYPE` reference to the data type requires a manual implementation of possible typing changes.

```
CLASS some_class DEFINITION ...
  PUBLIC SECTION.
    METHODS some_method
      CHANGING some_parameter TYPE some_type.
    ...
ENDCLASS.

CLASS some_class IMPLEMENTATION.
  METHOD some_method.
    DATA save_parameter TYPE some_type.
    save_parameter = some_parameter.
    ...
  ENDMETHOD.
  ...
ENDCLASS.
```

Listing 6.10 TYPE Reference to the Data Type of an Interface Parameter

Good Example

Compared to Listing 6.10, Listing 6.11 shows the improved declaration of the helper variable that now directly refers to the interface parameter with `LIKE` so that possible typing changes are automatically accepted.

```
  ...
  METHOD some_method.
    DATA save_parameter LIKE some_parameter.
    save_parameter = some_parameter.
    ...
  ENDMETHOD.
  ...
```

Listing 6.11 LIKE Reference to an Interface Parameter

6.1.7   Table Work Areas

Background

A table work area is a structured data object of a flat structure type, a database table type, or a view type of the ABAP Dictionary that is declared using the TABLES or NODES statements.[9]

From the data type view, the two statements

► **TABLES** table_wa.

► **NODES** table_wa.

are the same as

► **DATA** table_wa **TYPE** table_wa.

That means that data objects with the same name and type as the corresponding data types from the ABAP Dictionary are declared. This is supplemented with further meanings of TABLES and NODES. For all meanings, refer to the ABAP Keyword Documentation. The essential properties are as follows:

► TABLES and NODES declare so-called interface work areas which multiple programs of a program group share (see Section 6.5.6, Internal and External Procedure Calls).

► TABLES declares interfaces to classical dynpros and selection screens.

► NODES declares an interface to logical databases.

In addition, you can also use table work areas that have been declared with TABLES as implicit work areas in obsolete abbreviated forms of Open SQL or even older statements for database accesses (see Section A.12, Data Storage).

Rule

[⚙] **Rule 6.7: No Table Work Areas Except for Classical Dynpros**

Only use the TABLES statement in the global declaration part of function groups to communicate with classical dynpros. The NODES statement is no longer required outside of wrappings of logical databases.

---

9 NODES also allows for additional ABAP Dictionary types.

Details

The TABLES statement is not allowed within classes anyway and the NODES statement can only be syntactically created in the global declaration part of an executable program that is linked to a logical database. However, the last aspect is no longer allowed according to Rule 3.3, Accept the Standard Settings for Program Attributes.

Because obsolete database accesses (see Section A.12, Data Storage) that require the TABLES statement and shared data areas between programs (see Section A.2.2, Interface Work Areas) are not allowed, there's no need for using the TABLES statement except for the declaration of an interface to classical dynpros (see the following exception).

Exception

If dynpro fields in classical dynpros are defined with a reference to flat structures in the ABAP Dictionary, you must declare the global data objects of the ABAP program that have the same names using the TABLES statement. Otherwise, the data objects of the ABAP program are not linked to the dynpro fields, and their content cannot be accessed. For more information on the usage of classical dynpros, refer to Chapter 5, Section 5.3, User Interfaces.

Furthermore, TABLES is also required for the declaration of specific work areas when handling function codes of selection screens.

Note

That the TABLES statement is restricted to this last technical requirement, that is, the communication with classical dynpros and selection screens, can also be derived from other rules of these guidelines. However, because the usage of the TABLES statement instead of DATA still enjoys great popularity among experienced ABAP developers, Rule 6.7 explicitly stresses its prohibition.

6.1.8 Literals

Background

A literal is a data object that is defined in the source code of a program and completely determined by its value. Possible literals include the following:

- ▶ **Numeric literals**
  Sequence of digits with an optional plus/minus sign. The data type is either i or p.

- ▶ **Character literals**
  - ▶ Text field literals, which are enclosed in single quotes ('). The data type is c.
  - ▶ String literals, which are enclosed in back quotes (`). The data type is string.

Numeric literals do not support decimal separators or scientific notations with mantissa and exponent. To express such numeric values, you must use character literals (see Section 6.2.4, Specifying Numbers).

Rule

Rule 6.8: Avoid Literals in Operand Positions

Avoid the direct specification of values in the source code using literals. Instead, declare constants with these values. This applies particularly to numeric values.

Details

In the source code, some values are needed at various positions. It is therefore not useful to directly specify these values in the source code because you then have to adapt several statements if the value changes. If you introduce an appropriate constant instead, the value can be centrally adapted in the source code.[10] This can considerably facilitate the maintenance and further development of the program.

It also makes sense to create a corresponding constant for values that are only used in one statement. The name of the constant provides semantics for the value, which increases the understandability of the source code.

Numeric literals that occur in the source code without obvious semantic meaning are generally referred to as "magic numbers." They should be avoided in ABAP programs. For character literals, the translatability also plays a role (see Section 6.7.1, Storing System Texts).

---

10 Of course, literals are allowed as a value specification for the declaration of constants.

Exception

In specific situations, however, using a constant can also affect the legibility. In this case, it makes more sense to specify a literal, for example:

- ▶ `CALL FUNCTION 'MY_FUNC'.`
- ▶ `IF sy-subrc = 0.`
- ▶ `READ TABLE ... INDEX 1.`
- ▶ `ADD 1 TO counter.`

These examples clearly indicate the semantic meaning of the literals. The translatability is of no importance either here.

Another area where character literals can be used in a beneficial and comprehensive way is dynamic programming. Here, parts of statements or entire programs are generated, which is hardly possible without character literals. As of Releases 7.0 EhP2 and 7.2, character string templates provide considerably enhanced options for the use of literal texts.

Bad Example

Listing 6.12 shows the specification of the mathematical constant π in operand positions by using the same literal several times, which makes the program too complex and prone to typos.

```
DATA: radius        TYPE decfloat34,
      circumference TYPE decfloat34,
      area          TYPE decfloat34.

...

circumference =
  2* '3.14159265358979323846264383279503' * radius.
area =
  '3.14159265358979323846264383279503' * radius ** 2.
```

Listing 6.12 Magical Numbers

Good Example

Listing 6.13 shows the declaration of a constant for which the literal with the value π is required only once and its use in the corresponding operand positions.

```
CONSTANTS pi TYPE  decfloat34
             VALUE '3.14159265358979323846264383279503'.
```

```
DATA: radius        TYPE decfloat34,
      circumference TYPE decfloat34,
      area          TYPE decfloat34.

...

circumference = 2 * pi * radius.
area          = pi * radius ** 2.
```

Listing 6.13 Numeric Constant

6.1.9   Strings

Background

Strings are dynamic data objects of variable length (see Section 6.6.3, Using Dynamic Data Objects). There are text strings of the `string` data type and byte strings of the `xstring` data type in which you can store character or byte strings.

In contrast to text and byte fields of a fixed length (`c`, `x` data types)[11], the length of strings adapts to the content automatically. Strings are deep data objects that are internally managed by references. For this, the following additional memory is required:

- For strings whose length is less than 30 characters or 60 bytes, the additional memory requirement is approximately between 10 and 40 bytes depending on the string length.

- For longer strings, the additional memory requirement is approximately 50 bytes, irrespective of the string length.

In the case of assignments between strings, so-called *sharing* applies. This means that only the internal reference is copied first. Sharing is canceled if the source or target object is accessed for modification.

Rule

[⚙] **Rule 6.9: Use Strings for Character and Byte String Processing**

Use strings for the internal storage and processing of character and byte strings instead of fields of a fixed length.

---

11 Other data types, such as n, d, and t, are also treated as text fields in many operand positions.

Details

Strings are more flexible than fields of a fixed length and usually help you save memory space, because no unnecessary space is occupied by blanks or zeros and because sharing is implemented for assignments. Furthermore, *trailing blanks* are always significant in text strings. In text fields trailing blanks are simply ignored in many operand positions (but not in all), which may be quite confusing at times.

Exception

In the following cases, fields of a fixed length should be used instead of strings:

▶ The length of the field is critical, for example, for templates or for interfaces to screen fields.

▶ Despite sharing, the additional administration effort exceeds the benefits (see Rule 6.50, Consider the Ratio of Administration and Application Data), which may be particularly the case for very short strings. If it is obvious that a certain length is never exceeded, you can also use short fields of a fixed length.

▶ Structures that only contain character-type components are supposed to be treated like a single text field. This is not possible for structures that contain text strings (see also Rule 6.19, Avoid Implicit Casting).

Bad Example

Listing 6.14 shows an internal table for storing an HTML page whose line type is a text field of the fixed length 255. Most of the memory space of the internal table, however, is probably wasted for blanks.

```
TYPES html_line TYPE c LENGTH 255.

DATA html_table TYPE TABLE OF html_line.

APPEND '<HTML>' TO html_table.
...
APPEND '<BODY>' TO html_table.
...
APPEND '</BODY>' TO html_table.
APPEND '</HTML>' TO html_table.
```

Listing 6.14 Internal Table with Text Fields of a Fixed Length

Good Example

Listing 6.15 shows the example from Listing 6.14 but uses text strings. The memory space gained should exceed the additional administration effort considerably. As an alternative to using an internal table, you can also concatenate the HTML page in a single text string; however, this decreases the legibility, for example, in the ABAP Debugger.

```
DATA html_table TYPE TABLE OF string.

APPEND `<HTML>` TO html_table.
...
APPEND `<BODY>` TO html_table.
...
APPEND `</BODY>` TO html_table.
APPEND `</HTML>` TO html_table.
```

Listing 6.15 Internal Table with Strings

6.1.10 Start Values

Background

When you declare a data object with the DATA statement, you can use the VALUE addition to define a value with which the data object is populated when it is created. If you don't use the VALUE addition, the system uses the type-specific initial value. If you use the CONSTANTS statement, you must always specify the VALUE addition. If you want to use the type-specific initial value here, you can implement this by specifying the VALUE IS INITIAL addition.

If the defined start value doesn't correspond to the type and length of the data object, a conversion takes place during the program generation.

Rule

[⚙] | **Rule 6.10: Start Values Must Correspond to the Data Type of the Data Object**

Only specify start values with the VALUE addition whose type, content, and length correspond to the data type of the declared data object.

Details

A type-specific specification of a start value is not always possible because ABAP doesn't support type-specific literals (see Section 6.1.8) for all potential data types. In all cases where a conversion is vital, you should select the content of literals that are used as start values and their length in such a way that the actual value exactly corresponds to the expectations that you have when reading the source code.

Tip

For more information on start values in combination with numeric types, refer to Rule 6.15, Use a General Notation for Numeric Values.

Bad Example

The unbiased reader of Listing 6.16 would probably expect that the `high_noon` constant contains value 120000. Actually, however, the constant contains the value 092000 because the value of the numeric literal is considered a number in seconds and 12,000 seconds correspond to 9:20 a.m. of the next day.

```
CONSTANTS high_noon TYPE t VALUE 120000.
```

Listing 6.16 Unexpected Start Value

Good Example

Listing 6.17 enhances Listing 6.16 by replacing the numeric literal with a text field literal. Now, the `high_noon` constant contains the expected value, 120000.

```
CONSTANTS high_noon TYPE t VALUE '120000'.
```

Listing 6.17 Type-Specific Start Value

6.1.11 Data Objects for Truth Values

Background

Truth values are results of logical expressions. A truth value is either true or false. Currently, ABAP doesn't support a Boolean data type and therefore no data objects for truth values. The result of a logical expression can thus not be directly assigned to a data object.

It has become a common practice to express the truth value "true" as 'X' and the truth value "false" as a blank (' '). As of Releases 7.0 EhP2 and 7.2, there are Boolean functions that have logical expressions as arguments and return the value 'X' or a blank depending on the result.

To make it easier to use truth values that are expressed according to this convention, the `abap` type group contains the `abap_bool` data type of the elementary type (c) of length 1 as well as constants `abap_true` of value 'X' and `abap_false` of value

' ' instead of a real Boolean data type. In addition, there is also the `abap_unde-fined` constant of value ' - '.

Rule

[⚙] ███ Rule 6.11: Use the abap_bool Data Type for Truth Values ███

To explicitly handle truth values, use the `abap_bool` type as a workaround for a real Boolean data type. A data object that is declared in this way is not supposed to contain other values than the corresponding constants, `abap_true` and `abap_false` (as well as `abap_undefined`).

Details

The `abap_bool` type and the `abap_true` and `abap_false` constants clearly indicate that truth values are used.

Rule 6.8, Avoid Literals in Operand Positions, states that you shouldn't just use the 'X' and ' ' literals. State queries via the IS INITIAL and IS NOT INITIAL predicates or using the `space` constant are also not useful because to understand them, you have to be familiar with the technical values of `abap_true` and `abap_false` which don't play a role in the context of real Boolean data objects.

The `abap` type group additionally contains a third constant for the `abap_bool` type, namely, `abap_undefined`. However, the implementation of three-value logic makes only sense in exceptional cases and should therefore also only be used in exceptional cases. In this case, note that `abap_undefined` doesn't contain the initial value for variables of the `abap_bool` type. The initial value is always the value of `abap_false`. If required, the value of `abap_undefined` can be defined as the start value via the VALUE addition when declaring a truth value.

Bad Example

Listing 6.18 shows an inappropriate emulation of Boolean data objects, which do not exist in ABAP.

```
DATA is_found TYPE c LENGTH 1.
...
is_found = 'X'.
...
IF is_found IS NOT INITIAL.
    ...
ENDIF.
```

Listing 6.18 Inappropriate Emulation of Boolean Data Objects

Good Example

Listing 6.19 shows the recommended emulation of Boolean data objects, which do not exist in ABAP.[12]

```
DATA is_found TYPE abap_bool.
...
is_found = abap_true.
...
IF is_found = abap_true.
   ...
ENDIF.
```

Listing 6.19 Appropriate Emulation of Boolean Data Objects

6.2 Assignments, Calculations, and Other Accesses to Data

In the case of assignments (see also Section 4.6.4, Assignments and Calculations, in Chapter 4), the content of a data object is transferred to another data object. If the data objects are compatible, the content is copied unchanged. If the data objects are incompatible, and there is a suitable conversion rule, the content is converted. Assignments usually use the assignment operator (=, see Rule 4.19).

A calculation is made in a calculation expression (in Chapter 4, see Section 4.6.5, Calculation Expressions), which is executed in an operand position or on the right side of the equals sign of the COMPUTE statement. If necessary, the result of a calculation expression is converted to the data type of the operand position or of the result of the COMPUTE statement. In arithmetic expressions, the calculation is executed in a calculation type, which depends on the data types of all operands, including the result.

6.2.1 Assignments Between Different Types

Background

ABAP allows for the direct value assignment between data objects of different data types. A prerequisite is that there is a suitable conversion rule and that the content

---

12 As of Releases 7.0 EhP2 and 7.2, you no longer have to load type groups, such as the abap type group in this case, explicitly using the TYPE-POOLS statement (see Section A.2.1, Declaring Type Groups).

of the source field is a useful value for the data type of the target field. If the system cannot find a suitable conversion rule, or if the content of the source field is not appropriate, an exception is triggered.

Such conversion are not only used in direct assignments but also in a lot of operand positions and especially in arithmetic calculations if the given operand doesn't contain the data type that is expected for this position.

Rule

[⚙] **Rule 6.12: Avoid Conversions**

If possible, assign values between compatible data objects of the same data type.

Details

Type conversions involve additional runtime and may not always lead to the result intended by the developer. Consequently, you should only carry out conversions between data objects of different data types if they cannot be avoided. You should particularly avoid conversions if the conversion rule provides unexpected results (see Section 6.2.3, Using Conversion Rules).

Bad Example

Listing 6.20 shows an arithmetic calculation with two unnecessary conversions. The '1' text field literal needs to be converted to the i calculation type first. Then, the result of the calculation of the i type needs to be converted to the n data type. Such conversions lead to measurable longer runtimes.

```
DATA index TYPE n LENGTH 4.

...

DO ... TIMES.
  index = sy-index - '1'.
  ...
ENDDO.
```

Listing 6.20 Unnecessary Conversions

Good Example

Compared to Listing 6.20, Listing 6.21 shows improved code without conversions.

```
DATA index TYPE i.

...

DO ... TIMES.
  index = sy-index - 1.
  ...
ENDDO.
```

Listing 6.21 Type-Specific Assignments

6.2.2 Avoiding Invalid Values

Background

For performance reasons, the ABAP runtime environment doesn't check for each assignment whether the target field contains a valid value after the assignment. Particularly for target fields of the n, d, and t data types, the conversion rules allow for any alphanumeric value for the result of an assignment. But only the following values are valid values:

- For the n type only digits
- A calendar date in the YYYYMMDD format for the d type
- A time in the HHMMSS format for the t type

You must pay particularly attention to the fact that the initial value of the d data type (00000000) is an invalid date itself and that this initial value is generated — and not the zero point of date calculations (value 00010101) — when the number 0 is converted to the d data type.[13]

Rule

Rule 6.13: Assign Valid Values Only   [⚙]

Populate the data objects of the n, d, and t data types in assignments and calculations with valid values only.

---

13 As of value 1, all numbers are interpreted as the number of days since 01/01/0001 for date calculations. When being converted to a number, date 01/01/0001 consequently becomes zero but not vice versa.

Details

The correct behavior of statements that use variables of the n, d, and t types can be ensured for valid values only. Because the initial value for variables of the d type is no valid value itself, you should always define a suitable valid start value using the VALUE addition.

In the case of arithmetic calculations with date fields, you must therefore bear in mind that a result of the value 0 when assigned to a target field of the d data type also creates an invalid initial value, which means that you may have to handle such a result with particular care.

If you don't populate the data objects of the critical data types yourself and the robustness of a program compensates possible performance problems, you should check the content of the data objects for validity before using them.

Tip

To ensure a secure use of date and time fields and of calculations that are based on them, you should work with *timestamps*, which enforce valid values. The CONVERT DATE and CONVERT TIME STAMP statements are provided for conversions, and the CL_ABAP_TSTMP class can be used for calculations. As of Releases 7.0 EhP2 and 7.2, also the EXACT addition for the MOVE statement enables you to ensure that fields of the n, d, and t types are solely populated with valid values.

Bad Example

Listing 6.22 shows a trap in which you may get caught when using conversion rules in ABAP without care. The literals can be copied to the date fields without generating an exception. These date fields then contain the values 07092009 and 16092009. Unfortunately, these are interpreted as invalid dates 0709/20/09 and 1609/20/09. During the calculation, they are converted to 0 and the result is 0 instead of 9, as you would expect when looking at this example.

```
DATA: date1  TYPE d,
      date2  TYPE d,
      result TYPE i.

date1 = '07092009'.
date2 = '16092009'.
result = date2 - date1.
```

Listing 6.22 Invalid Values in Date Fields

Good Example

Listing 6.23 shows a date calculation, which has the expected result, 9, due to the valid values in the date fields.

```
DATA: date1  TYPE d,
      date2  TYPE d,
      result TYPE i.

date1 = '20090907'.
date2 = '20090916'.
result = date2 - date1.
```

Listing 6.23 Valid Values in Date Fields

Listing 6.24 shows how the validity of the date fields can be checked before the calculation if the fields are not populated in the same program.

```
IF date1 <> 0 AND date2 <> 0.
  result = date2 - date1.
ELSE.
  ...
ENDIF.
```

Listing 6.24 Checking the Validity of Date Fields

6.2.3   Using Conversion Rules

Background

ABAP provides numerous conversion rules for assignments between data objects of different data types. These rules govern assignments between

- Elementary data objects
- Elementary data objects and structures
- Structures
- Internal tables
- Reference variables

Only 2 of the 144 possible assignments between data objects of the 12 different elementary data types are not allowed (from d to t and vice versa). All other assignments are allowed — and almost every assignment has its own conversion rules. You particularly require rules for assignments between data objects of the same data type if different technical properties, such as length or number of decimal places, are allowed. As of Releases 7.0 EhP2 and 7.2, the EXACT addition is provided for the MOVE statement. It only allows for conversions that lead to valid values and if no values are lost.

Rule

Rule 6.14: Avoid Unexpected Conversion Results

Only assign such data objects to each other whose content corresponds to the data type of the target field and leads to an expected result. You shouldn't exploit every ABAP conversion rule to its full extent.

Details

The ABAP conversion rules are based on the philosophy that assignment should be allowed between as many combinations of values as possible without generating exceptions. In this context, ABAP behaves quite differently from other programming languages in which assignments between different data types are usually handled more strictly and special conversion routines or explicit casting for specific requested conversions are provided.

Although it is certainly comfortable to be able to readily assign all possible data objects to each other, this also provides disadvantages. Section 6.2.2, Avoiding Invalid Values, already indicated the possibility of generating invalid values. Another example is implicit casting, which takes place during assignments between elementary data objects and structures or during assignments between incompatible structures. This is further explained in Rule 6.19, Avoid Implicit Casting.

However, even if no invalid values but valid target values are generated from invalid source values, this does not necessarily meet the expectations of the reader and can considerably restrict the maintainability of the program. An example here is how an invalid content in the source field is handled when a character type is assigned to a byte type. Instead of terminating the assignment with an exception, the system simply transfers hexadecimal zeros as of the first invalid character.

A solution is provided in Releases 7.0 EhP2 and 7.2, which contain the EXACT addition for the MOVE statement (for so-called loss-free assignments). This addition triggers an exception in such cases. Even though this is a bit late in the day, you could consider the behavior of an assignment with the EXACT addition the normal, expected behavior while other, unexpected behaviors represent an implementation of special rules, which — alas — is the standard behavior in ABAP.

Bad Example

Those who are not familiar with all details of the ABAP conversion rules would probably expect an exception for the assignment of the text to the numeric text in Listing 6.25. Actually, only the digits of the text are considered so that the target field receives value 00000043 instead of value 00000007, which you could also expect.

```
DATA: text     TYPE string,
      num_text TYPE n LENGTH 8.
...
text = '4 Apples + 3 Oranges'.
...
num_text = text.
```

Listing 6.25 Conversion of Invalid Values to Valid Values

Good Example

Listing 6.26 corrects Listing 6.25 by using the EXACT addition for the MOVE statement, which is available as of Releases 7.0 EhP2 and 7.2. In the example illustrated, this addition triggers an exception.

```
...
text = '4 Apples + 3 Oranges'.
...
TRY.
    MOVE EXACT text TO num_text.
  CATCH cx_sy_conversion_error.
    ...
ENDTRY.
```

Listing 6.26 Exception for Invalid Values

6.2.4   Specification of Numbers

Background

Because there are no specific literals for numbers with decimal places or with mantissa and exponent, these must be expressed through character literals if required. The following notations are possible here:

▶ **Mathematical notation**
   This is a sequence of digits with exactly one point as the decimal separator and

optionally with a plus/minus sign in front of the digits, which can be separated from the digits with a blank, such as

```
- 1234.56
```

▶ **Commercial notation**
This is a sequence of digits with exactly one point as the decimal separator and optionally with a plus/minus sign after the digits, which can be separated from the digits with a blank, such as

```
1234.56-
```

▶ **Technical scientific notation**
This is an uninterrupted sequence of a mantissa (an optional plus/minus sign, digits with exactly one point as the decimal separator), a character e or E, and an exponent (an optional plus/minus sign and further digits), such as

```
-1.23456E03
```

Rule

[⚙] **Rule 6.15: Use a General Notation for Numeric Values**

Create numerical information in character strings that is supposed to be used for an assignment to a numeric data object in such a way that it is accepted for all possible target types. The plus/minus sign should always be in front of the digits, and blanks mustn't be contained.

Details

When converting a character string to a numeric variable, the notations that are accepted depend on the type of the target variable:

▶ If the type of the target variable is decfloat16 or decfloat34 (as of Releases 7.0 EhP2 and 7.2), all three notations are accepted.

▶ If the type of the target variable is f, all three notations are accepted. The mathematical and commercial notations are only accepted, however, if the plus/minus sign isn't separated from the digit sequence with one or several blanks and no blanks are in front of the digits.

▶ If the type of the target variable is p or i, only the mathematical notation and the commercial notation are accepted.

To maintain the legibility of a program and ensure that numerical information that is stored in a character string can be converted to as many numeric data types as possible, you should always use the mathematical notation without blanks between the plus/minus sign and the digit sequence, if possible. This notation also corresponds to other standards, such as the canonical representation of XML schema data types.

Bad Example

Listing 6.27 shows the initialization of a generically typed parameter with a commercial notation where the plus/minus sign is separated with a blank. If an actual parameter is transferred with another type than `f`, the assignment accordingly returns value `-1000`. If an actual parameter of the `f` type is used, the returned value is `+1000`.

```
CLASS class DEFINITION.
  PUBLIC SECTION.
    METHODS calculate_something
      EXPORTING number TYPE numeric.
ENDCLASS.

CLASS class IMPLEMENTATION.
  METHOD calculate_something.
    number = '1000 -'.
    ...
  ENDMETHOD.
ENDCLASS.
```

Listing 6.27 Unfavorable Numeric Notation

Good Example

Listing 6.28 shows an assignment with a general notation, which is well legible and returns the same result for all numeric data types, namely, `-1000`.

```
METHOD calculate_something.
  number = '-1000'.
  ...
ENDMETHOD.
```

Listing 6.28 General Numeric Notation

6.2.5 Selecting the Numeric Type

Background

To store numbers and for calculations, ABAP provides different numeric types with various properties and value ranges, such as:

- Signed 4-byte integers (type i)[14]
- Packed numbers in the BCD format (Binary Coded Decimals, type p)
- Binary floating point numbers (type f)
- Decimal floating point numbers (types decfloat16, decfloat34, since Releases 7.0 EhP2 and 7.2)

The decimal floating point numbers meet the requirements for an exact processing of decimal numbers in large value ranges of which the p and f data types cover only a partial aspect, respectively.

Rule

[✓] **Rule 6.16: Select Suitable Numeric Types for Numbers and Calculations**

Select a numeric type in accordance with the values that are supposed to be represented in order to achieve the highest possible speed and accuracy. The following rule of thumb applies:

- i for integers
- p for fixed point numbers
- decfloat16 or decfloat34 for floating point numbers
- f in exceptional cases only

Details

The calculation speed and accuracy are generally contradictory requirements and depend on the data type of the data objects to be processed. Therefore, when selecting the numeric type, you must weigh these two requirements. These considerations must also include the value range that is supposed to be represented:

- If the values that are supposed to be represented are integers, you must usually use the i type. This provides for the highest possible calculation speed. Examples of such integers are counters, indexes, offsets, and time intervals. If the values that are supposed to be represented exceed the value range of the i type, you can use the p type without decimal places instead. The calculation speed is slower in this case, but the mapping of the decimal places is still exact (except

---

14 There are also 1-byte and 2-byte integers with the internal types, b and s. Such data objects, however, cannot be generated via a reference to an built-in ABAP type but via a reference to the predefined ABAP Dictionary types, INT1 and INT2.

for rounding errors). If this value range is still not sufficient, you can work with a floating point type (the `decfloat16` and `decfloat34` types since Releases 7.0 EhP2 and 7.2, previously only the `f` type).

▶ If you have to map nonintegral values that have a fixed number of decimal places, you can use the `p` type. But calculations with the `p` type are implemented in the ABAP kernel and not by the hardware. Examples for such nonintegral values are lengths, weights, or monetary amounts. If their value range is not sufficient, you can use the decimal floating point types, `decfloat16` and `decfloat34`, instead that are provided as of Releases 7.0 EhP2 and 7.2. The binary floating point type, `f`, is less suitable because it cannot map all decimal fractions. In addition to the unavoidable rounding errors, this further restricts the calculation accuracy.

▶ For nonintegral values with a variable number of decimal places or a large value range, you should use the decimal floating point types, `decfloat16` or `decfloat34`, as of Releases 7.0 EhP2 and 7.2. The latter has a larger number of decimal places and a larger value range but leads to increased memory consumption.

Prior to Releases 7.0 EhP2 and 7.2, for the third item of the preceding list only the binary floating point type `f` was available. Due to the hardware support that is available on all platforms, it enables fast calculations but is inferior to the new decimal floating point types as follows:

▶ The `f` type can only represent fractions with the power of two in the denominator (1/2, 1/4, 1/8, etc.) and their sums there of exactly. Other values are rounded according to this mapping. This rounding process doesn't correspond to the decimal rounding process (and thus usually doesn't meet the expectations of the developer or user). For example, value 0.815 is internally approximated as `8.1499999999999995E-01`. Rounding to two decimal places therefore returns 0.81 instead of the expected value 0.82.

▶ According to IEEE754, very large numbers can no longer be exactly represented if the difference between the largest and the smallest exponent is larger than 52 in the total of powers of two, which is used for this purpose. For example, 1E+23 is represented as `9.9999999999999992E+22`.

▶ A number of the `f` type cannot be rounded to a specific number of decimal places when the result is to be assigned to another number of the `f` type.

▶ Divisions by powers of 10, which often occur when converting metric units, for example, are not exact. `805 / 1000`, for instance, is `8.0500000000000005E-01`.

▶ Simple calculations, often have unexpected results. `123456.15 - 123455`, for example, returns `1.1499999999941792` as a result.

▶ According to IEEE 754, the conversion of binary floating point numbers to other number formats is not clearly defined. Consequently, when storing data on the database, the rounding behavior depends on the platform and how the numbers of the `f` type are represented in the database.

The decimal floating point types, `decfloat16` and `decfloat34`, don't have these problems. Both have a larger value range as the `f` type, and `decfloat34` has 34 instead of 16 decimal places. However, the following restrictions apply:

▶ Calculations with decimal floating point types are currently slower than calculations with the `f` type (the speed is similar to calculations with the `p` type).[15]

▶ The decimal floating point types are not supported by corresponding data types in all database platforms yet.[16] As a workaround, the ABAP Dictionary provides a set of predefined data types (`DF16_...`, `DF34_...`) that are based on existing types (`DEC` and `RAW`) and allow for various processing options.

The benefits of the decimal floating point types compensate the currently slow calculation speed in most cases. However, you might still use the `f` data type if you have stringent requirements on the performance and not too stringent requirements on the calculation accuracy. In this context, you must also bear in mind that the speed advantage currently provided by `f` for calculations may be outweighed by the fact that conversions of the `f` type to other numeric types are relatively slow (for more information on this, also refer to Rule 6.17, Avoid Unnecessary Rounding Errors).

Tip

For programs that are already created with decimal floating point types, the performance is increased the moment the used processor architecture supports decimal

---

15 So far, only the Power6 architecture by IBM provides hardware support for such decimal floating point calculations according to IEEE-754-2008. On other platforms, the calculations with decimal floating point numbers must be carried out on the software side in the ABAP kernel similarly to calculations with the `p` type.

16 So far, only IBM provides support for their databases.

floating point calculations and the ABAP runtime environment makes use of this hardware support. Then, calculations with decimal floating point numbers become faster than calculations with packed numbers.

Bad Example

Listing 6.29 shows a declaration of a binary floating point number with an assignment of the start value `0.815`. The true start value, however, is `8.1499999999999995E-01`.

```
DATA number TYPE f VALUE '0.815'.
```

Listing 6.29 Binary Floating Point Number

Good Example

Listing 6.30 shows a declaration of a decimal floating point number with an assignment of the start value `0.815`. The true start value is `8.15E-01` indeed.

```
DATA number TYPE decfloat34 VALUE '0.815'
```

Listing 6.30 Decimal Floating Point Number

6.2.6 Rounding Errors

Background

For value assignments between floating point numbers (the `f` type, the `decfloat16` and `decfloat34` types since Releases 7.0 EhP2 and 7.2) and fixed point numbers (the `i` and `p` types), rounding errors usually occur, which distort the value. The other way round, values that are assigned from the `p` (and `decfloat16`, `decfloat34`) type to the `f` type are also not always represented exactly (see Section 6.2.5, Selecting the Numeric Type).

Rule

Rule 6.17: Avoid Unnecessary Rounding Errors	[✓]
Due to the resulting rounding errors, avoid unnecessary or frequent conversions between floating and fixed point numbers.

Details

Within a program, the values of a number should be kept in a data object with the numeric data type of the highest required accuracy as long as possible. This particularly applies when storing interim results for calculations.

In no case should the requirements of data input or data output, such as the formatting on the screen or in a print list, affect the internal storage of numbers. If you must format a number with a specific number of decimal places, you shouldn't convert the actual value to a packed number. Instead, you should implement the appropriate formatting in a character-type field with the language elements provided for this purpose. As of Releases 7.0 EhP2 and 7.2, these are character string templates. Previously, this was the WRITE TO statement.

Bad Example

Listing 6.31 shows a calculation in which results are assigned to a numeric field that has been provided for output. Due to the carried out rounding, the result is 56.00 instead of 55.55.

```
DATA: output     TYPE p DECIMALS 2,
      percentage TYPE decfloat34,
      value      TYPE decfloat34.

percentage = '55.55'.
value      = '100.0'.

output = percentage / 100.
output = value * output.
```

Listing 6.31 Rounding Error

Good Example

Listing 6.32 corrects Listing 6.31 by separating data objects provided for calculations and a character-type data object for the formatted output.

```
DATA: result     TYPE decfloat34,
      percentage TYPE decfloat34,
      value      TYPE decfloat34.

DATA  output  TYPE c LENGTH 40.

percentage = '55.55'.
value   = '100.0'.

result = percentage / 100.
result = value * result.

WRITE result TO output DECIMALS 2 EXPONENT 0.
```

Listing 6.32 Exact Calculation

6.2.7 Division by Zero

Background

All common programming languages, including ABAP, don't allow for a division by zero and trigger an exception in these cases. However, in ABAP there is one unique case: The `cx_sy_zerodivide` exception is not triggered if the dividend in the division by zero is also 0. In this case, the division in ABAP returns 0 as a result.

Rule

Rule 6.18: Avoid a Division by Zero	[⚙]
Don't fully exploit the behavior that ABAP allows for a division by zero if the dividend itself is zero.

Details

The ABAP behavior is rather random and doesn't meet the observer's expectations. It should therefore not be fully utilized. You must either avoid divisions by zero using preconditions or explicitly trigger the corresponding exception for the `0/0` case.

Example

Listing 6.33 always triggers an exception if the dividend of a division is zero.

```
IF divisor <> 0.
   result = dividend / divisor.
ELSE.
   RAISE EXCEPTION TYPE cx_sy_zerodivide.
ENDIF.
```

Listing 6.33 Division by Zero

6.2.8 Casting

Background

Casting refers to the process of handling a data object by assuming a certain data type. This differs from the meaning of the concept in other programming languages, such as Java, where casting is understood as something that is referred to as conversion in ABAP.

Casting in ABAP is either explicit or implicit:

► Explicit casting is possible with the CASTING addition for the ASSIGN statement and for the ASSIGNING addition in statements for the processing of internal tables. Assignments between reference variables allow for *upcasts* and *downcasts*. Furthermore, obsolete explicit casting is possible for formal parameters and field symbols using the STRUCTURE addition (in Appendix A, see Section A.1.3, Typing of Formal Parameters).

► An implicit casting sometimes takes place for some special assignments or during the handling of operands at certain operand positions. A common example is the handling of flat structures with only character-type components as a single field of the c type.[17]

Rule

[⚙] **Rule 6.19: Avoid Implicit Casting**

Avoid implicit casting. If casting to another data type is required, you can usually explicitly implement this using ASSIGN ... CASTING.

Details

Potentially, implicit casting occurs if structures are used for the following:

► Value assignments between incompatible structures or structures and elementary data objects

► Comparisons between structures and elementary data objects

► Use of structures in operand positions where elementary data objects are expected

► Reading from the database using SELECT * ... INTO wa

► Use of the INCREMENT addition for the ASSIGN statement

The usage of implicit casting is prone to errors and leads to source code that is difficult to retrace. If you use the CASTING addition when handling field symbols, you can implement explicit casting, which is easier to retrace. The explicit casting option is indeed an important reason for using field symbols (see Section 6.6.6, Accessing Data Objects Dynamically).

---

17 Outside of Unicode programs, this even applies to any flat structures.

Bad Example

Listing 6.34 shows the assignment of a text string to a structure with only character-type components. The assignment implies an implicit casting, which is unwanted according to Rule 6.19, and the entire structure is treated as a text field of the c type and length 6.

```
TYPES: BEGIN OF structure,
          comp1 TYPE c LENGTH 2,
          comp2 TYPE c LENGTH 4,
       END OF structure.

DATA structure TYPE structure.

DATA text       TYPE string.

...

text = ...

structure = text.
```

Listing 6.34 Implicit Casting

Good Example

Listing 6.35 improves Listing 6.34 by assigning the structure to a field symbol of the c type. Here, explicit casting takes place. The handling of the structure as a character-type field is implemented through the character-type field symbol only.

```
...

FIELD-SYMBOLS <text> TYPE c.

...

ASSIGN structure TO <text> CASTING.

<text> = ...
```

Listing 6.35 Explicit Casting

6.2.9   Runtime Errors When Accessing Data Objects

Background

When using data objects, runtime errors can occur if the data object doesn't contain appropriate content or the access to the data object is not suitable. Examples include the following:

- Assignments of values outside the value range of a target variable.

- Use of values that cannot be converted to the required type.[18]

- Accesses to sections of data objects (subfield accesses). This includes either off-set/length accesses or the use of built-in subfield functions, such as `substring` (as of Releases 7.0 EhP2 and 7.2).

Rule

[✓] **Rule 6.20: Avoid Runtime Errors When Accessing Data Objects**

Avoid runtime errors, which can occur when accessing data objects. Robust applications should always be programmed accordingly.

Details

If you cannot ensure that the following accesses work without errors by appropriately filling data objects in a program, you must either check the necessary properties before the access or catch the potential exceptions (subclasses of `CX_SY_CONVERSION_ERROR` or `CX_SY_DATA_ACCESS_ERROR`) of this access.

Bad Example

Listing 6.36 shows a typical situation in which runtime errors can easily occur if `text` doesn't contain the subfield that is defined by `offset` and `length`.

```
DATA text TYPE string.
...
substring = text+offset(length).
...
```

Listing 6.36 Risk of Runtime Errors

Good Example

Listing 6.37 and Listing 6.38 show how Listing 6.36 can be modified to avoid runtime errors with precautionary measures or exception handling.

```
IF strlen( text ) > offset + length.
  substring = text+offset(length).
```

---

18 That means that a conversion rule exists, but that the content of the source field cannot be converted, for example, when you try to assign a character field whose content cannot be interpreted as a number to a numeric field.

```
ELSE.
   ...
ENDIF.
```

Listing 6.37 Excluding Runtime Errors with Precautionary Measures

```
TRY.
    substring = text+offset(length).
  CATCH cx_sy_range_out_of_bounds.
    ...
ENDTRY.
```

Listing 6.38 Excluding Runtime Errors with Exception Handling

6.2.10 Anonymous Containers

Background

Anonymous containers are character-type or byte-type data objects of the c or string type or the x or xstring type to which data objects of other types and particularly structures are assigned via casting (see Section 6.2.8) in order to store them persistently in these containers.

Rule

Rule 6.21: Do Not Use Character or Byte Fields as a Container [✓]

Do not store structured data in unstructured character-type or byte-type variables.

Details

The direct storage of structured data in unstructured character-type or byte-type data objects involves problems, particularly in the context of data exchanges via Remote Function Calls (RFC), input/output via the file system, or output on a printer. Due to a platform-specific byte order (*endianness*) or alignment requirements as well as different character sets (*codepage*), unexpected results can occur.

For example, if a container is stored and imported to an application server with a different byte order, problems occur if the container is used for content for which the byte order is critical. These are always the numeric fields of the i, decfloat16, decfloat34, and f types. In Unicode systems, the byte order of character-type data objects also depends on the platform.

It can be difficult enough even without such technical problems to import data in an appropriate way that has been stored in such a way. For this purpose, you usually have to implement another casting for the data type with which the data are stored in the container. Because the corresponding type information is not stored as well, it may be possible that such type-specific casting is not possible.

Tip

If you need to store data in an unstructured container, you can use the EXPORT ... TO DATA BUFFER statement to do so. Storing data in this way is robust against different platform properties. However, you cannot use EXPORT and IMPORT to directly process reference variables and instances referenced by them. As a workaround, you can serialize them for the storage via the CALL TRANSFORMATION statement.[19]

6.2.11 Passing Global Data by Reference

Background

In a local context you can normally directly access the data objects of superordinate more global contexts (see Section 6.1). For example, in a method, you can have write access to the attributes of the specific class and to the potential global data of the current program.

Therefore, if a more global data object is passed to a procedure by reference, access is granted there both through its name and the formal parameter.

Rule

[✓] | **Rule 6.22: Do Not Pass Global Data to Local Contexts by Reference**

Do not use global data as actual parameters for formal parameters of procedures if this is possibly changed directly in the procedure and the parameter is passed by reference.

Details

If a global data object that has also been passed by reference is changed in a procedure (method, see Rule 6.37), this also changes the formal parameter and vice versa. This is usually a behavior that wasn't anticipated when writing the procedure.

---

19 A class has to include the IF_SERIALIZABLE_OBJECT tag interface so that its objects can be serialized using CALL TRANSFORMATION.

Global data is supposed to be transferred only to formal parameters for which pass by value is declared (see Section 6.5.3) or to procedures that don't have any unwanted consequences for this data.

Bad Example

After the `do_something` method has been called in the `main` method in Listing 6.39, the `attr` attribute contains the unexpected value, `2.0`, because the first assignment to the `c_value` changing parameter, which has been passed by reference, also changes `attr`.

```
CLASS class DEFINITION.
  PUBLIC SECTION.
    METHODS
      main.
  PRIVATE SECTION.
    DATA
      attr TYPE p DECIMALS 2.
    METHODS
      do_something CHANGING c_value TYPE numeric.
ENDCLASS.

CLASS class IMPLEMENTATION.
  METHOD main.
    attr = '1.23'.
    do_something( CHANGING c_value = attr ).
  ENDMETHOD.
  METHOD do_something.
    ...
    c_value = floor( attr ).
    ...
    c_value = c_value + attr.
    ...
  ENDMETHOD.
ENDCLASS.
```

Listing 6.39 Passing an Attribute of the Same Class by Reference

Good Example

If the pass by reference method in the method declaration of `do_something` in Listing 6.39 is converted into a pass by value method, as shown in Listing 6.40, the `attr` attribute contains the expected value, `2.23`, after the method has been called.

```
. . .
    METHODS
      do_something CHANGING VALUE(c_value) TYPE numeric.
. . .
```

Listing 6.40 Passing an Attribute of the Same Class by Value

6.3   System Fields

An ABAP program can query the state of the ABAP runtime environment via so-called *system fields*. Technically, these system fields are a set of predefined variables, that is, of the components of the predefined structure, `sy`[20] of the `SYST` data type from the ABAP Dictionary, that are always available during program execution. You can find a tabular overview of all system fields that are released for usage and their meaning in the ABAP online documentation.

6.3.1   Access

Background

The system fields are supplied with values via the ABAP runtime environment. In a program, however, they behave like normal variables to which you can also assign values using the ABAP program. The reason for this is that not only the ABAP kernel but also the ABAP parts of the ABAP runtime environment have write access to system fields.

Rule

[⚙]   Rule 6.23: Do Not Write System Fields

Use only read access but never write access for system fields in an ABAP application program.

---

20 An exception is the `sy-repid` system field, which indicates the name of the currently executed program. This is a predefined constant and no longer a component of the predefined structure, `sy`.

Details

Because the values of the system fields are generally vital for a proper program execution, write access to system fields bears a lot of risks. Write operations in system fields can lead to a loss of critical information, which affects a correct program execution. Consequently, you mustn't overwrite system fields with the intention to influence the further course of the program or use them as a replacement for explicitly defined variables.

Moreover, you mustn't misuse system fields as implicit output parameters of procedures, irrespective of whether they have been explicitly set within the procedure due to a prohibited write access or as a result of a statement execution.

Exception

The only system fields whose content could be changed in an application program belong to the classical list processing, which should no longer be used according to Rule 5.20, Use SAP List Viewer.

Bad Example

Listing 6.41 shows a write access to the `sy-subrc` system field that is not seldom seen. The access illustrated here isn't harmful but also isn't useful because `sy-subrc` is always set to zero when a function module is called and adopts a different value only by handling a classical exception. The statement is therefore redundant.

```
sy-subrc = 4.
CALL FUNCTION ...
  ...
  EXCEPTIONS ...
CASE sy-subrc.
  ...
```

Listing 6.41 Write Access to a System Field

Good Example

Listing 6.42 corrects Listing 6.41 by omitting the write access.

```
CALL FUNCTION ...
  ...
  EXCEPTIONS ...
CASE sy-subrc.
  ...
```

Listing 6.42 Only Read Access to a System Field

6.3.2 Obsolete and Internal System Fields

Background

Not all of the system fields are supposed to be used in application programs. You can display all existing system fields as components of the SYST ABAP Dictionary structure (or as components of the sy structure in the ABAP Debugger). The description of the components indicates the respective meaning. System fields that are obsolete or restricted to internal usage only are clearly marked as such.

Rule

[⚙] **Rule 6.24: Do Not Use Obsolete or Internal System Fields**

Do not use system fields in an ABAP application program that are marked as obsolete or for internal purposes only in the ABAP Dictionary and in the ABAP documentation.

Details

The behavior of obsolete or internal system fields is not defined. ABAP application programs are therefore not allowed to make assumptions regarding the content of such system fields.

Bad Example

Listing 6.43 shows the — according to Rule 6.24 — prohibited use of the sy-fodec system field, which is defined as internal in the SYST structure, after the DESCRIBE FIELD statement in order to determine the number of decimal places of a data object.

```
DATA dobj TYPE p LENGTH 8 DECIMALS 2.

DATA type TYPE c LENGTH 1.
DATA decimals TYPE i.

DESCRIBE FIELD dobj TYPE type.
decimals = sy-fodec.
```

Listing 6.43 Using an Internal System Field

Good Example

Listing 6.44 shows how you can determine the decimal places properly using the corresponding addition of the DESCRIBE FIELD statement.

```
DATA dobj TYPE p LENGTH 8 DECIMALS 2.
```

```
DATA type      TYPE c LENGTH 1.
DATA decimals TYPE i.

DESCRIBE FIELD dobj TYPE type DECIMALS decimals.
```

Listing 6.44 Using an Allowed Language Element

6.3.3 Evaluation

Background

System fields describe general system states or are set specifically by individual statements. The content of system fields is only defined as it is described in the documentation of the system fields or in the documentation of ABAP statements that set system fields. In other contexts than described there, the content of system fields is not defined. Particularly statements for which no effect on system fields is documented can affect the content of specific system fields, such as sy-subrc (see Section 6.3.4, Return Value) in an undefined way. This holds especially true for statements that explicitly or implicitly call ABAP code when being executed.

Rule

> **Rule 6.25: Evaluate System Fields at the Right Place** [✓]
>
> Evaluate system fields only in contexts for which they are defined. If an ABAP statement sets a system field in accordance with its documentation, the field should be evaluated directly after the statement. You mustn't evaluate system fields after statements, however, for which no effect is documented.

Details

A system field should be evaluated directly after the statement that set the field so that it cannot be overwritten by other statements. The larger the distance between the considered ABAP statement and the evaluation of a system field, the higher the risk that this system field will be influenced by a different statement in the meantime.

If necessary, you should store the values of system fields in helper variables. This applies particularly to the general return value, sy-subrc (see Section 6.3.4), which is set by considerably many different statements. Additional common examples include the sy-index loop counter or the sy-tabix table index.

You should never evaluate statement-related system fields after statements that do not set these fields according to their documentation. As before, a common example is the evaluation of sy-subrc. If it isn't documented for a statement that it sets sy-subrc in a defined way, an evaluation after this statement bears a lot of risks. Either sy-subrc still has the previous value, or it is set in an undefined way by the statement. Both situations can lead to incorrect program behavior. Figure 3.5 in Chapter 3, ABAP-Specific Basic Rules, shows an example of this.

Tip

As of Release 7.0, the static methods of the CL_ABAP_SYST class also return important system states. In this case, the risk of previous overwriting in the program is excluded.

Bad Example

Listing 6.45 shows an example where sy-subrc is evaluated too late. Even if it is not documented for the statements between FIND and IF that they set sy-subrc, the value can be overwritten due to possible side effects.

```
FIND REGEX ... IN ...
...
... "other statements
...
IF sy-subrc = 0.
   ...
ENDIF.
```

Listing 6.45 Evaluation of a System Field That Is Too Late

Good Example

Listing 6.46 corrects Listing 6.45 by assigning sy-subrc to a helper variable directly after FIND. This variable is then evaluated in IF. It can also be required to assign sy-index or sy-tabix to a helper variable directly after DO or LOOP loop is entered.

```
FIND REGEX ... IN ...
find_subrc = sy-subrc.
...
... "other statements
...
IF find_subrc = 0.
   ...
ENDIF.
```

Listing 6.46 Timely Evaluation of a System Field

6.3.4 Return Value

Background

The most prominent system field is probably the `sy-subrc` return value, which indicates a successful execution of an ABAP statement or, if classical exceptions (in Chapter 5, see Section 5.2.2, Classical and Class-Based Exceptions) are used, of a procedure. A return value of 0 usually indicates a successful execution.

Rule

Rule 6.26: Evaluate the sy-subrc Return Value	[✓]
Evaluate the `sy-subrc` return value after every ABAP statement that sets it according to its documentation. But you should never evaluate `sy-subrc` after the execution of a statement for which it is not documented that it sets the return value.	

Details

The `sy-subrc` system field indicates if a statement is executed successfully or not. If the execution isn't successful, the program usually has to respond appropriately. If not, you can assume unexpected behavior of the program.

This rule further details Rule 6.25, Evaluate System Fields at the Right Place, which is more general, and is explained here again because the `sy-subrc` return value plays a significant role in this context. The `sy-subrc` system field must always be evaluated immediately and assigned to a helper variable, if necessary. You mustn't implement an evaluation after statements that don't set `sy-subrc` in a defined way because this can easily lead to wrong conclusions.

Exception

If a handling seems to be unnecessary because a statement is always executed successfully in the developer's opinion, this assumption should at least be ensured and documented with an assertion (in Chapter 5, see Section 5.2.9, Assertions).

Bad Example

Listing 6.47 shows how the work area of a `SELECT` statement is directly used for further processing without querying `sy-subrc`. The content of `wa`, however, is here usually undefined if the success of the database access is not ensured by querying `sy-subrc`.

```
SELECT ...
      INTO wa
      ...

... "work with wa
```

Listing 6.47 Missing Evaluation of sy-subrc

Good Example

Listing 6.48 corrects Listing 6.47 by checking the successful execution of the SELECT statement.

```
SELECT ...
      INTO wa
      ...
IF sy-subrc <> 0.
  ...
ENDIF
... "work with wa
```

Listing 6.48 Appropriate Evaluation of sy-subrc

6.3.5   Using System Fields as Actual Parameters

Background

The sy structure whose components represent the system fields exists only once in an internal session and is shared by all programs of this internal session. System fields are thus global for all programs of an internal session and their procedures.

Rule

[✓] **Rule 6.27: Do Not Use System Fields as Actual Parameters**

Never use system fields as actual parameters, especially not for passing by reference.

Details

This rule tightens Rule 6.22, Do Not Pass Global Data to Local Contexts by Reference. Because system fields are set implicitly, you need to be even more careful. If the value of a system field changes implicitly within a procedure, the value of the parameter that has been passed by reference and that refers to this system field also changes. A procedure will never be prepared for such a behavior.

You should even not pass system fields by value because a procedure may be switched to pass by reference during further development without the user of the procedure being notified. The only secure method is to assign the value of a system field to a normal variable and then use this variable as the actual parameter when calling the procedure.

Bad Example

When taking a look at the do_something method in Listing 6.49, you'd expect that the index parameter in the loop contains the unchanged value that was passed to the procedure. Actually, however, index references sy-index, which is set to the current loop counter in the DO loop.

```
CLASS class DEFINITION.
  PUBLIC SECTION.
    METHODS main.
  PRIVATE SECTION.
    METHODS do_something IMPORTING index TYPE i.
ENDCLASS.

CLASS class IMPLEMENTATION.
  METHOD main.
    DO 2 TIMES.
      do_something( sy-index ).
    ENDDO.
  ENDMETHOD.
  METHOD do_something.
    DO 3 TIMES.
      ... index ... .
    ENDDO.
  ENDMETHOD.
ENDCLASS.
```

Listing 6.49 Using a System Field as an Actual Parameter

Good Example

Listing 6.50 corrects the call of the do_something method from Listing 6.49 by passing a helper variable with the corresponding value instead of transferring sy-index.

```
...

CLASS class IMPLEMENTATION.
  METHOD main.
```

```
    DATA index TYPE sy-index.
    DO 2 TIMES.
      index = sy-index.
      do_something( index ).
    ENDDO.
  ENDMETHOD.
  ...
ENDCLASS.

...
```

Listing 6.50 Using a Helper Field as an Actual Parameter

6.3.6 Using System Fields on the User Interface

Background

Because system fields are defined via the `syst` structure in the ABAP Dictionary, you can technically use them for the definition of input fields for dynpros or in Web Dynpro.

Rule

[✓] **Rule 6.28: Do Not Use System Fields on the User Interface**

Never use system field types to define input or output fields for dynpros or selection screens of application programs.

Details

This rule is derived from Rule 2.1, which addresses the SoC, and Rule 6.5, which considers the usage of data types. System fields are merely technical, and their semantic properties (documentation and other texts), which are defined in the ABAP Dictionary, do not allow for an appropriate use in user dialogs of application programs.

Tip

Similarly, you can apply Rule 6.5, Use Semantically Appropriate Data Types Only, also to the usage of components of the `SYST` structure for the typing of interface parameters of procedures. The semantic meaning of a system field, which is then expressed in the short text, generally doesn't correspond to the meaning of the parameter.

Bad Example

Figure 6.2 displays an input field for the language of a document output on a classical dynpro that is declared with reference to the `syst-langu` data type of the `sy-langu` system field as well as the corresponding F1 help in the Performance Assistant. The display of the help clearly indicates that `syst-langu` is not suited for language fields in the user dialog because the field help describes the behavior of the `sy-langu` field within a program and not the meaning of the language field within the respective application.

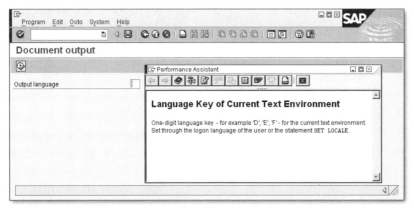

Figure 6.2   F1 Help for an Input Field with Reference to a System Field

Good Example

In Figure 6.3, the reference of the input field to the system field is replaced by a reference to a semantically appropriate data type of the ABAP Dictionary.

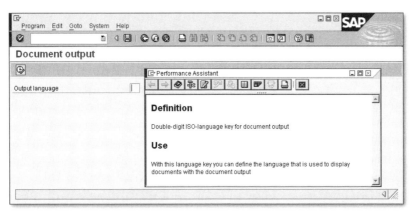

Figure 6.3   F1 Help for an Input Field with Reference to a Specific Data Type

6.3.7 Using System Fields in Operand Positions

Background

In statements that affect the content of system fields, the operands are usually first evaluated and then the system fields set. However, in some complex statements, it is possible that a statement sets a system field before all operand positions have been evaluated.

Rule

[✓] **Rule 6.29: Do Not Use System Fields in Statements That Set the Fields**

For robustness reasons, do not use system fields as operands of statements that set these system fields.

Details

Because it is not always defined if a specific system field is set in a statement before or after an operand is evaluated, the content of a system field is always supposed to be copied to a helper variable, and only this copy is supposed to be used within the respective statement. This contributes to your own security and to the retraceability for the readers of a program.

Tip

The usage of functional methods in operand positions should also be mentioned in this context because they usually affect critical system fields as well. Be careful when using system fields in operand positions of the same statement.

Bad Example

Listing 6.51 shows the use of the `sy-tabix` system field in a `READ` statement that sets the system field. No problems are known for the example illustrated here, but you should strictly adhere to Rule 6.29, also for legibility reasons.

```
LOOP AT itab1 ... WHERE ...
  ...
  READ TABLE itab2 ... INDEX sy-tabix.
  ...
ENDLOOP.
```

Listing 6.51 System Field in an Operand Position

Good Example

Listing 6.52 adds robustness to Listing 6.51 by assigning the value of the `sy-tabix`
system field to a helper variable before it is used.

```
LOOP AT itab1 ... WHERE ...
  index = sy-tabix.
  ...
  READ TABLE itab2 ... INDEX index.
  ...
ENDLOOP.
```

Listing 6.52 Helper Field for a System Field in an Operand Position

6.4 Internal Tables

An internal table is a dynamic data object (see Section 6.6.3, Using Dynamic Data
Objects) that consists of a sequence of lines of the same data type. The data type
of an internal table is a table type that comprises the following basic properties of
every internal table:

▶ **Line type**
The line type can be any kind of data type. Particularly tables of elementary
types, tables of structures, tables of tables, and tables of references are
feasible.

▶ **Table category**
The table category defines the type of storage and of the primary access. The
possible table categories are as follows:

  ▶ *Standard tables* that are managed with a primary table index and cannot have
  a unique primary table key.

  ▶ *Sorted tables* that are managed with a primary table index and can have a
  unique or non-unique primary table key according to which they are
  sorted.

  ▶ *Hashed tables* whose primary table key must always be unique and which
  manage their lines using a hash algorithm. Hashed tables don't have a primary table index.

▶ **Primary table key**
Each internal table has a primary table key. A table key consists of columns of
the internal table whose content identifies table lines. Depending on the table
type, the key can be either unique or non-unique.

Internal tables allow for a processing of variable data sets (a variable number of lines) with a fixed structure (the line type) in the memory of the program's internal session. Content of an internal table can be accessed either sequentially with loop processing using `LOOP` or by accessing individual lines (e.g., with `READ TABLE`).

Two alternatives are possible for accessing individual lines:

- Specifying a key (table key or free key)
- Specifying a line index

Access via the primary key is possible for all three table categories. Optimized for an access via the primary key, however, are only sorted and hashed tables. In standard tables, a primary key access uses a linear search. Access via the primary line index is only possible for standard and sorted tables.

As of Releases 7.0 EhP2 and 7.2, an internal table can have further *secondary keys* (see Section 6.4.2) in addition to its primary keys. These secondary keys extend and optimize the access options for the individual table categories.

6.4.1   Selecting the Table Category

Background

The table category defines the internal management of an internal table as well as the primary access type:

- Standard tables are managed via a primary table index. When inserting or deleting table lines, only the table index is reorganized but not the table lines itself. If you only append (`APPEND`) or delete lines at the end, a reorganization of the table index is not required. Access via the primary key, however, is not optimized. Instead, a linear search across all lines is carried out.

- Sorted tables are also managed via their primary key index, which is stored sorted according to the primary table key. Consequently, the table index must usually be reorganized when you insert or delete table lines. During access via the primary key, a binary search is performed, which results in a logarithmic dependency of the time requirement on the number of lines.

- Hashed tables are based on a hash function. They are therefore optimized for access via the primary table key and attain a constant access time, irrespective of the number of lines. In return, the hash values require additional memory space and don't allow for non-unique primary table keys. There is no primary table index, and a respective index access is not possible.

Standard tables and sorted tables can be summarized under the term *index tables*. An index access is always the fastest way to access table entries. Prerequisite for an index access is, of course, that the value for the index specification has been determined in advance. This usually requires a previous key access, for example, via READ TABLE, where the sy-tabix system field is set.

Rule

Rule 6.30: Use the Appropriate Table Category	[✓]
Select the table category according to the primary requirements. As a rule of thumb, if the tables are large, the following selection criteria apply: ▸ Mainly index accesses: standard tables ▸ Index accesses and key accesses: sorted tables ▸ Only key accesses: hashed tables	

Details

Particularly for tables with a lot of lines, you have to select the appropriate table category carefully. The following recommendations are mainly derived from the processing speed requirements:

▸ **Standard tables**
This table category can always be used if the primary access types are sequential processing or index access. You should fill standard tables by appending lines using APPEND and implement the other accesses using an index specification (INDEX addition of the respective statements). Ideally, the filling process is decoupled from other accesses. After explicit sorting has taken place, you can also use an optimized key access (free key) using BINARY SEARCH, which enables you to identify an entry point for sequential processing (LOOP), for example. However, if key accesses are the primary access type for an internal table, at least large standard tables (more than 100 lines) aren't the appropriate table category because of the linear search.

▸ **Sorted tables**
This table category is useful if both a fast key access and an index access are necessary and if the lines are supposed to be sorted already during the filling of the table. Furthermore, sorted tables are also suited for partially sequential processing in a LOOP loop, where left-most parts of the table key are specified in the WHERE condition. Finally, sorted tables with a non-unique key are the only alternative to hashed tables if no unique key can be defined.

▶ **Hashed tables**

This table category is useful if key accesses are the central operation for table entries, if the tables are large, and if a unique key can be defined.

In addition to the processing speed, memory requirements can also play an important role. If this is supposed to be optimized according to 6.50, Consider the Ratio of Administration and Application Data, you must also take into account the administration costs of the table categories.

▶ Standard tables and sorted tables (*index tables*), which are managed via a table index, incur the least administration costs (6 bytes for each line on average, see Section 6.6.5). As long as the logical order in the table index corresponds to the physical order in the table body, a standard table doesn't generate any line-related administration costs at all. This is the case if you always append lines after the last line or only delete the last line.

▶ Hashed tables require considerably more space for their administration data than index tables (18 or 30 bytes for each line on average, see Section 6.6.5).

Depending on the length of the key and the number of lines in an internal table, the access via a sorted key can be as fast as or even faster than using a hashed table. In such a case — and if the memory space is critical — you should work with a sorted table instead of a hashed table.

The rules mentioned here can be qualified if you use secondary keys (see Section 6.4.2, Secondary Keys) because the overall costs need to be considered then.

6.4.2 Secondary Keys

Background

Since Releases 7.0 EhP2 and 7.2, you can declare secondary keys for internal tables. The following options are possible:

▶ Sorted keys, which can be non-unique or unique

▶ Hash keys, which can be unique only

These keys are named when they are declared and can be created for any table type.[21] A secondary table index is internally created for each sorted secondary key, which enables index access to hashed tables also. When accessing internal

---

21 The primary key, which has had no name so far, is assigned a predefined name (`primary_key`) so that it can also be explicitly addressed now.

tables, you must specify which table key or index is supposed to be used. Without explicit specification, the internal table is accessed via the primary key or primary index by default.

The access to an internal table via secondary keys is always optimized and thus usually increases the performance for read accesses significantly for which no optimized key access was feasible previously. On the other hand, secondary keys also incur additional administration costs owing to memory consumption as well as to runtime. Additional runtime costs occur if a secondary table index needs to be updated after changes to the content of the table.[22] The administration costs for a secondary key are as high as for the respective primary table keys (see Section 6.6.5, Administration Costs of Dynamic Memory Objects), that is, 6 bytes for each line for each secondary index and 18 or 30 bytes for each line for each hash key on average. On average, another 8 bytes for each line are required if the table has at least one non-unique sorted secondary key. Additional memory costs are generated if a secondary key needs to be updated after the content of the internal table has been changed. These memory costs are in the same order of magnitude as the preceding ones and also depend on the number of lines.

Rule

Rule 6.31: Use Secondary Keys Efficiently	[✓]
Use secondary keys sparingly and only in such cases where their benefits exceed the extra costs.	

Details

The internal management of secondary keys in internal tables can involve a lot of effort with regard to the memory consumption and necessary updates. They are useful for accelerating read accesses in the following cases:

▶ The standard scenario for the beneficial use of secondary table keys is a very large internal table that is populated once and whose content is rarely changed. In this case, the runtime costs for the administration of the secondary keys are generated only when the internal table is created or rarely and are more than compensated through the more efficient, frequent read access.

---

22 The ABAP runtime environment delays these runtime costs as much as possible until they are actually required (*lazy update* and *delayed update*).

▶ One reason why a secondary key can also be useful for small internal tables is that unique table entries can be ensured with regard to certain components. The extra costs for the secondary key can then be justified. This applies particularly to standard tables whose primary keys can never be unique.

When using secondary keys, the following should be noted:

▶ Secondary hash keys should generally not contain too many components in order to not place too much load on the system through additional hash management. For secondary keys with numerous components, you should use sorted keys.[23]

▶ For the mere read access where unique table entries don't have to be ensured, it is usually sufficient to use non-unique sorted secondary keys. The read access is as fast as for unique keys or nearly as fast if duplicate entries exist. Updates after table modifications are only processed if necessary.

▶ If lines of an index table are deleted via secondary key accesses, the primary index of the table must be updated. This cannot be optimized for standard tables. Instead, a linear search needs to be carried out.

You shouldn't use secondary table keys in the following situations:

▶ For small internal tables (less than 50 lines), the performance advantage of the read access is usually outweighed by memory and administration costs.

▶ For tables that are often accessed for modifications, the costs for the updates of the secondary keys can outweigh the performance advantage of the read access. Especially in the case of *delayed updates* and *lazy updates,* update costs may be generated for those read accesses for which the optimization was actually intended so that no effect or a negative effect is registered.

Tip

It is relatively easy to provide secondary keys retroactively to optimize the performance for existing internal table types in ABAP programs but particularly also for table types that are defined in the ABAP Dictionary.[24] In such cases, you should usually only define non-unique sorted keys. Otherwise, programs that use tables

---

23 This also holds true for primary keys.

24 Bear in mind that you must — contrary to database accesses — explicitly specify the secondary key of an internal table in ABAP statements if it is to be used. Otherwise, it is not evaluated.

of this type and populate them with non-unique lines with regard to these components no longer function properly.

You also need to consider that the `sy-tabix` system field is supplied from the assigned secondary index if sorted secondary keys are used. If this value is used for the next index access to the internal table, the same table index must be explicitly used there. If used implicitly, it would be interpreted as a specification for the primary index.

Bad Example

Listing 6.53 shows an access to a large hashed table via a free key that doesn't correspond to the table's primary key. This access therefore requires a linear search, which is quite time-intensive.

```
DATA itab TYPE HASHED TABLE OF dbtab
  WITH UNIQUE KEY col1 col2 ...

  "fill itab with a large amount of data
  ...

READ TABLE itab
          WITH KEY col3 = ... col4 = ...
          ASSIGNING ...
```

Listing 6.53 Linear Search for an Access via a Free Key

Good Example

Listing 6.54 optimizes the example from Listing 6.53 by adding a secondary table key to the declaration of the table. This key replaces the free key for the access. Sequential processing in the order defined with this key is also possible now.

```
DATA itab TYPE HASHED TABLE OF dbtab
  WITH UNIQUE KEY col1 col2 ...
  WITH NON-UNIQUE SORTED KEY second_key
    COMPONENTS col1 col2 ...

  "fill itab with a large amount of data
  ...

READ TABLE itab
          WITH TABLE KEY second_key
          COMPONENTS col3 = ... col4 = ...
          ASSIGNING ...

...
```

```
LOOP AT itab USING KEY second_key.
  ...
ENDLOOP.
```

Listing 6.54 Optimized Search du to Access via a Secondary Key

6.4.3   Initial Memory Allocation

Background

Internal tables are stored in individual blocks in the memory. The runtime environment automatically allocates an appropriate initial memory area for the table's data by default. If the initial memory area is no longer sufficient, the system creates additional blocks up to a certain threshold value according to an internal duplication strategy. After that, all additional blocks are requested with a constant size between 8KB and 16KB.

The INITIAL SIZE addition enables you to specify a number of table lines for the declaration of an internal table to override the system-set number of initially allocated lines.

Rule

[⚙] **Rule 6.32: Manipulate the Initial Memory Allocation for Nested Tables Only**

Use the INITIAL SIZE addition for the declaration of internal tables in nested tables only if this prevents an unnecessary allocation of a large amount of memory.

Details

It doesn't make sense to use the INITIAL SIZE addition for outer tables or tables that are not nested because the automated memory allocation of the runtime environment leads to the desired result. For nested inner tables, the automated memory allocation can result in excessive memory consumption if more memory is allocated for numerous inner tables than they actually use. If the number of entries in the inner tables is already known, you can set the initial main memory allocation precisely using INITIAL SIZE.

Tip

Instance attributes of classes that are declared as internal tables can also be considered nested tables. If you can expect numerous instances of a class with tabular attributes, it may be useful to specify INITIAL SIZE here as well.

Bad Example

Listing 6.55 shows the declaration of a nested table. Here, the initial memory allocation is wrongly specified for the outer large table and not for the inner small table.

```
TYPES small_table TYPE STANDARD TABLE OF ...
  WITH NON-UNIQUE KEY ...

TYPES: BEGIN OF line_structure,
          ...
          int_table TYPE small_table,
          ...
       END OF line_structure,
       big_table TYPE SORTED TABLE OF line_structure
                WITH UNIQUE KEY ...
                INITIAL SIZE 10000.
```

Listing 6.55 Wrong Specification of the Initial Memory Allocation

Good Example

Listing 6.56 shows the declaration of a nested table. Here, as recommended in Rule 6.32, the initial memory allocation is specified for the inner small table and not for the outer large table.

```
TYPES small_table TYPE STANDARD TABLE OF ...
  WITH NON-UNIQUE KEY ...
  INITIAL SIZE 4.

TYPES: BEGIN OF line_structure,
          ...
          int_table TYPE small_table,
          ...
       END OF line_structure,
       big_table TYPE SORTED TABLE OF line_structure
                WITH UNIQUE KEY ...
```

Listing 6.56 Correct Specification of the Initial Memory Allocation

6.4.4 Sorted Filling

Background

The APPEND statement for appending a line to an internal table has a SORTED BY addition, which can be used to fill a standard table with sorted data. The following prerequisites must be met:

▶ The value specified for the INITIAL SIZE addition (see Section 6.4.3, Initial Memory Requirement) must be greater than zero.

▶ You must only use the APPEND statement with the SORTED BY addition to fill the internal table.

If these prerequisites are met, a ranking list is generated, which contains at the most as many lines as INITIAL SIZE specifies. The lines are sorted in descending order after the component that is listed after SORTED BY.

Rule

[⚙] **Rule 6.33: Do Not Generate Ranking Lists via Sorted Filling**

Do not use the SORTED BY addition of the APPEND statement to generate ranking lists. Use the SORT statement instead.

Details

The APPEND statement with the SORTED BY addition is no longer used to simply append lines as it name implies but executes a complex process, which only generates a ranking list if the prerequisites are met. If these prerequisites are not met, the process outputs results that are very difficult to retrace. Moreover, you can only sort by one column here.

The SORT statement is more robust, more powerful, and easier to retrace for this task.

Bad Example

Listing 6.57 shows the creation of a ranking list with APPEND SORTED BY, which is no longer recommended according to Rule 6.33. The ranking list contains the 10 largest distances from a table of flights. For this purpose, the INITIAL SIZE addition must be specified for the declaration of the ranking list table.

```
...

DATA distance_list TYPE TABLE OF spfli-distance
                INITIAL SIZE 10.

FIELD-SYMBOLS <spfli_wa> LIKE LINE OF spfli_tab.

...

LOOP AT spfli_tab ASSIGNING <spfli_wa>.
```

```
APPEND <spfli_wa>-distance TO distance_list
        SORTED BY table_line.
ENDLOOP.
```

```
. . .
```

Listing 6.57 Creating a Ranking List Through Sorted Filling

Good Example

Listing 6.58 shows a robust creation of the same ranking list from Listing 6.57 using the SORT statement as recommended in Rule 6.33.

```
. . .
```

```
DATA distance_list TYPE TABLE OF spfli-distance.

FIELD-SYMBOLS <spfli_wa> LIKE LINE OF spfli_tab.
```

```
. . .
```

```
SORT spfli_tab BY distance DESCENDING.

LOOP AT spfli_tab TO 10 ASSIGNING <spfli_wa>.
  APPEND <spfli_wa>-distance TO distance_list.
ENDLOOP.
```

```
. . .
```

Listing 6.58 Creating a Ranking List Through Sorting

6.4.5 Aggregated Filling

Background

The COLLECT statement enables you to insert lines into an internal table in an aggregated way. If a line with the corresponding primary key already exists in the target table, the values of numeric components are added to the values in the existing table line. Otherwise, the system inserts a new line in the table.

Rule

Rule 6.34: Do Not Use Aggregated Filling for Standard Tables   **[⚙]**

Use the COLLECT statement for hashed tables or sorted tables with a unique key only. Do not use it for standard tables.

283

Details

The COLLECT statement is based on unique entries with regard to the primary key and a stable key management. Not all internal table categories are therefore similarly suited for processing via COLLECT.

▶ If the COLLECT statement is used in combination with a standard table, the system first needs to set up a specific internal hash management for this table. This temporary hash management can be invalidated via change operations for the table. After such a change operation, the next COLLECT statements must use a linear search, which drastically slows down processing. In addition, the primary key of a standard table is never unique.

▶ You can use COLLECT for sorted tables and hashed tables without any problems, because — in contrast to standard tables — they always have a stable key management, which can be used by COLLECT. To ensure that COLLECT functions properly for sorted tables, the primary key must be unique.[25] For hashed tables, it is always ensured that the key values are unique.

6.4.6 Output Behavior

Background

Internal tables can be read sequentially (LOOP AT) or by accessing individual lines (READ TABLE). In both cases, you can define one of the following output behaviors:

▶ The INTO addition copies the line content to an appropriate data object.

▶ The ASSIGNING addition assigns the currently read line to a field symbol (see Section 6.6.6), which enables you to directly address the line.

▶ The REFERENCE INTO addition sets a data reference (see Section 6.6.6, Accessing Data Objects Dynamically) to the currently read line.

Besides for read operations, the ASSIGNING and REFERENCE INTO additions can also be used for the APPEND, COLLECT, INSERT, and MODIFY statements. In this case, they generate references to the currently processed line.

---

25 For sorted tables with non-unique keys, the table should only be filled with COLLECT, which can hardly be ensured.

Rule

Rule 6.35: Select an Appropriate Output Behavior

When reading lines of internal tables, select an appropriate output behavior. The following rule of thumb applies:

▸ Copy to a work area if the line type is narrow and the read line is not supposed to be modified.

▸ Assign to a field symbol if the line type is wide or deep and the read line is supposed to be modified.

▸ Set a data reference if the line type is wide or deep and a reference to the read line is supposed to be passed somewhere else.

Details

The criteria for selecting the output behavior are the processing speed, on the one hand, and what is supposed to be done with the read line, on the other hand:

▸ If the content of the read line is supposed to be modified, you should usually use the ASSIGNING addition. This allows for direct access to the line via the field symbol's *value semantics* and saves you later MODIFY operations (see Rule 6.51).

▸ If you require a reference to the read line that should be processed via *reference semantics*, use the REFERENCE INTO addition (see Rule 6.51).

▸ If the content of the read line is not supposed to be modified, you can use any of these procedures. Regarding performance, the line type of the table assumes the central role here. If the table line is wide or contains deep components (e.g., strings or other tables), read processes are usually faster if you use ASSIGNING or REFERENCE INTO instead of INTO. As above, Rule 6.51 is the determining factor for selecting which of the two you should use.

If you work with tables whose lines are flat and don't occupy more than approximately 1KB, copying with INTO is faster (at least for the READ statement) than configuring the administration that is required for dynamic access. For the LOOP statement, these costs are generated only once so that using ASSIGNING or REFERENCE INTO makes always sense as of a certain number of lines. INTO, in contrast, should always be used if the target area is supposed to be changed *without* this affecting the internal table.

Besides the processing speed, the retraceability of the source code is also critical. If you adhere to the recommendations mentioned, reading a table with the ASSIGNING addition (but also REFERENCE INTO) indicates that the table content is potentially changed. Reading with the INTO addition indicates that the table won't be modified.

Bad Example

Listing 6.59 shows the assignment of lines of an internal table to a work area with the goal to modify the read lines. For this modification, however, an additional statement, MODIFY, is required, and two unnecessary copy operations are performed for each loop pass.

```
LOOP AT itab INTO wa.
  ...
  wa = ...
  MODIFY itab FROM wa.
ENDLOOP.
```

Listing 6.59 Using a Work Area Unnecessarily

Good Example

Listing 6.60 corrects Listing 6.59; here, a field symbol is used for direct modifying access to the read lines. No unnecessary copy costs are generated.

```
LOOP AT itab ASSIGNING <fs>.
  ...
  <fs> = ...
ENDLOOP.
```

Listing 6.60 Addressing a Table Line via a Field Symbol

6.4.7 Loop Processing

Background

In addition to the statements for processing individual lines of internal tables, there are also statements that can address and change the whole table body. Examples include the following:

- All types of assignments of whole internal tables
- Deletion of a whole internal table using CLEAR or FREE
- Usage in target areas, such as SELECT INTO TABLE

In a loop over the internal table, these types of accesses to the table body lead to problems.

Rule

| Rule 6.36: Do Not Change the Whole Table Body in a Loop Pass | [✓] |

In a loop over an internal table, you mustn't perform accesses to a table that change the whole table body at once.

Details

Inside loops, modifying accesses to the whole table body usually result in a runtime error, but at least in unexpected program behavior. If this is possible to statically determine, the system outputs a syntax error within classes and for LOOP loops with a statically determinable secondary key if the mentioned table operations are implemented. Otherwise, for compatibility reasons, the syntax check solely indicates this in a syntax warning.

Tip

This rule mainly serves to make you more aware of the problem. If you only deploy ABAP Objects according to Rule 3.1 or consider all warnings of the syntax check according to Rule 3.6, Rule 6.36 should be automatically met.

6.5   Modularization Units

The key modularization units or callable units within an ABAP program are referred to as *processing blocks*. In this context, you distinguish between *procedures* on one side and *dialog modules* and *event blocks* on the other side. While dialog modules and event blocks are called from the dynpro flow logic or from the event processing of the ABAP runtime environment, procedures are provided for a direct call from an ABAP program. In addition to processing blocks, you can also create *macros* as callable units.

- Procedures include the following:
  - Methods
  - Function modules
  - Subroutines

Only procedures support a parameter interface and have a local data context (in Chapter 4, see Section 4.4.2, Local Declarations).

▶ Dialog modules and event blocks (see Section 6.5.8, Dialog Modules and Event Blocks) don't have a parameter interface and usually also don't have local data context.

▶ Macros (see Section 6.5.9, Macros) are something in between real callable units and source code modularization (in Chapter see Section 4.5, Source Code Organization).

6.5.1 Function Modules and Subroutines

Background

Function modules and subroutines are the procedures of the structured programming model (in Chapter 5, see Section 5.1.2, Modularization) that have already existed before the introduction of ABAP Objects.

▶ Function modules in function groups are independent repository objects that the structured model provides for external calls (see Section 6.5.6, Internal and External Procedure Calls) or for the provision of reusable functions.

▶ In the pre-ABAP Objects era, subroutines could be created in any programs and were provided in the structured model for internal calls (see Section 6.5.6) or for the internal modularization of programs.

With the implementation of ABAP Objects, methods have assumed these two roles.

Rule

[⚙] **Rule 6.37: No Implementations in Function Modules and Subroutines**

Only use function modules and subroutines when they're technically necessary. In these cases, do not implement the required function. Instead, call appropriate (local) methods.

Details

This rule is directly derived from Rule 3.1, Use ABAP Objects. According to this rule, only methods are supposed to be created. Only if using a method is technically not possible (in Chapter 3, see Section 3.1, ABAP Objects as a Programming Model), can you create other types of procedures:

▶ Function modules for RFC, updates, and accesses to classical dynpros or selection screens

▶ Subroutines for `PERFORM ON COMMIT`/`ROLLBACK` and `GENERATE SUBROUTINE POOL`

These are only supposed to be used to wrap method calls to ensure that ABAP Objects is also used in such cases.

All rules of these programming guidelines that refer to procedures (such as Section 6.5.2, Type of the Formal Parameters of Procedures, and the following) thus actually refer to methods because — strictly speaking — no other procedures with nontrivial code are supposed to occur. If you strictly adhere to Rule 6.37, all rules that refer to implementations of procedures can consequently hardly be applied to function modules and subroutines because they only serve to wrap calls. For example, function modules and subroutines should no longer contain any of the local declarations that are addressed in Rule 4.13.

If you cannot meet Rules 3.1 and 6.37, for example, because existing legacy function modules and subroutines need to be maintained or enhanced and you cannot switch to methods, the rules of these programming guidelines that refer to procedures also apply to function modules and subroutines, of course.

6.5.2   Type of the Formal Parameters of Procedures

Background

The parameter interface of a procedure consists of formal parameters and defines possible exceptions of the procedure (in Chapter 5, see Section 5.2.2, Classical and Class-Based Exceptions). The following types of formal parameters are possible:

▶ **Input parameters**
Are defined for methods and function modules using `IMPORTING` and for subroutines using `USING`.

▶ **Output parameters**
Are defined for methods and function modules using `EXPORTING`.

▶ **Input/output parameters**
Are defined for methods, function modules, and subroutines using `CHANGING`.

▶ **Return values**
Are defined for methods using `RETURNING`.

The actual behavior of a formal parameter, however, partly only derives from the combination of the parameter type and the transfer type (see Section 6.5.3, Transfer Type of Formal Parameters).

Rule

[✓] Rule 6.38: Select the Appropriate Formal Parameter Type

Select a formal parameter type that corresponds to the parameter semantics:

- ▶ Input parameters for parameters that are evaluated but not changed in the procedure
- ▶ Output parameters or return values for parameters that are not evaluated but changed in the procedure
- ▶ Input/output parameters for parameters that are evaluated and changed in the procedure

Details

For the user of a procedure, the parameter types provide important information on their usage in the procedures and indicate a certain behavior of the procedure. If you don't select the appropriate parameter type, the risk of an inappropriate use increases.

- ▶ Mere input parameters should always be of the IMPORTING type (or USING for subroutines).[26]

- ▶ Mere output parameters should always be of the EXPORTING or RETURNING type.

- ▶ Parameters that are evaluated and changed should always be of the CHANGING type. You should particularly not exploit the fact that an EXPORTING parameter (or a USING parameter in the case of subroutines) technically behaves like a CHANGING parameter (see Section 6.5.4, Passing Output Parameters by Reference) in a procedure (method, see Rule 6.37).

Input parameters or input/output parameters that are not necessarily required for the execution of a procedure should be defined as optional via OPTIONAL or by specifying a DEFAULT value. Otherwise, calling programs are forced to pass unnecessary parameters and create helper variables especially for this purpose.

A narrow parameter interface of a procedure that adheres to Rule 4.23, Restrict the Number of Statements in Procedures, only requires a few input parameters

---

26 In this context, bear in mind that you can write to input parameters that have been defined with USING for pass by reference without this leading to a syntax error as in the case of input parameters that have been defined using IMPORTING for methods or function modules. Yet another reason to not use subroutines (see Appendix A., Section A.1.1, Subroutines).

and one return value. But this cannot be implemented really consistently and is therefore not formulated as a rule here.

Tip

Another parameter type are table parameters that can be declared for function modules and subroutines using TABLES. Basically, they have the same effects as input/output parameters for internal tables. This parameter type is obsolete and should no longer be used (more on this and on exceptions of this rule for RFMs can be found in Appendix A, Section A.1.2, Table Parameters).

Bad Example

Listing 6.61 shows a formal parameter that is declared as an output parameter using EXPORTING but is used in the method as an input/output parameter declared with CHANGING. This doesn't correspond to the semantics that a calling program expects.

```
CLASS class DEFINITION.
  PUBLIC SECTION.
    METHODS do_something
      EXPORTING e_parameter TYPE ...
ENDCLASS.

CLASS class IMPLEMENTATION.
  METHOD do_something.
    "evaluate e_parameter
    ...
    "set e_parameter
    ...
  ENDMETHOD.
ENDCLASS.
```

Listing 6.61 Wrong Declaration of an Input/Output Parameter

Good Example

Listing 6.62 corrects Listing 6.61 by declaring the parameter as an input/output parameter with CHANGING according to its use.

```
CLASS class DEFINITION.
  PUBLIC SECTION.
    METHODS do_something
      CHANGING c_parameter TYPE ...
ENDCLASS.
```

```
CLASS class IMPLEMENTATION.
  METHOD do_something.
    "evaluate c_parameter
    ...
    "set c_parameter
    ...
  ENDMETHOD.
ENDCLASS.
```

Listing 6.62 Correct Declaration of an Input/Output Parameter

6.5.3 Transfer Type of Formal Parameters

Background

Parameters can be passed to procedures either by reference or by value.

► **Pass by reference**
  In the case of pass by reference, a reference to the actual parameter is transferred to the procedure when it is called. The procedure then works with the actual parameter. No local data object is created for the formal parameter. Input parameters that are passed by reference cannot be changed in the procedure (exception: USING parameters of subroutines).

► **Pass by value**
  In the case of pass by value, a type-specific local data object is created as a copy of the actual parameter for the formal parameter. The system initializes output parameters and return values when the procedure is started. Input parameters as well as input/output parameters receive the value of the actual parameter. A changed formal parameter is only passed back to the actual parameter if the procedure ends free of errors.

IMPORTING parameters that are passed by reference are protected from explicit changes within the procedure. This is not the case for parameters passed by value. RETURNING parameters always have to be passed by value.

Rule

[✓] **Rule 6.39: Select the Appropriate Transfer Type**

When selecting the transfer type, consider both speed and security:

► Pass by value for small amounts of data for security reasons
► Pass by reference for large amounts of data for performance reasons

Details

Passing by reference generally has a higher performance than pass by value because no values need to be copied. This speed advantage can be noticed especially in the case of large parameters, such as internal tables or strings, or in mass data processing. In the case of small, flat parameters, the passing by value usually doesn't lead to problems because the copy costs incurred are not high here. Furthermore, for strings and internal tables, so-called sharing[27] takes place in the case of pass by value. Consequently, only references are passed also here. The time-intensive copy process is skipped if the data objects involved are only accessed with read access, such as in the case of EXPORTING parameters that are filled within a procedure (method, see Rule 6.37), and aren't modified by the calling program after the transfer.

Despite the speed advantage, passing by reference can lead to problems due to the following aspects:

▶ EXPORTING parameters that are passed by reference are not initialized automatically. Therefore, such parameters are not supposed to be read until the value has been assigned to them (see Rule 6.40).

▶ Write accesses to EXPORTING and CHANGING parameters that were passed by reference directly work with the actual parameters. Their values are also modified if the procedure (method, see Rule 6.37) is left early due to an exception.

▶ IMPORTING parameters that are passed by reference change if the actual parameter changes during the execution of the procedure. The actual parameter can change, for example, if it is a global variable (see Rule 6.22) or a system field (see Rule 6.27).

If passing by value isn't problematic with regard to performance, that is, if small amounts of data are transferred or sharing can be used, you should use this approach for security reasons. If the speed is a problem, you should work with

---

27 For assignments between strings or internal tables and for pass by value of such data types, only the internal references are transferred to the string or table body due to performance reasons. Sharing is not canceled until one of the internal tables or strings that are involved is accessed for modification. Only then does the actual copy process take place. Excluded from sharing are nested tables or tables whose line types contain *boxed components* (as of Releases 7.0 EhP2 and 7.2).

passing by reference. In this case, the potential risks in the implementation of the procedure (method, see Rule 6.37) must be considered (see Rule 6.40).

Example

Refer to Figure 3.8 in Chapter 3. Here, an internal table is passed by reference due to performance reasons, while an elementary parameter is passed by value due to robustness reasons.

6.5.4 Passing Output Parameters by Reference

Background

When parameters are passed to a procedure by reference, this procedure directly uses the data object that has been passed as a parameter. Its value is consequently determined by the calling program of the procedure. This behavior must be considered particularly for EXPORTING parameters whose value is — in contrast to the case of pass by value — not initialized when the procedure is called. After the procedure has started, an output parameter that was passed by reference has the value of the supplied actual parameter.

Rule

[✓] **Rule 6.40: Use Output Parameters by Reference Method Correctly**

Do not evaluate EXPORTING parameters that are passed by reference in a procedure (method, see Rule 6.37) until a value has been explicitly assigned.

Details

Because the value of an output parameter that has been passed by reference is undefined from the procedure's perspective, it cannot be evaluated within the procedure in a useful manner. Therefore, no assumptions can be made regarding the content of the parameter until the first value has been assigned to it.

If such a parameter is an internal table or a string, a simple write access is not sufficient. First, an initialization must be done. For example, if new lines are supposed to be inserted in an internal table that is supposed to be output by reference, its current content needs to be deleted first. Due to passing by reference, you cannot be sure that the table is actually empty when the procedure is started.

The same applies to strings that are filled via concatenation operations within the procedure.

Tip

If the described properties are to be exploited for writable parameters that have been passed by reference in a procedure (method, see Rule 6.37), that is, a read access is supposed to be implemented prior to the write access or an existing dynamic data object is supposed to be extended, you must select the appropriate formal parameter type according to Rule 6.38, that is, input/output parameter (CHANGING parameter).

Exception

Strictly speaking, you must only initialize optional output parameters that have been passed by reference if the parameter is connected to an actual parameter when called.[28] This can be determined using the IS SUPPLIED query. The obsolete query, IS REQUESTED, in contrast, is no longer supposed to be used (in Appendix A, see Section A.5.3, Checking the Binding of Actual Parameters).

Example

Listing 6.63 shows how an internal table is returned by reference for performance reasons.[29] The tabular output parameter is explicitly initialized at the beginning of the method before new lines are inserted.

```
CLASS class DEFINITION.
  PUBLIC SECTION.
    CLASS-METHODS get_some_table
      EXPORTING e_some_table TYPE table_type.
ENDCLASS.

CLASS class IMPLEMENTATION.
  METHOD get_some_table.
    DATA new_line LIKE LINE OF e_some_table.
    CLEAR e_some_table.
    ...
```

---

28 For formal parameters that have been passed by reference and that aren't connected to an actual parameter when called, the system generates an initial local data object just as it does in the case of pass by value.

29 It can thus not be declared as a RETURNING parameter.

```
    INSERT new_line INTO TABLE e_some_table.
    ...
  ENDMETHOD.
ENDCLASS.
```

Listing 6.63 Initializing an Output Parameter

6.5.5 Typing of Formal Parameters

Background

The typing of formal parameters can be complete or generic. Formal parameters of methods must be, and formal parameters of function modules and subroutines should be, explicitly typed using the TYPE or LIKE addition. When you connect actual parameters to formal parameters, the system checks whether the data type of the actual parameter corresponds to the typing of the formal parameter.

▶ Complete typing completely defines the data type of a formal parameter and applies to both dynamic access and static access to formal parameters.

▶ Generic typing doesn't completely define the data type of a formal parameter. Instead, the actual data type of the supplied actual parameter is copied. For dynamic access to such a formal parameter, the properties of the actual parameters apply. For static access, the properties that are defined via the typing apply.

For generic typing, a set of predefined generic types is available in ABAP, which are only provided for typing of formal parameters and field symbols.[30] These include: any, any table, c, clike, csequence, data, decfloat, hashed table, index table, n, numeric, object, simple, sorted table, standard table, table, x, and xsequence. Self-defined table types without completely specified table key are also generic.

Rule

[✓]   **Rule 6.41: Be as Specific as Possible When Typing Formal Parameters**

Be only as generic as necessary when typing formal parameters. Completely generic types (any) should be the exception rather than the rule.

---

30 A different usage can either lead to errors or to an implicit completion of the missing properties with default values.

Details

Absolute type security within a procedure can only be achieved with complete typing. It should always be used when providing a generic service is not a defined goal. It is much easier to carry out tests for non-generic services than for generic services (see Rule 2.3, Adhere to Existing Product Standards or Check Their Adherence).

A generically typed procedure interface usually involves more implementation effort within the procedure (method, see Rule 6.37) to avoid runtime errors (see Rule 6.47). The following principle consequently applies to the provision of generic interfaces: as less generic typing as possible and as much generic typing as necessary. You should particularly use specific generic types, such as `numeric` or `csequence`, instead of `any` or `data`, for example, if services are involved that are supposed to process numeric values or character strings.

Generic typing can also be a pitfall when you're not aware that you've used generic typing instead of complete typing because only the technical type properties but no component names, for example, are checked when an actual parameter is connected. This can lead to different behavior than expected.

Tip

These rules for typing also apply to field symbols (see Section 6.6.6, Accessing Data Objects Dynamically).

Bad Example

The example in Listing 6.64 shows the mentioned trap in which you can get caught especially when working with table types if the table key is not completely specified in their declaration (in a program or in the ABAP Dictionary). Due to the missing key specification, the table type that is used to type the formal parameter of `sort_itab` is generic. While the first static sorting is successful, the second SORT statement fails and triggers a runtime error. For the dynamic component specification, the properties of the actual parameter apply to the formal parameter, and the actual parameter doesn't have the `col2` component (this can also be determined in the ABAP Debugger).

```
CLASS class DEFINITION.
  PUBLIC SECTION.
    TYPES: BEGIN OF struc,
             col1 TYPE type1,
             col2 TYPE type2,
```

```
            END OF struc,
            itab TYPE STANDARD TABLE OF struc.
    METHODS: main,
            sort_itab CHANGING c_itab TYPE itab.
ENDCLASS.

CLASS class IMPLEMENTATION.
  METHOD main.
    TYPES: BEGIN OF struc,
            col1 TYPE type1,
            col3 TYPE type2,
          END OF struc.
    DATA itab TYPE STANDARD TABLE OF struc
                WITH NON-UNIQUE KEY col1 col3.
    ...
    sort_itab( CHANGING c_itab = itab ).
  ENDMETHOD.
  METHOD sort_itab.
    SORT c_itab BY col1 col2.
    SORT c_itab BY ('COL1') ('COL2').  "<- Runtime error!
  ENDMETHOD.
ENDCLASS.
```

Listing 6.64 Unwanted Generic Typing

Good Example

Listing 6.65 shows a very simple correction of the typing in Listing 6.64. Because the primary table key is completely specified, the used type is no longer generic, and the dynamic sorting functions like the static sorting.

```
    ...
    itab TYPE STANDARD TABLE OF struc
        WITH NON-UNIQUE KEY col1 col2.
    ...
```

Listing 6.65 Complete Typing

6.5.6   Internal and External Procedure Calls

Background

When a procedure is called, you distinguish between *internal* and *external* procedure calls. An internal call calls a procedure of the same program, while an external call calls a procedure of a different program. The major difference between internal and external procedure calls is that the corresponding program may have to be loaded first for an external call. For internal calls, the program is already loaded, of course. Possible external calls for which a program may have to be loaded are calls of the following elements:

- Methods of global classes in class pools
- Function modules in function groups
- Subroutines in all programs that can contain subroutines (PERFORM...IN PROGRAM)
- Methods of local classes for which the name of the class is dynamically specified using an absolute type name (\PROGRAM= ... \CLASS=...\)

The programs that are loaded within an internal session form *program groups*. There is always a *main program group*; several *additional program groups* may also exist. Each program group contains a main program and may also contain other programs that have been loaded due to external use[31].

If shared resources are accessed in an externally called procedure, the information concerning which program group the corresponding program was loaded into is critical. Whether a program forms a specific program group when loaded or is loaded to an existing program group mainly[32] depends on the program type:

- Class pools and function groups and therefore the external calls of methods of global classes or of function modules always form a new program group when being loaded.
- If subroutines or the methods of local classes of program types other than class pools and function groups are externally called, the programs are loaded to the program group of the calling program when being loaded.

Rule

Rule 6.42: Call Only Appropriate Procedures Externally
Call only such procedures externally that are provided for this purpose. The methods of global classes and function modules are intended for external calls. Subroutines and methods of local classes are not provided for external calls.

---

31 The loading is not always a result of a call but can also take place due to other references to components of external programs, such as a reference to a visible data type of a global class.

32 Actually, it is the introductory statement that is decisive here.

Details

The only procedures that are intended for external calls are visible methods of global classes and function modules. The main programs of these procedures are always main programs of their program groups, and it is always defined that the procedure uses the resources of this program group.

The external call of subroutines and the dynamic invoke of methods in local classes of other programs, however, are problematic. Usually, subroutines and local classes are supposed to be used internally within their program. When developing them, you cannot anticipate that they are also externally called.[33] They should therefore always be treated as private components of their program, even though they are technically public.

Furthermore, the assignment to a particular program group is not statically defined. Because the call sequence can depend on user actions or data contents, the program of the called procedure can sometimes belong to the main program group and to an additional program group at other times. Therefore it is not fixed to which program group the shared resources belong. These are as follows:

- **Classical dynpros (including selection screens and classical lists) and GUI status**
  The classical dynpros and GUI status are always shared within a program group, namely those of the main program of a program group. For example, the CALL SCREEN statement in an externally called procedure always calls a dynpro of the main program of the program group and not a dynpro of the main program of the procedure. The response to user actions in the dynpro that has been called in this way is also handled within the main program of the program group.

- **Interface work areas**
  Interface work areas are defined using the TABLES and NODES statements as table work areas (see Section 6.1.7, Table Work Areas) or using the obsolete statement, DATA ... COMMON PART (in Appendix A, see Section A.2.2, Interface Work Areas). They are created only once for each program group and are shared by the main program and the loaded additional programs.

---

33 No problems occur when an already loaded program deliberately passes a reference to an object of a local class to another program.

Tip

Except for the warning regarding the dynamic invoke of methods of local classes of other programs, this rule is basically supposed to raise the awareness of problems when using existing programs. In new programs, the creation of new subroutines (in Appendix A, see Section A.1.1, Subroutines) and the usage of shared resources (see Rule 6.7, No Table Work Areas Except for Classical Dynpros, and Section A.2.3, Table Work Areas) are obsolete to a large extent anyway. Solely the use of classical dynpros or selection screens (and therefore also of the GUI status and table work areas, see Section 5.3, User Interfaces, in Chapter 5) can lead to the problems mentioned.

Example

The example in Listing 6.66 demonstrates the assignment of interface work areas to program groups in the case of external calls of subroutines. The `dbtab` table work area, which is declared in the `sapssubr` program, is shared either with `sapmprog` or with `saplfugr`. If `share` has the value `FUGR`, `saplfugr` and `sapssubr` share the table work area. Otherwise, `sapmprog` and `sapssubr` share this work area. So you cannot rely on a certain assignment.

```
**********************************
PROGRAM sapmprog.
TABLES dbtab.
...
IF share = 'FUGR'.
  CALL FUNCTION 'FUNC'.
ENDIF.
...
PERFORM sub IN PROGRAM sapssubr.
**********************************

**********************************
FUNCTION-POOL saplfugr.
TABLES dbtab.
...
FUNCTION func.
  PERFORM sub IN PROGRAM sapssubr.
ENDFUNCTION.
**********************************

**********************************
PROGRAM sapssubr.
```

```
TABLES dbtab.
...
FORM sub.
  ...
ENDFORM.
***********************************
```

Listing 6.66 Shared Table Work Area in Different Programs of a Program Group

6.5.7   Exiting Procedures

Background

You can exit procedures either regularly using the `END...` statement or one of the following statements:

▶ `RETURN`

▶ `EXIT`

▶ `CHECK log_exp`

These statements end a procedure properly, that is, the system passes output parameters for which passing by value is specified and returns values to the assigned actual parameters. In addition, you can terminate the processing of a procedure as follows whereby the actual parameters are not supplied with values:

▶ Calling another unit (program, dynpro) without returning to the procedure

▶ Triggering an exception or sending a dialog message if an error occurs (in Chapter 5, see Section 5.2, Error Handling).

Rule

> **Rule 6.43: Exit Procedures with RETURN Only**
>
> Use the `RETURN` statement to properly exit a procedure (method, see Rule 6.37) early.

Details

The `RETURN` statement serves to exit procedures and always has this result. The behavior of the `EXIT` and `CHECK` statements (conditional exit), in contrast, is context-dependent: Within a loop, only the loop is left, outside a loop, the surrounding procedure is left. This ambiguity limits the legibility of source code. Loops are consequently supposed to be left via `EXIT` and `CHECK` only, and procedures are supposed to be left via RETURN. Only RETURN enables you to exit a procedure in a loop context.

Tip

In addition to the statements mentioned, RETURN, EXIT, and CHECK, there are further statements (REJECT, STOP) that enable you to exit specific event blocks (see Section 6.5.8, Dialog Modules and Event Blocks). Inversely, RETURN, EXIT, and CHECK can also be used to leave other processing blocks in addition to procedures. In both cases, you must consider the particular behavior of the ABAP runtime environment regarding the left processing block. Because other processing blocks are only supposed to contain one method call according to Rule 3.1, Use ABAP Objects, or Rule 6.44, No Implementations in Dialog Modules and Event Blocks, these cases should no longer occur in new programs.

Exception

An exception to the rule that states that only RETURN to exit procedures is supposed to be used are CHECK statements that are located at the beginning of a procedure and that check the prerequisites for the execution of the procedure there. Using the CHECK statement in such a way doesn't restrict the legibility and is thus allowed. However, this exception doesn't apply to other positions within a procedure that are outside loops.

Bad Example

Listing 6.67 shows how a method is left early with a CHECK statement whose meaning cannot be identified by simply looking at it. You have to know that CHECK leaves the procedure if its logical expression is wrong so that a double negation is necessary.

```
METHOD some_method.
  ...
  CHECK is_finished = abap_false.
  ...
ENDMETHOD.
```

Listing 6.67 Conditionally Exiting a Method via CHECK

Good Example

Listing 6.68 corrects and simplifies Listing 6.67 by implementing a conditional exit with an IF control structure that is easy to read.

```
METHOD some_method.
  ...
  IF is_finished = abap_true.
    RETURN.
  ENDIF.
  ...
ENDMETHOD.
```

Listing 6.68 Conditionally Exiting a Method via RETURN

6.5.8 Dialog Modules and Event Blocks

Background

In addition to procedures, there are two further types of processing blocks. These, however, do not have a parameter interface and do not allow for a declaration of local data:[34]

▶ **Dialog modules**
Dialog modules are introduced using the MODULE statement and ended using the ENDMODULE statement. They are the functional interface between classical dynpros and their ABAP program and are called from the dynpro flow logic.

▶ **Event blocks**
Event blocks are introduced by the corresponding keyword and implicitly ended by the next processing block. The processing of such an event block is triggered by the ABAP runtime environment when the corresponding event occurs. Event blocks are available for

  ▷ Loading a program (LOAD-OF-PROGRAM)

  ▷ Reporting events that occur during the processing of an executable program (with a logical database) (INITIALIZATION, START-OF-SELECTION, GET, END-OF-SELECTION)

  ▷ Selection screen events (AT SELECTION-SCREEN ...)

  ▷ List events of the classical list processing (AT LINE-SELECTION, AT USER-COMMAND)

---

34 Exceptions are AT SELECTION-SCREEN and GET. These exceptions should not be utilized, however.

Rule

Rule 6.44: No Implementations in Dialog Modules and Event Blocks [✿]

Only use dialog modules and event blocks if they're technically necessary. Do not implement the required function there. Instead, call appropriate (local) methods.

Details

Due to the missing option for declaring local data in dialog modules and event blocks, you cannot implement reasonable program logic. Therefore, dialog modules and event blocks — provided that they are still necessary according to Rule 3.1, Use ABAP Objects — are supposed to contain only one method call. If ABAP Objects is used consistently, only the following elements are required still today:

- `LOAD-OF-PROGRAM` or `INITIALIZATION` as the program constructor in those cases in which other program types than class pools are used (in Chapter 3, see Section 3.2.1, Program Type).

- Dialog modules and `AT SELECTION-SCREEN` when classical dynpros and selection screen are processed (see Rule 5.19).

- `START-OF-SELECTION` in executable programs for background processing (in Chapter 3, see Section 3.2.1) For legibility reasons, you must always specify the statement explicitly (although it is optional in a lot of situations).

Although syntactically possible, you should never specify an event block several times within a program.

Tip

Using `LOAD-OF-PROGRAM` in a function group can be considered analogous to using a static constructor in a global class. In executable programs, you can use `INITIALIZATION` instead if the parameters that may have been transferred via `SUBMIT` are supposed to be evaluated.

Example

Listing 6.69 shows the PAI modules of the `DEMO_CR_CAR_RENTAL_SCREENS` function group from the `SABAP_DEMOS_CAR_RENTAL_DYNPRO` package whose screens are illustrated in Figure 5.1 in Chapter 5. These dialog modules follow Rule 6.44. They do not contain own implementations but call methods of a local class of the function group.

```
MODULE cancel INPUT.
  screen_handler=>cancel( ).
ENDMODULE.

MODULE user_command_0100 INPUT.
  screen_handler=>user_command_0100( ).
ENDMODULE.

MODULE customers_mark INPUT.
  customer_table=>mark( ).
ENDMODULE.

MODULE reservations_mark INPUT.
  reservation_table=>mark( ).
ENDMODULE.
```

Listing 6.69 PAI Modules Without Specific Implementation

6.5.9   Macros

Background

A macro defines a statement sequence between `DEFINE` and `END-OF-DEFINITION` for program-internal reuse. The statement sequence can be integrated anywhere in the program by specifying the macro name. A macro can contain up to nine place holders (`&1` to `&9`) instead of ABAP words and operands or parts of operands, which have to be replaced by concrete words when integrating the macro.

Rule

[⚙] **Rule 6.45: Use Macros in Exceptional Cases Only**

Use mainly procedures (methods, see Rule 6.37) instead of macros.

Details

Macros are often used as callable units instead of real procedures. This is rarely useful, however. On the one hand, macros don't have a specific context, on the other hand, they cannot be executed step-by-step in the ABAP Debugger. Consequently, troubleshooting is almost impossible in programs that use comprehensive or complex macros. Therefore, a macro can by no means replace a real procedure.

Moreover, macros were previously not used as a replacement for procedures only but also to implement frequently recurring declarations of structured data. Today, standalone types should be used instead of macros for this purpose, of course (see Rule 6.1).

In some situations, the use of macros can still be justified. This is the case in the presence of simple, recurring statement patterns. Here, a macro can be considered a means for design-time generation. The good example in this section illustrates such a macro use. In such a context, using a macro can be better than using a procedure for the following reasons:

▸ The statement sequence that the macro contains is sufficiently simple and obvious so that the missing debugging option plays only a minor role.

▸ The syntax check statically checks the statements for correctness. If you used the otherwise required dynamic language elements in a procedure, errors (in this case, incorrectly specified names) would not be determined until runtime. In addition, dynamic accesses would be more time-consuming (see Section 6.6, Dynamic Programming Techniques).

▸ Compared to formulating all individual statements, the source code remains clearer if you use such macros, particularly if the statement sequence is repeated numerous times. The risk of trivial typos is reduced because you have to create and maintain less source code that is very similar. You can retroactively change the logic with a minimum of effort.

In other words, in such specific cases, the use of macros can also increase the correctness and maintainability of source code. However, macros that contain non-trivial control structures are always a maintenance problem because they cannot be executed step-by-step in the ABAP Debugger. If you thus want to use macros, you should use them only sparingly, and they should contain only a few lines because it is almost impossible to analyze errors in macros.

Tip

Besides in the source code of a program, macros can also be stored in type groups or in the TRMAC database table for reuse in different programs. A common example is the break macro from the TRMAC table. However, you are not supposed to define new macros in type groups or in the TRMAC table.

Bad Example

Listing 6.70 shows an example where a macro insufficiently replaces a real procedure. In the example shown, the macro could also be used only once in a context because the `wa` work area can be declared there only once as well. Here, a partly dynamic procedure would make more sense.

```
DEFINE get_data.
  DATA wa TYPE &1.
  SELECT SINGLE *
         FROM &1
         INTO wa
         WHERE &2 = &3 AND
               &4 = &5.
END-OF-DEFINITION.

get_data spfli carrid 'LH' connid '0400'.
```

Listing 6.70 A Macro Replaces a Procedure

Good Example

Listing 6.71 shows an example where it makes sense to use a macro. Some simple statement sequences (assignments of which each is enclosed in `IF`) are supposed to be repeated quite often, and the names of the operands used follow some regularity. This functionality could also be implemented otherwise, for example, via a procedure that accesses the variables with dynamic means or by formulating each individual `IF` block. Using a small macro in this case, however, increases the legibility and maintainability of the program.

```
TYPES: BEGIN OF value_and_flag,
         value TYPE string,
         flag  TYPE c LENGTH 1,
       END OF value_and_flag.

TYPES: BEGIN OF structure,
         component_up   TYPE value_and_flag,
         component_down TYPE value_and_flag,
         ...
         component_top  TYPE value_and_flag,
       END OF structure.

DATA struct TYPE structure.

DEFINE macro_set_value_if_flag_is_set.
  IF struct-component_&1-flag  = abap_true.
     struct-component_&1-value = &2.
  ENDIF.
```

```
END-OF-DEFINITION.

...

macro_set_value_if_flag_is_set up    'ABC'.
macro_set_value_if_flag_is_set down 'IJK'.
...
macro_set_value_if_flag_is_set top  'XYZ'.

...
```

Listing 6.71 Reasonable Use of a Macro

6.6 Dynamic Programming Techniques

Dynamic programming techniques cover the usage of all language elements whose effects or significance cannot be determined until the runtime of a program.

6.6.1 Using Dynamic Programming Techniques

Using dynamic programming techniques basically includes the following:

▸ Accessing dynamic memory objects, that is, dynamic data objects (strings and internal tables) as well as instances of classes and anonymous data objects

▸ Dynamically accessing data objects via reference variables and field symbols[35]

▸ Dynamically invoking procedures or entire programs

▸ Generically creating data types and using them to create anonymous data objects

▸ Generically creating programs in which parts of the statements are specified using dynamic tokens, or entire programs are created at runtime

In this sense, handling reference variables can also be considered a dynamic technique. The dynamic type (the object to which the reference refers) can be more specific than the static type of the variable, which entails polymorphic behavior and becomes apparent during assignments in the form *upcasts* or *downcasts*.

---

35 To a certain extent, this also includes accessing generically typed formal parameters in procedures (see Section 6.5.5, Typing of Formal Parameters).

Rule

[■]

Only use dynamic programming techniques when this is necessary and reasonable. Use only as many dynamic language elements as required to carry out the assigned task.

Detail

The advantage of dynamic programming techniques is the increased flexibility when creating programs. Dynamic programming techniques enable you to develop flexible and generic services that meet various requirements. The price you have to pay for this advantage is that dynamic programming techniques may decrease the static checkability, legibility, maintainability, testability, performance, and security.[36]

This section describes various dynamic programming techniques. From using strings, which is strongly recommended (see Rule 6.9); to using internal tables, which are one of the foundations of ABAP programming (see Section 6.4, Internal Tables); to generating entire programs, which you shouldn't do (see Rule 6.52). The more dynamics, the more comprehensive the precautionary measures that you have to take when using these techniques. Already the simple access to data objects involves a corresponding partial aspect, which was addressed in Rule 6.20. The rules in this section extend such specific rules and provide a more general framework.

You should basically always consider the following aspects when deploying dynamic techniques:

▶ Programs that work with dynamic techniques are usually more complex and harder to understand than programs that use only static techniques. This has a negative effect on maintainability.

▶ The risk of exceptions or runtime errors increases considerably because in dynamic programming, a lot of checks, which are carried out already during the compilation in other cases, can only be performed at runtime.

▶ Checking the dynamic parts at runtime can reduce the processing speed because the checks have to be repeated each time the parts are used again.

---

36 Security standards (see Chapter 2, Section 2.3, Correctness and Quality) can even completely prohibit risky dynamic programming techniques.

▶ More tests are required because numerous states of a dynamic program and possible errors situations need to be checked.

Of course, the significance of these aspects differs for the various dynamic programming techniques. For example, a program that uses strings is by no means more complex than a program that works only with text fields. Nevertheless, some details must already be taken into account here.

6.6.2 Runtime Errors During Dynamic Processing

Background

When you use dynamic techniques, various exception situations can occur, which can never occur when you use the corresponding static techniques because of their static checkability.

Rule

Rule 6.47: Avoid Runtime Errors During Dynamic Processing	[✓]
Respond appropriately to all possible error situations when using dynamic techniques.	

Details

The different dynamic techniques also require different reactions to the possible exception situations. Examples include the following:

▶ When accessing *dynamic data objects*, you mustn't violate their current limitations (see Rule 6.20). For internal tables, for example, you mustn't specify line numbers for which no line exists.

▶ Before *dynamically accessing* data objects via data references or field symbols, you must ensure that these are connected to a data object and check this connection using IS BOUND or IS ASSIGNED, if necessary. After the access, you should check the return value for a successful execution, if possible.

▶ For the *dynamic invoke*, you must catch exceptions that are triggered due to non-existent programs, classes, or procedures or due to inappropriate parameters.

▶ In case of a dynamic token specification, for example, a dynamic WHERE condition in Open SQL or internal tables (since Releases 7.0 EhP2 and 7.2), you must catch possible exceptions and respond accordingly.

▸ If complete programs are generically developed, you have to check the generated programs using the `SYNTAX-CHECK` statement.

These examples illustrate how the use of dynamic techniques can lead to more complex and less clear code due to the numerous possible exception situations. Of course, the more the mentioned techniques are combined, the more complex and less clear the code becomes. Therefore, you should always adhere to the general Rule 6.46.

Tip

If you cannot respond to particular error situations, for example, because no exception that can be handled exists, you must ensure that this error situation never occurs and verify this in comprehensive test scenarios.

Bad Example

The seemingly well legible source code section from Listing 6.72 uses almost only dynamic operands and tokens. Neither the ABAP Compiler nor the reader can know the content of the specified variables at runtime. An error in one of these variables results in a termination of the program.

```
READ TABLE where_clauses ASSIGNING <where_clause> WITH ...
DELETE FROM (dbtab_name) WHERE (<where_clause>).
IF sy-subrc = 0.
  CALL METHOD (class_name)=>(method_name).
ENDIF.
```

Listing 6.72 Dynamic Programming Without Error Handling

Good Example

Listing 6.73 corrects Listing 6.72 with an appropriate error handling — this reduces the legibility, of course. Here, it is additionally considered that an initial dynamic `WHERE` condition means that no restrictions are imposed. As shown here, this case has to be explicitly avoided. Otherwise, the entire table content will be deleted.

```
UNASSIGN <where_clause>.
READ TABLE where_clauses ASSIGNING <where_clause> WITH ...
IF sy-subrc <> 0.
  RAISE EXCEPTION ...
ENDIF.
ASSERT <where_clause> IS ASSIGNED.
```

```
IF <where_clause> IS NOT INITIAL.
  TRY.
      DELETE FROM (dbtab_name) WHERE (<where_clause>).
    CATCH cx_sy_dynamic_osql_error.
      ...
  ENDTRY.
  IF sy-subrc = 0.
    TRY.
        CALL METHOD (class_name)=>(method_name).
      CATCH cx_sy_dyn_call_error.
        ...
    ENDTRY.
  ENDIF.
ENDIF.
```

Listing 6.73 Dynamic Programming with Error Handling

6.6.3 Using Dynamic Data Objects

Background

Dynamic data objects are a subgroup of dynamic memory objects (see Section 6.6.4, Memory Consumption of Dynamic Memory Objects) and nothing more than our well known

▶ Strings and

▶ Internal tables

The data type statically defines all properties for dynamic data objects — except for the memory consumption. Although they are internally managed via references, they are addressed with their names, and value semantics applies, which means that the de-referenced internal reference is always used for access.

Rule

Rule 6.48: Use Appropriate Dynamic Data Objects [✓]

To store dynamic amounts of data transiently when using dynamic data objects, always select the type that corresponds best to the content and the desired access:

▶ Strings for data that cannot be divided

▶ Internal tables for data that can be divided

To avoid memory bottlenecks for large amounts of data, other approaches can be required as well.

Details

When using dynamic data objects, the selection of the type is a basic decision. The natural rule is as follows:

▶ Data that can be handled in one piece are stored as a character or byte string (`string` or `xstring` data type).

▶ Structured data or data that are divided into individual sections in a natural way are stored as lines of an internal table.

If the goal is to store a very large amount of data as dynamic data objects, the considerations need to be more differentiated. Data objects of the `string` and `xstring` types must be stored in one piece in the memory, while the content of internal tables is stored in blocks. This can more easily lead to resource bottlenecks when strings are used because sufficient memory space may be available but cannot be used to include a string of the requested length due to its fragmentation (see Section 6.6.4, Memory Consumption of Dynamic Memory Objects). In these cases, it makes more sense to store the data as an internal table instead of storing the data in one piece in a string.

The `EXPORT` statement for storing data in a cluster supports both storage types, for example: `EXPORT ... TO DATA BUFFER` stores the cluster in one long byte string, while `EXPORT ... TO INTERNAL TABLE` distributes the cluster across numerous lines of an internal table. For the reason mentioned previously, the last variant is more secure if the cluster is supposed to include a very large amount of data.

Tip

Strings and internal tables are directly built-in in the ABAP language as data types and the corresponding access statements. In other programming languages, however, they are often implemented as libraries (e.g., string classes, container classes). In ABAP, it is usually neither required nor useful to define specific classes to store strings or table-type data (in Chapter 5, see Section 5.1, Object-Oriented Programming). Nevertheless, it can make sense to wrap internal tables in classes to release more memory when data are deleted (see Section 6.6.5, Administration Costs of Dynamic Memory Objects).

6.6.4 Memory Consumption of Dynamic Memory Objects

Background

In dynamic memory objects, the actual data is addressed via references. Dynamic memory objects are always deep. The following dynamic memory objects are available:

- Table bodies of internal tables that are addressed via internal table references
- Text or byte strings that are addressed via internal string references
- Anonymous data objects that have been created with `CREATE DATA` and are addressed via data references in data reference variables
- Instances of classes that have been created with `CREATE OBJECT` and are addressed via object references in object reference variables

The maximum overall size and number of all dynamically managed memory objects of an internal session are generally defined by the maximum memory space that the session can request for the program execution.

Besides the available memory space of the application server, there are two additional technical limitations that limit the possible size of individual dynamic memory objects.

- For the size of a string in bytes[37] and the number of lines in an internal table, the upper limit is 2^{31}-1.
- The memory for both the content of a string and the hash management of an internal hashed table must be provided in one piece. Therefore, the `ztta/max_memreq_mb` profile parameter is relevant for these two memory object types. It defines how much memory can be requested in one piece at most. A maximum size for strings and a limitation for the line number for hashed tables can be directly derived from this.[38]

Any attempt to exceed one of these limits results in a runtime error with program termination.

---

37 In a Unicode system, each character of a character string occupies 2 bytes.

38 This limitation doesn't depend on the width of the table lines because only the hash management and not the table content itself must be provided in one piece in the memory. Currently, the limitation is the highest power of two that is less than or equal to an eighth of the value specified by the profile parameter. For example, if the profile parameter specifies 250MB, a hashed table can contain approximately 16 million lines.

Rule

Rule 6.49: Avoid Memory Bottlenecks

When using dynamic memory objects, ensure that the program isn't terminated due to a lack of memory.

Details

Memory limits are fixed limitations that cannot be deactivated programmatically. To avoid memory bottlenecks, you should consider the following:

▶ The limits of the available physical memory when developing a program

▶ The given technical limits for strings and hashed tables

The only way to prevent memory limits from being exceeded is to programmatically limit the data that are loaded to the memory. This applies to the processing of large amounts of data but also to the creation of objects. The latter can result in memory bottlenecks if either too large or too many small objects are created. Furthermore, *memory leaks*, that is, unused but not released memory, can be the cause of memory problems.

Processing Large Amounts of Data

If large amounts of data need to be processed that are stored in a persistent storage in one piece but do not fit into the available memory, you must read and process them either in packages or sequentially. A common language element for this purpose is the `PACKAGE SIZE` addition for reading large amounts of data to internal tables with the `SELECT` Open SQL statement.

As of Releases 7.0 EhP2 and 7.2, memory-saving processing of large strings (*Large Object, LOB*) in database tables is also possible. *Locators* enable you to access subfields of strings in database tables; *streaming* allows for a sequential and gradual transfer of data into the memory. Both concepts were introduced to ABAP to avoid memory bottlenecks.

Releasing Memory

Dynamically managed memory provides the major benefit that it can be released. To avoid memory leaks and possibly resulting memory bottlenecks, you should use this option and delete no longer required data and objects:

▶ You can delete strings using the `CLEAR` statement.

- You can delete internal tables using CLEAR or FREE. FREE releases the entire memory space, while the initial memory requirement of the table[39] remains reserved when CLEAR is used.

- Anonymous data objects and instances of classes are deleted by the Garbage Collector after *all* reference variables that refer to these object have been initialized. Here, you must ensure that all references are actually identified during the initialization. This is not always trivial, particularly in the case of complex object networks. This involves concepts such as *directed graphs* and *strongly connected components*, which are not further discussed here, but in "Analyze Memory-Related Problems in Your ABAP-Programs in Less Time and with Less Effort using the ABAP Memory Inspector" in the 2004 November/December issue of the SAP Professional Journal.

To analyze memory problems and detect memory leaks, you can use the Memory Inspector and the memory analysis of the ABAP Debugger. Among other features, they display rankings of all dynamically managed memory objects with regard to their memory consumption.

Tip

In this context, note that statically managed data objects can also involve unnecessary memory consumption, for example, large flat structures with unused or initial components whose initial values require a lot of memory space. Particularly character strings that contain only blanks are a significant factor in Unicode systems with 2 bytes for each blank. It can become considerably critical if such structures are combined with dynamic techniques; that is, if they are used as lines of internal tables, for example. So-called *boxed components* were therefore introduced with Releases 7.0 EhP2 and 7.2. They support initial value sharing for initial substructures so that the initial value of a substructure is created only once in memory. For structures with substructures that have a sparse fill level, this can reduce memory consumption and copy costs significantly.

Bad Example

Listing 6.74 shows how all data of a very large database table is read into an internal table. Here, a direct risk of memory bottlenecks is given.

---

[39] The size of the initial memory requirement is generally appropriately selected by the ABAP runtime environment itself but can also be predefined using the INITIAL SIZE addition (see Section 6.4.3, Initial Memory Requirement).

```
SELECT *
      FROM very_large_table
      INTO TABLE ...
```

Listing 6.74 Importing All Data of a Database Table into an Internal Table

Good Example

Listing 6.75 corrects Listing 6.74 by adding the `PACKAGE SIZE` addition, which restricts the maximum size of the internal table to a secure level.

```
SELECT *
      FROM very_large_table
      INTO TABLE ... PACKAGE SIZE 1000.
  ...
ENDSELECT.
```

Listing 6.75 Importing All Data of a Database Table into an Internal Table in Packages

6.6.5 Administration Costs of Dynamic Memory Objects

Background

Unfortunately, the flexibility provided by dynamic memory objects does also incur costs. The administration of these objects leads to internal costs, which are reflected in additional memory consumption and, in the worst case, can be the cause of too high memory consumption.

The overall memory consumption of a dynamic memory object is comprised of a consumption for the actual objects and a consumption for the administration data. The administration data consists of a reference with a fixed size of 8 bytes and a header, which contains the address of the actual data as well as further administration information.[40] The size of the header is dynamic and depends on the memory object type as follows:

- *String headers* of strings whose length is less than 30 characters or 60 bytes occupy between 10 and 40 bytes depending on the string length. For longer strings, the memory consumption of the header is approximately 50 bytes, irrespective of the string length.

- *Table headers* occupy about 150 bytes (32-bit architecture) or 200 bytes (64-bit architecture).

---

40 The reference only refers to a header and not directly to the object.

- *Object headers* of anonymous data objects and instances of classes occupy about 30 bytes, irrespective of the object.

The headers are created when dynamic data objects are supplied with content or when objects are created. When a dynamic data object (string or internal table) is initialized, only the actual content is deleted, and the header is kept for reuse.[41] If the Garbage Collector deletes an object, the object header is also deleted.

For internal tables, in addition to the administration data in the header, which is mainly independent of the number of lines, more memory is required for each line, for example, for index or hash management. This memory is not created in the table header, but in parallel to the table body. Depending on the table type, every table has at least a primary index (standard tables, sorted tables) or hash management (hashed tables). The costs of these are as follows:

- 6 bytes on average for each table line for the primary index.

- 18 bytes on average for each table line for the hash management as long as the DELETE or SORT statements are not used to access the table. After such an access, 30 bytes on average are required for each table line.

For each additional secondary table key (as of Releases 7.0 EhP2 and 7.2), the memory consumption increases by the memory required for the secondary key management (secondary index or secondary hash management) (see Section 6.4.2, Secondary Keys).

Rule

Rule 6.50: Consider the Ratio of Administration and Application Data [✿]

When using dynamically managed memory objects, bear in mind that you also require memory for administration purposes in addition to memory for the actual data. Compared to the application data, this administrative proportion shouldn't be too large.

Details

Although the memory management of dynamic memory objects is generally invisible for the developer and cannot be controlled by him, the administration costs should also be considered during the design and development phases to ensure that they don't become disproportionately high compared to the actual data con-

---

41 Only the FREE statement partly deletes table headers that are too large.

tent. For internal tables, for example, the administration costs consist of a proportion that is mainly independent of the number of lines and a proportion for each line. Consequently, tables with only a few lines but also tables with very narrow lines are unfavorable. A sorted table of integers, for instance, always uses more memory for its administrative information than for the actual application data. Hashed tables involve even more administration effort for each line.

Furthermore, the so-called *fill level* of complex data objects assumes a significant role. If the application data is stored in only a few large memory objects, the administrative proportion usually doesn't play a role. However, if complex data objects (structures, internal tables) have various deep components, you have to be careful: A disproportionate amount of memory space is lost for tables with many relatively small strings or for nested tables that contain relatively small tables, for example. Basically, you have to distinguish among the following three cases:

▶ **Complex data objects with a sparse fill level**
Such a data object contains many deep components of which a majority is initial.

▶ **Complex data objects with a duplicative fill level**
Such a data object contains many deep components of which a majority refers to the same application data via a reference variable or via sharing.

▶ **Complex data objects with a low fill level**
Such a data object contains many deep components that refer to different objects, strings, or internal tables, which contain only some application data or are empty.

Deep data objects with a fill level that is sparse or duplicative can usually be used without problems. But for complex data objects with a low fill level, a disproportion of administration and application data can easily occur. ABAP is inappropriate for an intense use of data objects with a low fill level.

At a low fill level, you can possibly consider a class wrapping as an alternative to internal tables because the extra costs for objects are comparatively low and because objects can be completely deleted from the memory (unlike dynamic data objects). This is an exception to the note in Section 6.6.3, Using Dynamic Data Objects.

Tip

Besides the ratio of administration and application data, the ratio of the memory that is allocated for application data and the actually used memory is also interesting for internal tables (see Section 6.4.3, Initial Memory Consumption).

Example

The DEMO_MEMORY_USAGE program (included in the system since Releases 7.0 EhP2 and 7.2) of the sample library that is integrated in the ABAP Keyword Documentation illustrates the administration costs of deep components with low data content.

6.6.6 Accessing Data Objects Dynamically

Background

Field symbols and data references serve to access data objects whose name and attributes are only known at runtime.

▶ **Field symbols**
A field symbol is a symbolic name for a data object to which you can assign memory areas using the ASSIGN statement or, if internal tables are processed, using the ASSIGNING addition. Fields symbols are declared with FIELD-SYMBOLS. They are typed either generically or completely and can be used in place of data objects in all appropriate operand positions. For typing, the same rules apply as for formal parameters of procedures (see Rule 6.41, Be as Specific as Possible When Typing Formal Parameters). When accessing field symbols, value semantics applies, which means that the assigned memory content is addressed directly. Field symbols are thus always handled like dereferenced pointers.

▶ **Data references**
A data reference is the content of a data reference variable that is declared via REF TO and points to any data objects or parts of data objects. You need data references to create anonymous data objects using CREATE DATA. They can also be filled, however, using the GET REFERENCE statement or, if internal tables are processed, using the REFERENCE INTO addition for existing data objects. A data reference variable is either completely generic or completely typed. When accessing data reference variables, reference semantics applies, which means that the data reference itself is addressed. To access the referenced memory con-

tent, you must explicitly dereference a data reference variable using the dereferencing operator (->*).

Field symbols and data references are closely linked because only completely typed data reference variables can be dereferenced in any operand position. Completely generic data reference variables (REF TO data) can be dereferenced in the ASSIGN statement only.

You can declare data reference variables in the same context as all other data objects (see Section 6.1.3, Declaration of Variables), especially also as attributes of classes. Field symbols, in contrast, can only be declared within procedures (methods, see Rule 6.37) or in the global declaration part. However, according to Rule 6.3, the latter is no longer allowed.

Rule

[⚙] | **Rule 6.51: Use Field Symbols and Data References Appropriately**

Use field symbols and data references for the purpose that matches their semantics best:

- ▸ Field symbols for value access (value semantics)
- ▸ Data references for working with the references (reference semantics)

Details

Both field symbols and data references can be understood as pointers to memory areas. The main difference here relates to the different access semantics.

- ▸ Due to their value semantics, field symbols are to be used if the focus is on the access to referenced data. For this purpose, field symbols provide specific functions, which are not available for data references:

  - ▸ Dynamic access to attributes of classes and objects

  ```
  ASSIGN (class_name)=>(attr_name) ...
  ASSIGN oref->(attr_name) ...
  ```

  - ▸ Dynamic access to structure components

  ```
  ASSIGN ... COMPONENT ...
  ```

  - ▸ Explicit casting

  ```
  ASSIGN ... CASTING ...
  ```

▶ Dereferencing of generic data reference variables

```
ASSIGN dref->* ...
```

▶ Due to their reference semantics, data references are to be used if the focus is on the handling of references to data objects. Data references are vital for the generation of anonymous data objects or complex dynamic data structures, such as trees or chained lists in the internal session or in the Shared Objects memory. Furthermore, data references are the preferred element to implement explicit sharing between any data objects and pass pointers to data objects to and from procedures.

Note

Actually, data reference variables are better suited for programs that are based on ABAP Objects according to Rule 3.1 because they have the same semantics as object reference variables and therefore represent a more modern programming concept (in Chapter 3, see Section 3.3, Modern ABAP). Field symbols, instead, provide more functions than data references and can thus not always be replaced by them. Consequently, the usage of field symbols for dynamic accesses to data objects is still recommended, although the sole use of data references would be favorable for consistency and simplicity reasons.

Bad Example

Listing 6.76 shows a loop for an internal table in which the system is supposed to directly access the current line according to Rule 6.35. If a generic data reference variable is used for this purpose, you also need a field symbol for its dereferencing.

```
METHOD some_method.
  "IMPORTING i_itab TYPE INDEX TABLE
  DATA dref TYPE REF TO data.
  FIELD-SYMBOLS <fs> TYPE data.
  ...
  LOOP AT i_itab REFERENCE INTO dref.
    ASSIGN dref->* TO <fs>.
    <fs> = ...
  ENDLOOP.
  ...
ENDMETHOD.
```

Listing 6.76 Detour via a Data Reference

Good Example

Listing 6.77 simplifies Listing 6.76 by directly using a field symbol, which is required to directly access table lines via a data reference anyway. The direct use of the field symbol thus also follows Rule 2.2, Adhere to the KISS Principle.

```
METHOD some_method.
  "IMPORTING i_itab TYPE INDEX TABLE
  FIELD-SYMBOLS <fs> TYPE data.
  ...
  LOOP AT i_itab ASSIGNING <fs>.
    <fs> - ...
  ENDLOOP.
  ...
ENDMETHOD.
```

Listing 6.77 Direct Use of a Field Symbol

6.6.7 Generic Programming

Background

The highest level of dynamics is achieved in generic programming, that is, by dynamically generating source code. The following techniques are available here:

▶ **Dynamic token specification**
For the dynamic token specification, individual operands or entire parts of statements (clauses) are specified as character-type data objects, which are usually enclosed in parentheses and must contain source code that is syntactically correct at runtime. Important examples include the following:

  ▶ Dynamic access to attributes of classes.

  ▶ Dynamic invoke of procedures, particularly methods.

  ▶ Dynamic type specification for the generation of anonymous data objects. Here, you can also use types that were constructed via *Runtime Type Services (RTTS)* at runtime.

  ▶ Dynamic specifications of clauses when accessing internal tables or in Open SQL.[42]

The dynamic token specifications are often used in the context of dynamic accesses to data objects (see Section 6.6.6, Accessing Data Objects Dynamically).

---

42 The dynamic WHERE clause for internal tables is provided as of Releases 7.0 EhP2 and 7.2.

▶ **Program generation**

In the program generation, complete programs are prepared as the content of internal tables and then generated. You distinguish between the following types:

▸ Transient program generation using GENERATE SUBROUTINE POOL where the generated programs are only available in the internal session of the current program

▸ Persistent program generation using INSERT REPORT where the generated programs are stored as repository objects

Rule

Rule 6.52: Avoid Program Generation
Consider program generation the last resort for generic programming. Especially in application programs, you should first fully utilize other dynamic techniques, such as the dynamic token specification, Runtime Type Services (RTTS), and dynamic access to data objects.

Details

The program generation provides many conceptual problems, for example, the checking, testing, and maintenance of the generated programs. Moreover, transiently generated programs can be security risks because you cannot statically check them. The generation of programs is usually very runtime intensive and resource consuming. Therefore, you should avoid program generation wherever possible and implement other dynamic techniques instead:

▶ The dynamic token specification provides the advantage that only parts of the statements are dynamic and that the remaining parts can be statically checked.

▶ Runtime Type Services (RTTS)[43] can be deployed as follows:

▸ At runtime, they determine the type properties of data objects (*Runtime Type Information, RTTI*). The RTTI capabilities exceed those of the DESCRIBE FIELD statement significantly.

---

43 Runtime Type Services are implemented through a hierarchy of type classes whose root is CL_ABAP_TYPEDESCR. For more information, refer to the corresponding class documentations and to the ABAP Keyword Documentation.

▶ They define types at runtime (*Runtime Type Creation, RTTC*). You should use RTTC if the other options of the CREATE DATA statement are not sufficient for the intended use, for example, for designing new structures.

Today, these techniques combined with field symbols and data references (see Section 6.6.6, Accessing Data Objects Dynamically) are sufficient for most of the tasks that could only be solved with program generation in older releases.

Exception

Only if the other means for the desired dynamic control of a program are actually not sufficient, can you use program generation as a makeshift device. Another reason can be the processing speed. For program generation, you can possibly ensure that checks and the generation incur costs less frequently than for other dynamic techniques for which costs may be generated in regular intervals.[44] The previously mentioned conceptual problems, however, remain so that you should carefully consider all aspects.

Unlike application programs, system programs do normally more frequently depend on program generation and its language elements. Examples include the generation of proxy classes for Web Dynpro or Web services. Also the ABAP Editor itself uses nothing else than statements such as READ REPORT and INSERT REPORT.

Tip

Generated programs should also always correspond to the guidelines introduced here. For example, in a generated subroutine pool, the program logic should be implemented/generated as a local class (see Rule 3.1, Use ABAP Objects). This generated function is then called according to Rule 6.37, that is, via a single subroutine that serves as an entry point to the generated local classes (see Listing 6.78).

To avoid as many risks as possible, it may make sense to store templates with a correct syntax, which also adheres to other aspects of the guidelines, in the repository, and use READ REPORT to load them as a template for dynamically generated programs in which only small parts are modified or supplemented at runtime.

---

44 But usually, a full program generation has less performance than a dynamic token specification. Therefore, you gain only if you can restrict the number of generations.

Subroutines in generated subroutine pools are an exception to Rule 3.1, which states that subroutines should no longer be created, and to Rule 6.42, which defines that subroutines shouldn't be called externally.[45]

Bad Example

Listing 6.78 shows an unnecessary program generation. The only reason for the generation of the program is the dynamic read access to a database table. For this purpose, the name of the database table and the line type of the internal table to which data is imported is replaced by the value of a parameter in the source code of the program that is supposed to be generated. To create the internal table, an actually proscribed macro (see Rule 6.45) is used for the sake of simplicity. The subroutine of the generated subroutine pool solely contains, as recommended, the call of a method of a local class, which contains the actual implementation. Instead of populating the program table line by line, you could have created a corresponding program in the repository here and loaded it using READ REPORT.

```
PARAMETERS dbtab TYPE c LENGTH 16.

DATA table TYPE REF TO data.
FIELD-SYMBOLS <table> TYPE STANDARD TABLE.

DATA: source   TYPE TABLE OF string,
      program  TYPE string,
      mess     TYPE string.

DEFINE app.
  APPEND &1 TO source.
END-OF-DEFINITION.

app `program.`.
app `class main definition.`.
app `  public section.`.
app `    class-data`
app `      dyn_table type standard table of dyn_name.`.
app `    class-methods meth`.
app `      exporting table type ref to data.`.
app `endclass.`.
app `class main implementation.`.
app `  method meth.`.
```

---

45 You can directly access local classes of a generated subroutine pool via absolute type names. This, however, contradicts Rule 6.42, Call Only Suitable Procedures Externally.

```
app `    select *`.
app `           from dyn_name`.
app `           into table dyn_table.`.
app `    get reference of dyn_table into table.`.
app `  endmethod.`.
app `endclass.`.
app `form subr changing table type ref to data.`.
app `  main=>meth(`.
app `     importing table = table )`.`.
app `endform.`.

REPLACE ALL OCCURRENCES OF 'dyn_name'
       IN TABLE source WITH dbtab.
GENERATE SUBROUTINE POOL source NAME program MESSAGE mess.
IF sy-subrc = 0.
  PERFORM subr IN PROGRAM (program) CHANGING table.
  IF table IS BOUND.
    ASSIGN table->* TO <table>.
  ENDIF.
ELSE.
  ...
ENDIF.
```

Listing 6.78 Unnecessary Program Generation

Good Example

Listing 6.79 has the same result as Listing 6.78; that is, after a successful execution, the <table> field symbol refers to an internal table that is populated with the data of the dynamically specified database table. But in Listing 6.79, the specification is implemented much more efficiently through a generation of an anonymous data object and a dynamic token specification. If the target table cannot have the same structure as the database table, you must additionally use the Runtime Type Creation (RTTC). *ABAP Objects* (SAP PRESS, 2007) provides further examples of this.

```
PARAMETERS dbtab TYPE c LENGTH 20.

DATA table TYPE REF TO data.
FIELD-SYMBOLS <table> TYPE STANDARD TABLE.

TRY.
    CREATE DATA table TYPE TABLE OF (dbtab).
    ASSIGN table->* TO <table>.
    SELECT *
```

```
        FROM (dbtab)
        INTO TABLE <table>.
  CATCH cx_sy_create_data_error cx_sy_dynamic_osql_error.
    ...
ENDTRY.
```

Listing 6.79 Dynamic Token Specification

6.7 Internationalization

Business software that will be deployed by globally active enterprises must meet specific requirements regarding adaptability (localizability), for example, considering different logon languages or deviating legal stipulations. The language aspect is referred to as *internationalization* in the SAP world and is a part of the *globalization* product standard (in Chapter 2, see Section 2.3, Correctness and Quality). When developing in ABAP, you must select translatable text sources but also consider the technical requirements for handling different character sets.

6.7.1 Storing System Texts

Background

In ABAP programs, texts are used as parts of processed data but also as a means to communicate with the user. The latter are called *system texts*, which are delivered with an ABAP application. The ABAP Workbench manages system texts in such a way that they can be translated from the original language into other languages independently of the actual development object (in Chapter 3, see Section 3.2.3, Original Language). The following are examples of translatable system texts:

- Texts and documentations of data elements in the ABAP Dictionary
- Short texts and documentations of the components of local classes
- UI texts of dynpros, in Web Dynpro applications and in menu entries
- Message texts
- Text pools of ABAP programs that include the text elements of the program, for example, text symbols
- Texts of the Online Text Repository (OTR)

In addition to translatable system texts, an ABAP program can also contain untranslatable texts. These are usually the character literals (see Section 6.1.8, Literals) and the comments that are stored as a part of the source code. Comments were already discussed in Chapter 4, Section 4.3, Comments.

Rule

[⚙] **Rule 6.53: Send Only Translatable System Texts to the User**

Specify all texts that a program uses to communicate with the user as translatable system texts. When you create translatable system texts, ensure that the length is sufficient for translations.

Details

This rule is not only critical for the use of programs in an international environment; it already plays a role when multilingual development groups collaborate (see Rule 3.4, Determine Original Language at Project Level). The prohibition of the use of character literals in the ABAP source code for all texts that are relevant for user dialogs is derived from this rule. You cannot translate character literals. Their content is independent of the respective logon language. Instead of character literals, you use text symbols or link character literals with text symbols. This is also checked in the extended program check (in Chapter 3, see Section 3.4.2, Extended Program Check).

When you create system texts, ensure that the length is sufficient. Usually, you cannot change the text length during the translation, and the translator relies on you providing sufficient space for a reasonable translation already during development. This aspect is very important for longer texts, particularly if the original language is English, because facts can normally be expressed in fewer words in English than in other languages. It can be the contrary for short texts, for example, "Feld" (German) and "field" (English), or for compounds that are written in two or more words in English.

Exception

For merely technical texts (such as HTML tags or regular expressions) that are not supposed to be translated, you can use character literals or literal content of character string templates (as of Releases 7.0 EhP2 and 7.2). These are to be marked as not relevant for translation for the extended program check using pseudo comments or pragmas (as of Releases 7.0 EhP2 and 7.2).

Bad Example

Figure 6.4 shows a typical error — which has been eliminated in the meantime, of course — where the developer for the UI texts ("Indexsuche," "Volltextsuche") in the original language (German) didn't provide enough space for the translation so that it had to be abbreviated.

Figure 6.4 System Texts with a Length That Has Been Defined Too Short

Good Example

Listing 6.80 shows how text parts that are relevant for the translation and text parts that are not relevant for the translation are supposed to be handled in the source code:[46] Technical texts that are not relevant for the translation are specified as character literals. Other texts are bound to a text symbol.

```
html_line = '<title>' && 'Some Title'(ttl) && '</title>'.
APPEND html_line TO html_body.
...
```

Listing 6.80 Texts in the Source Code

6.7.2   Translation-Friendly Message Texts

Background

Message texts as such are translatable system texts (see Section 6.7.1, Storing System Texts). You can use placeholders in the short and long texts of messages. The placeholder of a short text can either be defined uniquely with &i or anonymously with &. Here, i is a digit between 1 and 4.

---

46 The concatenation operator shown here (&&) is available as of Releases 7.0 EhP2 and 7.2. It has the same effect as the CONCATENATE statement. If the additions of the CONCATENATE statement are not important (e.g., SEPARATED BY), you should use the concatenation operator because this increases the legibility of the source code.

When the message is output with the `MESSAGE` statement, you can use the `WITH` `dobj1 ... dobj4` addition, which replaces the placeholders `&1` to `&4` and `&` of the short text with the content of the `dobj1, ..., dobj4` data objects. In this case, the content of the first data object replaces placeholder `&1` and the first `&`, that of the second `&2` and the second `&`, and so on. In addition, the content of the `dobj1, ..., dobj4` data objects is assigned to the `sy-msgv1` to `sy-msgv4` system fields respectively.

Rule

[⚙] **Rule 6.54: Do Not Use Anonymous Placeholders (&) in Message Texts**

Create placeholders in message texts with the unique names, &1, &2, &3, and &4 only.

Details

Because the syntax is different in the various languages, a translator may need to change the sequence of the replacement texts when translating message texts. However, she can only adapt the sequence of replacement texts if the different placeholders in the message texts have unique names. Instead of using the anonymous placeholder (&), you should work with the numbered placeholders, &1, &2, &3, and &4, in messages with multiple placeholders.

Tip

The same applies to all other constructs in which such placeholders are possible, for example, GUI titles of classical dynpros. In cases where text in text symbols is explicitly replaced by self-defined placeholders, the placeholders in the text symbol must have unique names and must be clearly identifiable for translators as placeholders that are not supposed to be translated.

Bad Example

A bad example of a message text would be as follows:

In Tabelle & wurde der Eintrag & nicht gefunden

If this message text was translated with

In table & the entry & was not found

everything would work fine. If it was translated with

The entry & was not found in table &

a `MESSAGE` statement would output the wrong text with English as the logon language.

Good Example

The following message texts corrects the bad example:

In Tabelle &1 wurde der Eintrag &2 nicht gefunden

A translation with

In table &1 the entry &2 was not found

as well as a translation with

The entry &2 was not found in table &1

outputs a reasonable text via the `MESSAGE` statement if English is used as the logon language.

6.7.3 Text Environment

Background

The text environment is a part of the runtime environment of an ABAP program and consists of a *language*, a *locale*, and a *system codepage*. All programs of an internal session have the same text environment.

By default, the text environment of an internal session is defined by the logon language and can be set programmatically by means of the `SET LOCALE` statement. The `sy-langu` system field contains the language of the current text environment.

Rule

> **Rule 6.55: If Possible, Do Not Modify the Text Environment Programmatically**   [⚙]
>
> Use the `SET LOCALE` statement in exceptional cases only, and undo a modification of the text environment in time.

Details

Services programmed in ABAP usually assume that the text environment is determined by the logon language of the current user and not by programmatic modifications of the text environment of an internal session.

333

If the text environment needs to be changed for a specific service due to the exceptions mentioned next, you must only implement this temporarily. That means that a modified text environment needs to be reset within the same program context to avoid unexpected behavior in other programs in the same internal session.

Exception

It can be necessary to programmatically change the text environment in the following cases:

▶ If texts are processed that have not been written in the logon language, such as when SORT ... AS TEXT is used for sorting or when TRANSLATE or a respective built-in function (as of 7.0 EhP2 and 7.2) is used to manipulate characters.

▶ If external files are accessed.

Bad Example

Listing 6.81 shows a modification of the text environment in a method without resetting the text environment before leaving the method. You now run the risk that you work with the wrong text environment after having left the method.

```
METHOD ...
  SET LOCALE LANGUAGE ...
  ...
ENDMETHOD.
```

Listing 6.81 Changing the Text Environment Without Resetting

Good Example

Listing 6.82 shows a modification of the text environment in a method, which is reset to its original state before the method is left.

```
METHOD ...
  DATA: env_lang    TYPE tcp0c-langu,
        env_country TYPE tcp0c-country.
  GET LOCALE LANGUAGE env_lang COUNTRY env_country.
  SET LOCALE LANGUAGE ...
  ...
  SET LOCALE LANGUAGE env_lang COUNTRY env_country.
ENDMETHOD.
```

Listing 6.82 Changing the Text Environment with Resetting

6.7.4 Character Set of Source Code

Background

ABAP source code is processed in the ABAP Workbench's ABAP Editor, which is an ABAP program itself. The ABAP Editor internally stores and processes the ABAP source code in a data object (internal table).

The processing of the source code therefore takes place in the current text environment of the developer, for which the corresponding codepage is used.

Rule

Rule 6.56: Use 7-Bit ASCII Characters in the Source Code Only [⚙]

Only use characters from the 7-bit ASCII character set in ABAP source code to avoid problems in systems with different codepages.

Details

The 7-bit ASCII character set only comprises characters that are also available in all other codepages. A restriction to this character set for characters that are used in source code ensures that the code can be processed and executed, irrespective of the logon language. In the worst case, source code that contains characters from other character sets is syntactically no longer correct in a system with a different codepage.

Because the ABAP words in ABAP statements consist solely of 7-bit ASCII characters anyway, this rule applies to names, literals, and comments.

Tip

Because you're only allowed to deploy Unicode programs according to Rule 3.3, Accept the Standard Settings for Program Attributes, Rule 6.56 is automatically adhered to for names. In non-Unicode programs, no syntax check is carried out with this regard. For comments, Rule 4.9, Comment Programs in English, applies. Consequently, there's no need to use country-specific special characters.

If it's obvious that a program is exclusively written for Unicode systems, Rule 5.56 is unnecessary at least for literals and comments. However, because you cannot ensure that a program may not be used in a non-Unicode system, you should always adhere to this rule for general robustness reasons.

6.7.5 Splitting Texts

Background

The characters of a character set are normally mapped in a codepage by a fixed number of bytes so that the memory always knows where a character begins and ends. However, there are codepages in which a character is combined of multiple separately stored characters.

- On the one hand, this is implemented via so-called *combining characters* of some non-Unicode codepages in non-Unicode systems where a sequence of characters results in a grapheme (the smallest unit of a writing system of a specific language).

- On the other hand, this also applies to the characters of the so-called *surrogate area* of the Unicode character set. These characters are represented by two consecutive 16-bit surrogates in the UTF-16 Unicode codepage. The surrogate area comprises, for example, some Chinese characters that are mainly used in Hong Kong.

Rule

[⚙]
> **Rule 6.57: Split Texts at Character Boundaries Only**
>
> If you use statements that split character strings, ensure that you don't split the strings in positions where compound characters or surrogates are located.

Details

The following operations are operations that split character strings:

- Subfield accesses via offset/length specifications or `substring` functions (as of Releases 7.0 EhP2 and 7.2)
- The `SPLIT` statement
- Every assignment to a character-type fields that is too short and where the original value is truncated on one side

If texts are involved that contain combining characters or surrogates, undefined characters that cannot be displayed can occur. If this risk is given, you can define an appropriate split position using the `SPLIT_STRING_AT_POSITION` method of the `CL_SCP_LINEBREAK_UTIL` class, if required.

6.7.6 Codepages for Files

Background

When you open text files on the application server using the OPEN DATASET statement, you can make the following specifications, which are critical for the internationalization:

▶ The ENCODING addition defines the *codepage* in which the contents of the file are to be handled.

▶ The WITH BYTE-ORDER MARK addition, which is only possible for UTF-8 files, defines that a *Byte-Order Mark* (BOM) is inserted at the beginning of the file when a text file is written.

If the codepage is not explicitly specified when a file is written, it is implicitly set (to UTF-8 in a Unicode system). If nothing is specified, no BOM will be set.

Rule

> **Rule 6.58: Write Text Files in UTF-8 and with Byte-Order Mark**   [✿]
>
> Open text files for output explicitly in the UTF-8 codepage. The byte-order mark is supposed to be inserted and considered for reading.

Details

When a file is read, the used codepage can hardly be identified in general. If the byte-order mark is inserted, however, a file is clearly defined as a UTF-8. Therefore, you should always specify the ENCODING UTF-8 WITH BYTE-ORDER MARK additions when opening a text output file with the OPEN DATASET statement. When such a text field is read, it is only supposed to be opened with the SKIPPING BYTE-ORDER MARK addition so that the byte-order mark is automatically skipped and doesn't occur in the read application data.

Exception

Files that are used for data exchange with applications that don't support a UTF-8 format must be output in an appropriate codepage.

Appendices

A   **Obsolete Language Constructs** 341

B   **Automatic Check of Naming Conventions** 365

C   **Table of Rules** 373

D   **Recommended Reading** 377

E   **The Authors** 379

"Nothing is cheap which is superfluous, for what one does need, is dear at a penny."
– Plutarch

A   Obsolete Language Constructs

As already mentioned, ABAP is a living programming language that is continuously further developed. To ensure downward compatibility, you cannot simply ban obsolete language elements because then existing ABAP programs might no longer function properly. For new developments, however, you mustn't use these obsolete language elements (see Rule 3.5, Do Not Use Obsolete Language Elements).

A statement or a statement addition only becomes obsolete if a more modern alternative is available that is faster, less prone to errors, or conceptually superior. It is therefore in the interests of the developer to no longer use obsolete language elements for new developments. The following overview will help the developer identify obsolete language elements as such.

Many of the statements or statement additions listed are already forbidden in ABAP Objects so that they shouldn't play a role in programs that adhere to Rule 3.1, Use ABAP Objects. The language elements that are prohibited in ABAP Objects are indicated by this icon in the overview provided next. **[✗]**

If a language element is prohibited in ABAP Objects, it can still be syntactically used within function modules, subroutines, or other processing blocks. If still required, other processing blocks should consequently contain nothing else than a method call according to Rules 6.37, No Implementations in Function Modules and Subroutines, and 6.44, No Implementations in Dialog Modules and Event Blocks. For existing programs that perhaps don't adhere to this rule yet, you can activate the Obsolete Statements (OO context) check in the extended program check (in Chapter 3, see Section 3.4.2, Extended Program Check), which carries out the same more stringent syntax check as within classes in other contexts.

Furthermore, there are some risky statements or execution variants of statements that can be used outside of Unicode programs only. In this book, however, selecting the Unicode Checks Active program attribute according to Rule 3.3, Accept the Standard Settings for Program Attributes, is absolutely mandatory. These constructs are consequently usually not further discussed here.

A.1   Procedures

A.1.1   Subroutines

[✗]
Obsolete Construct

Subroutines that are declared with FORM-ENDFORM are obsolete.

Reason

▶ Parameter interface weaknesses (position-related parameters, no write protection for input parameters passed by references, no need for explicit typing, no optional parameters).

▶ Subroutines cannot be protected from external calls and thus implicitly belong to the public interface of their program although they are provided for internal modularization only (see Rule 6.42, Call Only Appropriate Procedures Externally).[1]

Alternative

Methods of local and global classes.

Exception

Usage of subroutines in the context of PERFORM ON COMMIT, PERFORM ON ROLLBACK, and GENERATE SUBROUTINE POOL.

A.1.2   Table Parameters

[✗]
Obsolete Construct

Table parameters of function modules (and subroutines) that are declared with TABLES are obsolete.

Reason

The formal parameter is an internal table with an obsolete header line.

Alternative

CHANGING parameters that are typed as an internal table.

---

1 The introduction of the operational package concept for Release 7.2 enables you to protect subroutines at least from calls from outside of the package.

Formal parameters of Remote Function Modules (RFM) as long as basXML is not set as the RFC protocol. Because the classical binary RFC protocol is implicitly used for TABLES parameters instead of the xRFC protocol, which is usually deployed for deep types, the transfer of internal tables via TABLES parameters can be significantly faster than the transfer via CHANGING parameters.

A.1.3   Typing of Formal Parameters

Obsolete Construct   **[×]**

The typing of formal parameters of function modules (and subroutines) with the STRUCTURE addition is obsolete.

Reason

The STRUCTURE addition is used for both typing and casting.

Alternative

The TYPE addition for typing and the CASTING addition for ASSIGN for casting.

A.2   Declarations

A.2.1   Declaring Type Groups

Obsolete Construct

As of Releases 7.0 EhP2 and 7.2, the TYPE-POOLS statement is obsolete.

Reason

With this release, the ABAP Compiler supports demand-driven loading (load on demand) so that a type group is loaded automatically when one of its elements is addressed for the first time.

A.2.2   Interface Work Areas

Obsolete Construct   **[×]**

Shared data areas of programs that are declared using the BEGIN OF COMMON PART and END OF COMMON PART additions are obsolete.

Reason

Shared data areas are very prone to errors regarding both their maintainability and their function.

Alternative

Anonymous data objects or instances of classes that are shared by different programs.

A.2.3 Table Work Areas

[×] **Obsolete Construct**

In addition to the prohibition of TABLES and NODES according to Rule 6.7, No Table Work Areas Except for Classical Dynpros, table work areas that are declared with TABLES *... are completely obsolete.

Reason

The implicit use of table work areas for database accesses is prohibited (see Section A.12, Data Storage).

Alternative

Using implicit work areas.

A.2.4 Referring to Data Types

[×] **Obsolete Construct**

Referring to flat structures and database tables of the ABAP Dictionary using the LIKE addition is obsolete.

Reason

The LIKE addition can only be used to refer to data objects.

Alternative

Using the TYPE addition to refer to data types.

A.2.5 Declaring Field Symbols

[×] **Obsolete Construct**

Omitting explicit typing in the FIELD-SYMBOLS statement is obsolete.

Reason

Same handling as for formal parameters of methods.

Alternative

Explicit typing with TYPE or LIKE.

A.2.6 Typing Field Symbols

Obsolete Construct

The typing of field symbols using the STRUCTURE addition is obsolete.

Reason

The STRUCTURE addition is used for both typing and casting.

Alternative

The TYPE addition for typing and the CASTING addition for ASSIGN for casting.

A.2.7 Header Lines of Internal Tables

Obsolete Construct

The HEADER LINE addition for the declaration of header lines of internal tables is obsolete.

Reason

An internal table with a header line leads to two data objects with the same name within a context.

Alternative

Explicitly declared work areas with different names.

A.2.8 Declaring Internal Tables

Obsolete Construct [×]

Declaring internal tables with the OCCURS addition for TYPES, DATA, and so on is obsolete.

Reason

Standard tables with header lines are declared; their initial memory requirement (in Chapter 6, see Section 6.4.3, Initial Memory Requirement) is defined.

A.3 Object Generation

A.3.1 Anonymous Data Objects

[×]

Obsolete Construct
The ASSIGN LOCAL COPY OF statement, which generates an anonymous data object, is obsolete.
Reason
Replaced by a more general concept.
Alternative
Generating anonymous data objects using CREATE DATA.

A.4 Calls and Exits

A.4.1 Dialog Modules

Obsolete Construct
The CALL DIALOG statement for calling a dialog module is obsolete.
Reason
Dialog modules are obsolete.
Alternative
Calling methods of global class or of function modules (for classical dynpros, see Rule 5.19, Encapsulate Classical Dynpros and Selection Screens).
Note
Calling a dialog module opens a new internal session without changing the SAP LUW, which is not possible but also not necessary for other calls.

A.4.2 Function Module Exit

Obsolete Construct
The CALL CUSTOMER-FUNCTION statement for connecting a customer exit is obsolete.
Reason
Replaced by a more general concept.

Alternative

Calling a BAdI of the enhancement concept using `CALL BADI`.

A.4.3 External Subroutine Call

[✗] **Obsolete Construct**

The `PERFORM subr(prog)` variant for static external subroutine calls is obsolete.

Reason

Parenthesis syntax is reserved for a dynamic token specification.

Alternative

In exceptional cases where external subroutine calls are still accepted (see Rule 6.42, Call Only Appropriate Procedures Externally), you must use the `PERFORM form IN PROGRAM prog` variant.

A.4.4 Exiting Programs

Obsolete Construct

The `LEAVE` statement without additions is obsolete.

Reason

The `LEAVE` statement without addition leaves a program depending from how the program was called.

Alternative

Using additions that clearly control the behavior:
```
LEAVE PROGRAM
LEAVE TO TRANSACTION
LEAVE [TO] SCREEN
LEAVE LIST-PROCESSING
```

A.4.5 Exception Handling

Obsolete Construct

The `CATCH SYSTEM-EXCEPTIONS` statement for handling catchable runtime errors is obsolete (see Rule 5.15, Do Not Handle Catchable Runtime Errors).

Reason

Replaced by a more general concept.

Alternative

Catching the associated class-based exceptions in a TRY control structure.

A.5   Program Flow Control

A.5.1   Relational Operators

Obsolete Construct

The relational operators >< for not equal to, =< for less than or equal to, and => for greater than or equal to are obsolete.

Reason

Uncommon notations, risk of confusion.

Alternative

The relational operators <>, NE for not equal to, <=, LE for less than or equal to, and >=, GE for greater than or equal to (for more information on the selection of variants, see Rule 4.16, Use a Clear Notation).

A.5.2   Case Distinction

Obsolete Construct   [×]

Listing operational statements between CASE and WHEN is obsolete.

Reason

The semantics is unclear for the reader of the program.

Alternative

Placing the statements before CASE.

A.5.3   Checking the Binding to Actual Parameters

Obsolete Construct

The IS REQUESTED predicate for checking whether an actual parameter is bound to an output parameter of a procedure is obsolete.

Reason

Replaced by a more general concept.

Alternative

The IS SUPPLIED predicate.

A.5.4   Checking Changes of Data Objects

[✗]   **Obsolete Construct**

The ON CHANGE OF – ENDON control structure is obsolete.

Reason

Behavior that is prone to errors and based on an implicit global helper variable.

Alternative

Allowed control structures (IF, CASE) with explicit helper variables of the same context.

A.5.5   Loops for Memory Content

Obsolete Construct

The DO ... VARYING and WHILE ... VARY statements are obsolete.

Reason

Unwanted memory accesses.

Alternative

The ASSIGN statement with the INCREMENT addition (see also Rule 6.19, Avoid Implicit Casting).

A.6   Assignments

A.6.1   Subfield Access

[✗]   **Obsolete Construct**

The MOVE ... PERCENTAGE statement is obsolete.

Reason

Antiquated subfield access with questionable semantics.

Alternative

Subfield access with offset/length specifications or substring functions (as of Releases 7.0 EhP2 and 7.2).

A.6.2 Converting Packed Numbers

Obsolete Construct   **[✗]**

The PACK statement for the conversion of character-type fields to a packed number is obsolete.

Reason

The statement doesn't have its own conversion rule and is therefore superfluous.

Alternative

Assignment with MOVE or equals sign (=).

Note

The UNPACK statement supports a different conversion rule from a packed number to a character-type field than MOVE or the equals sign (=) and is consequently — compared to PACK — not obsolete.

A.6.3 Initialization

Obsolete Construct   **[✗]**

The WITH NULL addition of the CLEAR statement for filling with hexadecimal zeros is obsolete.

Reason

Byte-type operation on any data objects.

Alternative

Using CLEAR WITH val.

A.6.4 Temporary Storage of Data Objects

Obsolete Construct   **[✗]**

The LOCAL statement for the temporary storage of global variables is obsolete.

Reason

Using global variables is obsolete (see Rule 6.3, Do Not Declare Global Variables).

Alternative

Global variables are replaced by attributes of classes.

A.6.5 Casting

[×] **Obsolete Construct**

The TYPE and DECIMALS additions for the ASSIGN statement for explicit casting are obsolete.

Reason

Replaced by a more powerful concept.

Alternative

Using the CASTING TYPE addition.

A.6.6 Dynamic Assignment to a Field Symbol

[×] **Obsolete Construct**

The TABLE FIELD addition for the ASSIGN statement for restricting the assignable data objects to table work areas is obsolete.

Reason

Table work areas that are declared with TABLES are obsolete (see Rule 6.7, No Table Work Areas Except for Classical Dynpros).

Alternative

Not restricting the assignable data objects.

A.7 Calculation Statements

A.7.1 Component-Based Calculations

[×] **Obsolete Construct**

The ADD-CORRESPONDING, SUBTRACT-CORRESPONDING, MULTIPLY-CORRESPONDING, and DIVIDE-CORRESPONDING statements for calculations with structure components with an identical name are obsolete.

Reason

Prone to errors because the convertibility in a numeric type cannot be ensured for all components with an identical name.

Alternative

Explicit programming of the calculations.

A.7.2 Calculations with Memory Content

Obsolete Construct   **[×]**

The ADD THEN ... UNTIL ... and ADD FROM ... TO ... statements for adding memory sections are obsolete.

Reason

Dependent on the structure of the memory, prone to errors.

Alternative

The ASSIGN statement with the INCREMENT addition (see also Rule 6.19, Avoid Implicit Casting).

A.8   Processing Character and Byte Strings

A.8.1   Searching in Character and Byte Strings

Obsolete Construct

The SEARCH ... FOR ... statement for searching for substrings and patterns in character and byte strings is obsolete.

Reason

Replaced by a more powerful concept.

Alternative

Using the FIND SUBSTRING and FIND REGEX statements or search functions (as of Releases 7.0 EhP2 and 7.2).

A.8.2   Replacements in Character and Byte Strings

Obsolete Construct

The REPLACE ... WITH ... INTO ... statement for replacing substrings in character and byte strings is obsolete.

Replaced by a more powerful concept.

Using the REPLACE SUBSTRING and REPLACE REGEX statements or replacement functions (as of Releases 7.0 EhP2 and 7.2).

A.8.3 Creating the Nine's Complement

[×]

Obsolete Construct

The CONVERT DATE and CONVERT INVERTED DATE statements for the conversion of the digits of a character-type field to their nine's complement for sorting in descending order are obsolete.

Reason

Replaced by a more general concept.

Alternative

For sorting in descending order the DESCENDING addition for SORT, for composing the nine's complement the TRANSLATE statement or the predefined function, translate (as of Releases 7.0 EhP2 and 7.2).

A.8.4 Translating Characters and Numbers

Obsolete Construct

The TRANSLATE CODE PAGE and TRANSLATE NUMBER FORMAT statements for translating the internal display of characters (codepage) and numbers are obsolete and also prohibited in Unicode programs.

Reason

Replaced by more general concepts.

Alternative

Methods of the CL_ABAP_CONV_IN_CE and CL_ABAP_CONV_OUT_CE classes.

A.8.5 Text Editor

Obsolete Construct

The EDITOR-CALL statement for calling an editor to edit the character-type content of an internal table is obsolete.

Bad Example

Listing 6.83 shows how a text file is opened for a write process without explicitly specifying the codepage. In Unicode systems, UTF-8 is implicitly selected, but no byte-order mark is inserted.

```
OPEN DATASET dset
  FOR OUTPUT IN TEXT MODE
  ENCODING DEFAULT.
```

Listing 6.83 Opening a Text Output File Without BOM

Good Example

Listing 6.84 shows how a text file is opened for a write process with explicitly specifying the UTF-8 codepage and using the byte-order mark.

```
OPEN DATASET dset
  FOR OUTPUT IN TEXT MODE
  ENCODING UTF-8 WITH BYTE-ORDER MARK.
```

Listing 6.84 Opening a Text Output File in UTF-8 and with BOM

Using the TABLE OF addition. You can specify the initial memory requirement via the INITIAL SIZE addition (adhere to Rule 6.32, Manipulate the Initial Memory Requirement for Nested Tables Only).

A.2.9 Ranges Tables

[×]

Obsolete Construct

The RANGES statement for the declaration of a ranges table is obsolete.

Reason

The table declared has a header line.

Alternative

The RANGE OF addition for TYPES, DATA, and so on.

A.2.10 Addressing Data Objects

[×]

Obsolete Construct

The FIELDS statement for addressing a data object is obsolete.

Reason

Replaced by more general concepts.

Alternative

Pseudo comment "#EC NEEDED or pragma ##NEEDED (as of Releases 7.0 EhP2 and 7.2).

A.2.11 Loading Classes and Interfaces

Obsolete Construct

As of Releases 7.0 EhP2 and 7.2, the LOAD addition for CLASS DEFINITION and INTERFACE is obsolete.

Reason

With this release, the ABAP Compiler supports demand-driven loading (load on demand) so that a class or interface is loaded automatically when one of its elements is loaded for the first time.

Reason

Replaced by a more general concept.

Alternative

Using the `CL_GUI_TEXTEDIT` class.

A.9   Internal Tables

A.9.1   Processing Statements

Obsolete Construct   [×]

All abbreviated forms of statements that implicitly use the header line of an internal table are obsolete.

Reason

Header lines of internal tables are prohibited.

Alternative

Specifying explicit work areas.

A.9.2   Key Specifications

Obsolete Construct   [×]

The following variants of the `READ` statement are obsolete:

`READ TABLE itab.` with reading the key from the header line

`READ TABLE itab WITH KEY key ...` with casting a key

`READ TABLE itab WITH KEY = key ...` to specify the entire line

Reason

The variants use the header line, carry out implicit casting, and have been replaced by a more general concept.

Alternative

Using a table key or an allowed free key. Specifying the entire line using the `table_line` pseudo component.

A.9.3 Deleting a Table

Obsolete Construct

The REFRESH statement for deleting an internal table is obsolete.

Reason

The statement is superfluous because header lines are prohibited.

Alternative

Using the CLEAR or FREE statement.

A.9.4 Formatted Assignment

[×]

Obsolete Construct

The WRITE TO statement is prohibited for assigning content to lines of internal tables.

Reason

Replaced by more general concepts.

Alternative

Field symbols or data references serve to directly access table lines (see Rule 6.35, Select an Appropriate Output Behavior). As of Releases 7.0 EhP2 and 7.2, you can generally replace the WRITE TO statement with character string templates.

A.9.5 HR Infotypes

[×]

Obsolete Construct

The abbreviated form of the PROVIDE statement for simultaneously processing multiple internal tables for HR infotypes[2] is obsolete.

Reason

The statement is based on header lines.

Alternative

Long form of the PROVIDE statement (for experts only).

---

2 Especially set up structures of the ABAP Dictionary.

A.10   Dynpro Flow Logic

According to Rule 5.18, Use Web Dynpro ABAP, classical dynpros are to be used for new developments in exceptional cases only. The following constructs are no longer supposed to be used at all.

A.10.1   Comparing Values

Obsolete Construct
The `FIELD ... VALUES` and `FIELD ... SELECT` dynpro statements for comparing dynpro fields with value lists or with the results of a database access are obsolete.
Reason
No application logic in the presentation layer.
Alternative
Corresponding checks in the ABAP program.

A.10.2   Accessing Databases

Obsolete Construct
The `SELECT` dynpro statement for accessing the database is obsolete.
Reason
No access to persistent data from the presentation layer.
Alternative
Open SQL statement `SELECT` in the persistency layer.

A.10.3   Extending Subscreens

Obsolete Construct
The `CALL CUSTOMER SUBSCREEN` dynpro statement for integrating a subscreen as an extension is obsolete.
Reason
Replaced by a more general concept.

Alternative

Using the switch-controlled enhancement concept.

A.10.4 Step Loops

Obsolete Construct

The LOOP – ENDLOOP dynpro statements for defining step loops without a connection to table controls are obsolete.

Reason

Replaced by a more powerful concept.

Alternative

Usage only with the WITH CONTROL addition for assignments to a table control.

A.11   Classical List Processing

According to Rule 5.20, Use SAP List Viewer, classical lists are no longer to be used in live application programs. The following constructs are no longer supposed to be used at all.

A.11.1   Formatting

[✗]
Obsolete Construct

The DETAIL, SUMMARY, and INPUT list statements for formatting list outputs are obsolete.

Reason

Replaced by a more general concept.

Alternative

The INTENSIFIED OFF, INTENSIFIED ON, and INPUT ON additions of the FORMAT statement.

A.11.2   List Event

Obsolete Construct

The handling of the AT PFnn list event is obsolete.

Reason

Replaced by a more general concept.

Alternative

Handling the AT USER-COMMAND event.

A.11.3 Print Parameters

Obsolete Construct

The specification of individual print and archiving parameters for the NEW-PAGE PRINT ON and SUBMIT TO SAP-SPOOL statements is obsolete.

Reason

Replaced by a more powerful concept.

Alternative

Using the [SPOOL] PARAMETERS and ARCHIVE PARAMETERS additions to pass consistent structures.

A.11.4 Spool Request

Obsolete Construct   [×]

The NEW-SECTION list statement for creating a new spool request is obsolete.

Reason

Replaced by a more general concept.

Alternative

Using the NEW-SECTION addition of the NEW-PAGE PRINT ON statement.

A.11.5 Extreme Values and Calculations

Obsolete Construct   [×]

The MINIMUM, MAXIMUM, and SUMMING list statements, which evaluate values that have been output with WRITE, are obsolete.

Reason

Behavior that is prone to errors and based on implicit global helper variables.

Explicit programming. For minimum and maximum values, the predefined functions, nmin and nmax, are available as of Releases 7.0 EhP2 and 7.2.

A.12 Data Storage

A.12.1 Open SQL

[✗] **Obsolete Construct**

All abbreviated forms of Open SQL statements that implicitly use a table work area that has been declared with TABLES are obsolete.

Reason

The TABLES statement is to be used in the context of classical dynpros only (see Rule 6.7, No Table Work Areas Except for Classical Dynpros).

Alternative

Specifying explicit work areas of the same context.

A.12.2 Native SQL

[✗] **Obsolete Construct**

The PERFORMING addition for EXEC SQL for implicit cursor processing with an evaluation of the imported data per line in a subroutine and the corresponding EXIT FROM SQL statement are obsolete.

Reason

The called subroutine solely uses global data; subroutines are obsolete anyway.

Alternative

Explicit cursor processing with OPEN, FETCH, and CLOSE.

A.12.3 Data Cluster

[✗] **Obsolete Construct**

Using implicit names for the EXPORT TO MEMORY and IMPORT FROM MEMORY statements is obsolete.

Reason

Prone to errors because the specified names literally are used as IDs of the stored data.

Alternative

Explicit name specification, preferred with = (instead of FROM and TO; in Chapter 4, see Section 4.6.1, Alternative Language Constructs in Statements).

A.12.4 Data Clusters in the ABAP Memory

Obsolete Construct   [×]

Omitting the ID addition of the EXPORT TO MEMORY and IMPORT FROM MEMORY statements when writing and reading data clusters in the ABAP Memory is obsolete.

Reason

All programs of a call sequence implicitly use the same memory area.

Alternative

Specifying the ID addition.

A.12.5 Data Clusters in the Database

Obsolete Construct   [×]

The MAJOR-ID and MINOR-ID additions of the IMPORT FROM DATABASE statement when reading data clusters from database tables are obsolete.

Reason

The specified ID is not unique.

Alternative

Programmatically creating the required ID.

A.12.6 Work Area for Data Clusters

Obsolete Construct   [×]

Omitting the FROM wa or INTO wa addition of the EXPORT TO MEMORY and IMPORT FROM MEMORY statements when writing and reading data clusters in database tables or in the shared memory is obsolete.

Reason

Abbreviated forms are implicitly based on table work areas that are declared with TABLES and whose use is obsolete.

Alternative

Specifying an explicit work area.

A.12.7 Obsolete Database Accesses

[×] **Obsolete Construct**

The following ABAP statements for database accesses that do not belong to the scope of Open SQL are obsolete:

```
READ TABLE dbtab
LOOP AT dbtab
REFRESH itab FROM TABLE dbtab
MODIFY dbtab VERSION
DELETE dbtab VERSION
```

Reason

Replaced by a more powerful concept, dependent on the TABLES statement.

Alternative

Open SQL statements.

A.13   Contexts

Obsolete Construct

The context concept where cross-program instances, which represent dependencies between key fields and fields that can be derived from those, are generated on an application server is obsolete, including the corresponding statements, CONTEXTS, SUPPLY, and DEMAND.

Reason

Replaced by a more general concept.

Alternative

Using shared objects.

A.14   External Interfaces

A.14.1   XML Connection

Obsolete Construct

The OBJECTS addition for the CALL TRANSFORMATION statement for passing object references to transformations is obsolete.

Reason

Replaced by a more general concept.

Alternative

Using the PARAMETERS addition.

A.14.2   CPI-C Interface

Obsolete Construct   [×]

The COMMUNICATION statement for cross-system communication is obsolete.

Reason

Replaced by a more powerful concept.

Alternative

Remote Function Calls, which are based on the RFC interface.

A.14.3   JavaScript Connection

Obsolete Construct

The CL_JAVA_SCRIPT class for accessing the JavaScript Engine of the ABAP kernel is obsolete.

Reason

Unnecessary concept.

Alternative

The connection from JavaScript to ABAP will no longer be delivered in a future release without any replacement.

"Sometimes a tree is felled to catch a sparrow."
– Chinese Proverb

B   Automatic Check of Naming Conventions

As discussed in Chapter 4, Section 4.2, Naming, we consider the naming conventions that give priority to the technical properties of the named objects as an attempt to cure the symptoms and not the cause of a poor programming style. To a certain extent, they may help to facilitate the maintenance of poorly structured monolithic programs. In such cases, however, the maintenance problem to be solved is usually not due to the naming but due to the high complexity and missing separation of tasks. If you strictly adhere to the other guidelines presented in this book within the scope of development, such excessive naming conventions are therefore not required and don't contribute to the legibility of the programs.

Nevertheless, there is a consistent demand for such naming conventions. Obviously, the ability to automatically check them also plays a major role here. But the orientation of naming toward this criterion stands in contrast to the top priority of source codes that are oriented toward the human reader. Easy and unambiguously traceable program code is necessary if development and maintenance costs are to be kept within a reasonable limit. Naming conventions that can be tested automatically don't add to this goal necessarily.

Nonetheless — and for all those who want this — as of Release 7.0 SP13, the Code Inspector supports the implementation of naming conventions that are based on technical properties and predefines such a naming convention as a default setting.

B.1   Naming Conventions in the Code Inspector

You can find a check of naming conventions in the Code Inspector as an ENHANCED NAMING CONVENTIONS FOR PROGRAMS check in the PROGRAMMING CONVENTIONS branch.[1] Using this check, you can examine the naming of programs and the declarations contained therein. The default setting checks the adherence of a suggestion for a naming convention, which SAP created in response to the request of maintenance organizations in order to become familiar with the programs to be maintained more quickly.

The check of the naming convention is subdivided by tabs into the following areas:

▶ **Prefixes**
For type-specific prefix components.

▶ **General/Procedure Local**
For local declarations in procedures.

▶ **Only Functional Programming**
For entities of structured programming.

▶ **Only Object Oriented Programming**
For entities of object-oriented programming.

The following sections present the default setting of the subareas and thus the suggested naming convention. In the Code Inspector, the possible name components, for which a check is carried out, are specified with regular expressions that are not quoted literally here.

B.2 Type-Specific Prefix Components

Table B.1 lists the suggested naming convention and consequently the default settings for the type-specific prefix components.

Data Type	Prefix Component
Elementary types	e or v
Structures	s
Standard tables or tables that are generic with regard to the table category (INDEX or ANY TABLE)	t
Sorted tables	ts or t

Table B.1 Type-Specific Prefix Components

---

1 This check is next to an older, simpler check, Naming Conventions, which is less extensive.

B.4 Structured Programming

Table B.3 lists the prefixes for entities of the structured programming that are pre-defined by the suggested naming convention and thus the default setting. Again, the *[t]* specification must be replaced with the suitable type-specific prefix component from Table B.1.

Entity	Naming Convention
Function module parameter	i*[t]*_* for IMPORTING parameter
	e*[t]*_* for EXPORTING parameter
	c*[t]*_* for CHANGING parameter
	t*[t]*_* for TABLES parameter
Subroutine parameter	p*[t]*_* for USING parameter
	c*[t]*_* for CHANGING parameter
	t*[t]*_* for TABLES parameter
Program-global variables (DATA)	g*[t]*_*
Program-global field symbols (FIELD-SYMBOLS)	<g*[t]*_*>
Program-global constants (CONSTANTS)	gc*[t]*_*
Program-global selection criteria (SELECT-OPTIONS)	s_*
Program-global parameters (PARAMETERS)	p_*

Table B.3 Naming Conventions for Structured Programming

For program-global variables and constants, one prefixed namespace name (*prefix namespace*) is permitted, respectively.

In the tab for checking naming conventions for entities of structured programming, you can also enter specifications for the names of function groups and function modules, for executable programs and subroutines, as well as for program-global type declarations. The naming convention doesn't make any statement about these, and the Code Inspector doesn't implement any check in the default setting. Here again, you can enter your own convention if required.

▶ In this naming convention, the prefix p for USING parameters instead of the more general i (in Chapter 4, see Section 4.2.4, Program-Internal Names), which is actually intended for input parameters is somewhat surprising because it may be confused with program-global parameters. One suggestion here would be the convention mentioned in Section 4.2.4 for procedure parameters without separation by the types of procedure.

▶ Because in the programming guidelines the use of global data objects is only provided for the interfaces to classical dynpros and selection screens (see Rule 6.3, Do Not Declare Global Variables) anyway, a special convention s_ and p_ for selection criteria and parameters becomes unnecessary. Here, the use of g_, which is suggested in Section 4.2.4 for all program-global data seems to make more sense.

▶ If — as provided for in this naming convention — you must specify the data type in the interface parameters, this results in the redundant prefix, tt_, for TABLES parameters because these are always standard tables.

▶ For program-global field symbols, the same applies as for procedure-local field symbols: You usually don't need to know the context of the declaration of the field symbol.

B.5   Object-Oriented Programming

Table B.4 lists the prefixes for entities of the object-oriented programming that are predefined by the suggested naming convention and thus the default setting. Again, the *[t]* specification must be replaced with the suitable type-specific prefix component from Table B.1.

Entity	Naming Convention
Global class	cl_*
Local class	lcl_*
Global interface	if_*
Local interface	lif_*
Instance attribute (DATA)	m*[t]*_*
Static attribute (CLASS-DATA)	g*[t]*_*
Constants in classes and interfaces (CONSTANTS)	c*[t]*_*

Table B.4 Naming Conventions for Object-Oriented Programming

Entity	Naming Convention
Method parameters	i[t]_* for IMPORTING
	e[t]_* for EXPORTING
	c[t]_* for CHANGING
	r[t]_* for RETURNING
Event parameters	i[t]_*

Table B.4 Naming Conventions for Object-Oriented Programming (Cont.)

For global classes and interfaces, one prefixed namespace name (*prefix namespace*) is permitted, respectively.

In the tab for checking naming conventions for entities of object-oriented programming, you can also enter specifications for the names of types, methods, and events. The naming convention doesn't make any statement about these, and the Code Inspector doesn't implement any check in the default setting. Here again, you can enter your own convention if required. Furthermore, the check also allows for different conventions for the components of classes and interfaces, which is not used in the suggested convention or the default setting.

> **Notes**
>
> ▶ The specification of a g_ prefix for static attributes is problematic because it is actually reserved for program-global data objects (which are undesirable according to Rule 6.3, Do Not Declare Global Variables; in Chapter 4, see the example for Section 4.2.4, Program-Internal Names).
>
> ▶ The m_ prefix for instance attributes is unnecessary because you can always prevent confusions and hidings using the me-> self-reference.
>
> ▶ As discussed in Section 4.2.4, the lcl_ and lif_ prefixes are also not required unless a differentiation between local classes and interfaces is to be made from the user's point of view. Such a differentiation, however, is usually not required.

B.6   Assessment of the Naming Conventions

The naming convention checked here clearly shows the difficulties that arise if you try to express complex technical information in prefixes. To accommodate all technical information used here (data type, context, changeability, visibility, parameter type, transfer type, etc.) uniquely in a prefix, you require a notation with at least three digits for a meaningful combination of the individual dimensions. In this notation, each desired aspect must be assigned to a fixed position and be specified in full. For example, you could express a local elementary variable as `lev_`, a global constant structure as `gsc_`, and a tabular return value as `rtv_` (or `ltr_` or similar), whereas `l` really means local and `v` really means variable. However, it is questionable whether such extensive notations subserve the legibility of a program.

If — as has happened here — you try to express as much information as possible in prefixes with only one or two digits, the same position is simultaneously assigned with multiple technical aspects, and you quickly fall into a trap so that the naming conventions become incomprehensible (see `lv_` previously, which only seems to be easy to understand and `lcv_` previously, which is incomprehensible) or even nonunique (see `g_` for static attributes and global variables). The latter undermines the purpose of naming conventions to avoid confusions and hidings.

In Chapter 4, Section 4.2.4, Program-Internal Names, described that such naming conventions based on technical attributes are not required. Therefore, for program-internal entities, we recommend using only the minimal convention specified there with maximum one-digit prefixes, which is necessary to avoid confusion or hidings. If desired, the check of this convention can simply be defined in the Code Inspector in one of the two tests provided by overwriting the default setting.[4] However, you must always consider that the top goal in naming, that is, descriptive and meaningful names, cannot be checked automatically. We therefore question the informative value of such a check of a program with regard to the program quality, particularly if — as is often the case unfortunately — this is the only check relating to this matter.

---

4 Here, you must consider that no regular expression is permitted in the Naming Conventions check. But they are not required for the conventions suggested in Chapter 4, Section 4.2.4, Program-Internal Names.

C   Table of Rules

Rule 2.1:   Adhere to the SoC Principle 24
Rule 2.2:   Adhere to the KISS Principle 32
Rule 2.3:   Adhere to Existing Product Standards or Check Their Adherence ... 36
Rule 3.1:   Use ABAP Objects 42
Rule 3.2:   Select the Appropriate Program Type 53
Rule 3.3:   Accept the Standard Settings for Program Attributes 56
Rule 3.4:   Determine Original Language at Project Level 60
Rule 3.5:   Do Not Use Obsolete Language Elements 63
Rule 3.6:   Consider Syntax Warnings 67
Rule 3.7:   Use the Extended Program Check 70
Rule 3.8:   Use Default Check Variant of the Code Inspector 73
Rule 3.9:   Configure and Use the ABAP Test Cockpit Correctly 76
Rule 4.1:   No Mixed Uppercase and Lowercase in Names 81
Rule 4.2:   One Statement at Most per Program Line 84
Rule 4.3:   Use the Pretty Printer Consistently and Universally 86
Rule 4.4:   Do Not Use Full Line Width 89
Rule 4.5:   Use English Names 93
Rule 4.6:   Assign Descriptive Names 95
Rule 4.7:   Clarify the Type and Affiliation of Repository Objects in Names ... 102
Rule 4.8:   Prevent Confusion and Unintentional Hidings in
                 Program-Internal Declarations 106
Rule 4.9:   Comment Programs in English 115
Rule 4.10:   Comment Meaningfully 117
Rule 4.11:   Arrange Comments Correctly 120
Rule 4.12:   Implement Global Declarations Centrally 124
Rule 4.13:   Implement Local Declarations at the Beginning of the
                 Procedure 128
Rule 4.14:   Modularize Source Code Using Include Programs 131
Rule 4.15:   Do Not Use Include Programs Multiple Times 132
Rule 4.16:   Use a Clear Notation 135
Rule 4.17:   Use Chained Statements Only in Appropriate Positions 137
Rule 4.18:   Formulate Static Method Calls Without CALL METHOD 141
Rule 4.19:   Use Operator Notation 143
Rule 4.20:   Omit the COMPUTE Keyword 145
Rule 4.21:   Limit the Complexity of Expressions 147

Rule 4.22: Restrict the Nesting Depth of Control Structures 149

Rule 4.23: Restrict the Number of Statements in Procedures 150

Rule 4.24: Maintain Reasonable Class Sizes 151

Rule 4.25: Remove Dead Code 153

Rule 5.1: Utilize the Encapsulation Options as Much as Possible 156

Rule 5.2: Modularize Instead of Atomize 158

Rule 5.3: Do Not Use Static Classes 162

Rule 5.4: Avoid Deep Inheritance Hierarchies 166

Rule 5.5: Access Interface Components Using an Interface Reference
Variable 167

Rule 5.6: Position Local Declarations Appropriately 169

Rule 5.7: Declare the Instance Constructor in the Public Visibility
Section 171

Rule 5.8: Select a Proper Reaction to Error Situations 173

Rule 5.9: Use Class-Based Exceptions 175

Rule 5.10: Use the Appropriate Exception Category 179

Rule 5.11: Provide Appropriate Exception Texts in the Exception Class
and Only Use Those 181

Rule 5.12: Use Appropriate Exception Classes Only 183

Rule 5.13: Catch Exceptions or Forward Them Appropriately 185

Rule 5.14: Cleanup Before Forwarding 187

Rule 5.15: Do Not Handle Catchable Runtime Errors 189

Rule 5.16: Use Assertions 190

Rule 5.17: Use Messages Only for Error Handling in Classical Dynpros
and as Exception Texts 193

Rule 5.18: Use Web Dynpro ABAP 196

Rule 5.19: Encapsulate Classical Dynpros and Selection Screens 200

Rule 5.20: Use the SAP List Viewer 204

Rule 5.21: Ensure Accessibility 207

Rule 5.22: Plan Persistent Data Storage Carefully 208

Rule 5.23: Use Open SQL 211

Rule 5.24: Do Not Access Data of Other Clients 212

Rule 5.25: Implement the Explicit Buffering in the Shared Memory
Using Shared Objects 213

Rule 6.1: Use Standalone Data Types 218

Rule 6.2: Declare Data Types and Constants in the Appropriate Context 220

Rule 6.3: Do Not Declare Global Variables 224

Rule 6.4: Do Not Include Components of Structures 226

Rule 6.5: Use Semantically Appropriate Data Types Only 228

Rule 6.6: Declare Dependent Data Objects with Reference to Other Data Objects 230

Rule 6.7: No Table Work Areas Except for Classical Dynpros 232

Rule 6.8: Avoid Literals in Operand Positions 234

Rule 6.9: Use Strings for Character and Byte String Processing 236

Rule 6.10: Start Values Must Correspond to the Data Type of the Data Object 238

Rule 6.11: Use the abap_bool Data Type for Truth Values 240

Rule 6.12: Avoid Conversions 242

Rule 6.13: Assign Valid Values Only 243

Rule 6.14: Avoid Unexpected Conversion Results 246

Rule 6.15: Use a General Notation for Numeric Values 248

Rule 6.16: Select Suitable Numeric Types for Numbers and Calculations 250

Rule 6.17: Avoid Unnecessary Rounding Errors 253

Rule 6.18: Avoid a Division by Zero 255

Rule 6.19: Avoid Implicit Casting 256

Rule 6.20: Avoid Runtime Errors When Accessing Data Objects 258

Rule 6.21: Do Not Use Character or Byte Fields as a Container 259

Rule 6.22: Do Not Pass Global Data to Local Contexts by Reference 260

Rule 6.23: Do Not Write System Fields 262

Rule 6.24: Do Not Use Obsolete or Internal System Fields 264

Rule 6.25: Evaluate System Fields at the Right Place 265

Rule 6.26: Evaluate the sy-subrc Return Value 267

Rule 6.27: Do Not Use System Fields as Actual Parameters 268

Rule 6.28: Do Not Use System Fields on the User Interface 270

Rule 6.29: Do Not Use System Fields in Statements That Set the Fields 272

Rule 6.30: Use the Appropriate Table Category 275

Rule 6.31: Use Secondary Keys Efficiently 277

Rule 6.32: Manipulate the Initial Memory Requirement for Nested Tables Only 280

Rule 6.33: Do Not Generate Ranking Lists via Sorted Filling 282

Rule 6.34: Do Not Use Aggregated Filling for Standard Tables 283

Rule 6.35: Select an Appropriate Output Behavior 285

Rule 6.36: Do Not Change the Whole Table Body in a Loop Pass 287

Rule 6.37: No Implementations in Function Modules and Subroutines 288

Rule 6.38: Select the Appropriate Formal Parameter Type 290

Rule 6.39: Select the Appropriate Transfer Type 292

Rule 6.40: Use Output Parameters with the Pass by Reference Method Correctly 294

Rule 6.41: Be as Specific as Possible When Typing Formal Parameters 296

Rule 6.42: Call Only Appropriate Procedures Externally 299

Rule 6.43: Exit Procedures with RETURN Only 302

Rule 6.44: No Implementations in Dialog Modules and Event Blocks 305

Rule 6.45: Use Macros in Exceptional Cases Only 306

Rule 6.46: Use Dynamic Programming Techniques with Care 310

Rule 6.47: Avoid Runtime Errors During Dynamic Processing 311

Rule 6.48: Use Appropriate Dynamic Data Objects 313

Rule 6.49: Avoid Memory Bottlenecks 316

Rule 6.50: Consider the Ratio of Administration and Application Data 319

Rule 6.51: Use Field Symbols and Data References Appropriately 322

Rule 6.52: Avoid Program Generation 325

Rule 6.53: Send Only Translatable System Texts to the User 330

Rule 6.54: Do Not Use Anonymous Placeholders (&) in Message Texts 332

Rule 6.55: If Possible, Do Not Modify the Text Environment
Programmatically 333

Rule 6.56: Use 7-Bit ASCII Characters in the Source Code Only 335

Rule 6.57: Split Texts at Character Boundaries Only 336

Rule 6.58: Write Text Files in UTF-8 and with Byte-Order Mark 337

D   Recommended Reading

Dijkstra, Edsger W. On the role of scientific thought. In: Dijkstra, Edsger W., *Selected Writings on Computing: A Personal Perspective*. Springer-Verlag, Inc., 1982, pp. 60-66.

Feathers, Michael C. *Working Effectively with Legacy Code*. Prentice Hall 2007.

Gahm, Hermann. *ABAP Performance Tuning*. SAP PRESS, 2009.

Gamma, Erich; Helm, Richard; Johnson, Ralph; Vlissides, John. *Design Patterns. Elements of Reusable Object-Oriented Software*. Addison-Wesley, 1995.

Keller, Horst. *The Official ABAP-Reference*. 2nd ed. SAP PRESS, 2005.

Keller, Horst; Kluger, Gerd. Not Yet Using ABAP Objects? Eight Reasons Why Every ABAP Developer Should Give It a Second Look. In: *SAP Professional Journal,* Sept./Oct. 2004. (Vol. 8, Iss. 7).

Keller, Horst; Krüger, Sascha: *ABAP Objects: ABAP Programming in SAP NetWeaver*. 2nd ed. SAP PRESS 2007.

McConnell, Steve. *Code Complete. A Practical Handbook of Software Construction*. 2nd ed. Microsoft Press, 2004.

Schneider, Thomas. *SAP Performance Optimization Guide*. SAP PRESS, 2008.

E   The Authors

Horst Keller studied physics at the Darmstadt University of Technology, Germany, and received his doctorate in nuclear physics. After some time abroad at the University of Paris, France, he joined SAP AG in 1995. Horst Keller works in the TD Core AS&DM ABAP group at SAP. As a Knowledge Architect, he is responsible for documentation and rollout of ABAP and ABAP Objects. He also develops and maintains the programs for preparing and presenting the ABAP documentation, including the relating search algorithms. He has been author and editor of numerous ABAP books at SAP PRESS and of many other publications and workshops on this subject for numerous years.

Wolf Hagen Thümmel studied physics at the Karlsruhe University, Germany, and received his doctorate in experimental particle physics. In 2001, he joined SAP AG. He is currently a member of the TD Core AS&DM ABAP group and there focuses on language-related tools in the ABAP environment as well as in the area of mass checks for quality assurance. He assumes responsibility for ABAP checkpoint statements and the related tools, memory analyses, and parts of the ABAP Debugger. Wolf Hagen Thümmel also deals with topics regarding the complexity of ABAP programs. He is author of several ABAP-related publications in trade journals and handbooks on programming languages.

Index

4GL language, background, 158
?=, notation, 143
<, notation, 135
<=, notation, 135
=, notation, 135, 143
>, notation, 135
>=, notation, 135
=<, obsolete, 349
=>, obsolete, 349
><, obsolete, 349
&& -> see chaining operator, 90
=> -> see Class component selector, 109
-> -> see Instance component selector, 109
& -> see literal operator, 90
?TO, notation, 143

A

abap_bool
    background, 239
    use, 240
ABAP Database Connectivity -> see ADBC, 210
ABAP Dictionary
    Background, 220
    use, 221
abap_false
    background, 239
    use, 240
ABAP language element
    Background, 62
    Coexistence, 65
    Example, 161
    Use, 159
ABAP Objects
    Background, 41
    Example, 48
ABAP programming
    Classical, 25
    Object-oriented, 155
ABAP statement
    Arrangement, 83
    Example, 84, 85
    Notation, 135

ABAP Test Cockpit -> see ATC; ABAP Test Cockpit, 76
abap_true
    background, 239
    use, 240
abap_undefined
    use, 240
ABAP Unit
    Module test, 37
ABAP word
    Naming, 107
Abbreviated form (data cluster)
    Obsolete, 360, 361
Abbreviated form (internal table)
    Obsolete, 355
Abbreviated form (Open SQL)
    Obsolete, 360
Accessibility
    Product standard, 35, 207
Activatable assertion
    Use, 191
ADBC, 210
    Background, 210
    Use, 211
ADD
    Use, 143
ADD-CORRESPONDING
    Obsolete, 352
ADD FROM
    Obsolete, 353
Additional program group
    background, 299
ADD THEN
    Obsolete, 353
ALV, 204
    Background, 204
ALV list
    Example, 206
Anonymous container
    background, 259
Anonymous data object
    Background, 217
    dynamic memory object, 315
    example, 328

Application buffer
  Background, 213
  Example, 215
  Use, 214
Application logic
  Separation of concerns, 29
Arithmetic expression
  Example, 148
  Notation, 145
ASCII character set
  use, 335
ASSERT
  Background, 190
  Use, 191
Assertion
  Background, 173, 190
  Example, 191
  Use, 173, 194
ASSIGN
  dynamic access, 321
  use, 322
ASSIGN DECIMALS
  Obsolete, 352
ASSIGNING
  dynamic access, 321
  example, 286
  use, 285
ASSIGN LOCAL COPY OF
  Obsolete, 347
Assignment
  background, 241
  conversion rule, 245
  loss-free, 246
  Notation, 143
ASSIGN TABLE FIELD
  Obsolete, 352
ASSIGN TYPE
  Obsolete, 352
ATC
  Background, 76
  Example, 77
  Use, 76
AT LINE-SELECTION
  background, 304
Atomization
  Example, 160
AT PFnn
  Obsolete, 358
AT SELECTION-SCREEN

  background, 304
  use, 305
AT USER-COMMAND
  background, 304

B

Background, 94
Background processing
  Use, 45
BAdI
  Naming convention, 103
BETWEEN
  Notation, 135
Binary floating point number
  background, 250
  example, 253
  use, 251
Bit expression
  Notation, 145
Blank lines
  Use, 87
BOM
  OPEN DATASET, 337
  text file, 337
Boolean data type
  background, 239
Bound data type
  Background, 218
  Example, 219
Boxed component, 227
  Background, 227
  use, 317
Browser Control
  Use, 208
BSP
  Use, 196
Business Add-In -> see BAdI, 103
Business Server Pages -> see BSP, 196
Byte string
  background, 236

C

Calculation
  background, 241
  Notation, 143
Calculation expression
  Notation, 145

Calculation type
  background, 241
CALL CUSTOMER-FUNCTION
  Obsolete, 347
CALL CUSTOMER SUBSCREEN
  Obsolete, 357
CALL DIALOG
  Obsolete, 347
CALL FUNCTION IN UPDATE TASK
  Use, 44
CALL METHOD
  Rule, 141, 142
CALL SCREEN
  Background, 195
  Use, 45
CALL SELECTION-SCREEN
  Background, 195
  Use, 45
CALL TRANSACTION
  Program execution, 52
CALL TRANSFORMATION
  use, 260
Camel case style
  Example, 82
  Use, 81
CASE
  Complexity, 149
  Obsolete, 349
Case sensitivity
  Background, 80
  Example, 82
  Use, 81, 88
Casting
  background, 255
CASTING
  ASSIGN, 256
  example, 257
  implicit, 256
  use, 322
CATCH
  Background, 185
Catchable runtime error
  Background, 188
  Obsolete, 348
CATCH SYSTEM-EXCEPTIONS
  Background, 188
  Example, 189
  Obsolete, 348
  Use, 189
Chained statement

Background, 137
Use, 137
Chaining operator &&
  Use, 90
CHANGING
  background, 289
  example, 291
  Naming convention, 107
  use, 290
Character literal
  background, 234
  translatability, 329
  use, 235, 330
Character literal template
  use, 330
Character set
  background, 335
Character string expression
  Notation, 145
Character string template
  use, 254
CHECK
  background, 302
  example, 303
  use, 302
Checkpoint group
  Assertion, 190, 191
Class
  Complexity, 151
  Naming, 96
Class-based exception
  Background, 175
  Example, 177
  Forwarding, 185
  Handling, 185
  Use, 176
Class component
  Naming, 110
Class component selector
  Naming, 109, 110
Classical exception
  Background, 174
  Example, 177
  Use, 175
Classical list
  Background, 204
  Example, 205
  Use, 205
Class pool
  Local declaration, 169

Program type, 51
Rule, 53
Use, 54
Class reference variable
Background, 167
Use, 167
Class size
Background, 151
CLEANUP
Background, 186
Example, 187
Use, 187
CLEAR
use, 316
CLEAR WITH NULL
Obsolete, 351
Client handling
Background, 211
Example, 212, 213
CLIENT SPECIFIED
Use, 212
CL_JAVA_SCRIPT
CLASS DEFINITION, 171
Obsolete, 363
Code Inspector
Background, 72
Error, 73
Example, 74
Message, 73
Naming convention, 365
Pseudo comment, 73
Use, 73
Warning, 73
Codepage
text file, 337
COLLECT
background, 283
use, 284
Colon-comma logic-> see chained
statement, 137
Combining characters
background, 336
Comment
Arrangement, 120
Background, 115
Example, 119, 122
Pseudo comment, 121
translatability, 330
Use, 117, 148

Comment language
Background, 115
Example, 116, 117
Comment line
Background, 115
Commercial notation
background, 248
COMMON PART
Obsolete, 343
COMMUNICATION
Obsolete, 363
Compilation unit
Background, 131
Complete typing
background, 296
example, 298
Complexity
Background, 146
Class, 151
Control structure, 149
Dead code, 153
Function group, 152
Procedure, 150
COMPUTE
Example, 146
COMPUTE EXACT
use, 146
Constant
Background, 220
example, 223, 235
Naming, 96
use, 234
CONSTANTS
background, 220
constructor
METHODS, 171
Context
Naming convention, 111
CONTEXTS
Obsolete, 362
CONTROLS
use, 225
Control structure
Chained statement, 139
Comment, 120
Complexity, 149
Conversion
background, 241
example, 242

Conversion rule
  background, 245
CONVERT DATE
  Obsolete, 354
  use, 244
CONVERT TIME STAMP
  use, 244
Coverage Analyzer
  Test coverage, 37
CREATE addition
  CLASS DEFINITION, 171
CREATE AREA HANDLE
  Use, 214
CREATE DATA
  dynamic access, 321
  rule, 326
Customer namespace
  Name, 102
CX_DYNAMIC_CHECK
  Background, 179
  rule, 186
CX_NO_CHECK
  Background, 179
  rule, 186
CX_ROOT
  Rule, 186
CX_STATIC_CHECK
  Background, 178
  Rule, 186

D

DATA
  use, 225
Database access
  Background, 210
Database table
  Background, 208
  Use, 209
Data cluster
  Use, 209
DATA COMMON PART
  interface work area, 300
Data encapsulation
  ABAP Objects, 42
Data object
  Background, 217
  reference to, 230
Data reference

  dynamic access, 321
  example, 323
  rule, 322
  use, 323
Data type
  background, 217, 220, 228
  example, 229, 271
  Naming, 96
  Naming convention, 111
  reference to, 230
  rule, 228
Date field
  background, 243
  use, 244
Dead code
  Background, 153
  Complexity, 153
Decimal floating point number
  background, 250
  example, 253
  use, 251
Declaration
  Chained statements, 138
Default check variant
  Code Inspector, 73
DELETE dbtab
  Obsolete, 362
DEMAND
  Obsolete, 362
Dereferencing
  use, 323
DESCRIBE FIELD
  use, 325
DETAIL
  Obsolete, 358
Development language
  Background, 60
Dialog message
  Use, 193
Dialog module
  background, 288, 304
  Use, 45, 200
Dialog program
  Example, 202
  Separation of concerns, 23
Dialog transaction
  Program execution, 52
  Use, 45

DIVIDE
  Use, 143
DIVIDE-CORRESPONDING
  Obsolete, 352
DO
  Complexity, 149
Documentation
  Means, 37
  Product standard, 35
DO VARYING
  Obsolete, 350
Downward compatibility
  Background, 62
Dynamic access
  background, 309, 321, 324
  rule, 322
  use, 311, 322
Dynamic data object
  background, 313
  rule, 313
  use, 311
Dynamic invoke
  background, 309, 324
  use, 311
Dynamic memory object
  administration, 318
  background, 309
  example, 317, 318
  fill level, 320
  memory consumption, 315
Dynamic programming
  background, 309
  example, 312
  use, 310
Dynamic token specification
  background, 324
  example, 328
  use, 311, 325
Dynpro
  Background, 195
  Example, 197, 202
  use, 300
  Use, 197

E

eCATT
  Scenario test, 37
EDITOR-CALL

  Obsolete, 354
Encapsulation
  Background, 156
ENCODING
  OPEN DATASET, 337
END-OF-SELECTION
  background, 304
  Program execution, 53
English
  Comment language, 115
  Development language, 61
  Naming language, 92
  Use, 93
EQ
  Notation, 135
Error
  Code Inspector, 73
  Extended program check, 69
error_message
  Use, 193
Error message
  Use, 193
Error situation
  Handling, 172
Event
  ABAP Objects, 43
  Naming, 96
Event block
  background, 288, 304
  Use, 45
Event handler
  Naming, 97
EXACT
  COMPUTE, 145
  MOVE, 246
Exception
  Background, 172
  Naming, 97
  Use, 173
Exception category
  Background, 178
Exception class
  Background, 183
  Example, 184
  Use, 183
Exception handling
  Background, 174
  Remote Function Call, 177
Exception text

Background, 180
Example, 182
Exclusive buffer
Use, 214
Executable program
Program type, 51
Rule, 53
Separation of concerns, 24
Use, 54
EXIT
background, 302
use, 302
Exit message
Use, 194
EXPORT
Notation, 136
EXPORTING
background, 289
example, 291, 295
Naming convention, 107
pass by reference, 294
rule, 294
use, 290, 294
EXPORT TO DATA BUFFER
use, 260, 314
EXPORT TO INTERNAL TABLE
use, 314
Expression
Complexity, 147
Extended program check
Background, 69
Error, 69
Example, 71
Message, 69
Use, 70
Warning, 69
External procedure call
background, 298

F

FIELD (dynpro)
Obsolete, 357
FIELDS
Obsolete, 346
Field symbol
dynamic access, 321
example, 324
rule, 322

typing, 297
use, 322
FIELD-SYMBOLS
declaration, 225
Obsolete, 344
File
Background, 208
Use, 209
Final class
Use, 166
FIND
Notation, 136
Fixed point arithmetic
Program attribute, 56
Rule, 56
Fixed Point Arithmetic
Use, 57
Floating point number
background, 250
FORM
Obsolete, 342
Formal parameter
rule, 290, 292
transfer, 292
type, 289
typing, 296
FORMAT
Background, 195
FREE
use, 317
Functional correctness
Product standard, 35
Functional method
Naming, 97, 110
Function group
Complexity, 152
example, 226
Example, 45
Global declaration part, 127
Program type, 51
Rule, 53
Use, 54, 200
Function module
background, 287, 288
use, 300
Use, 45
Function pool
Program type, 51

G

Garbage Collector
  use, 317
GE
  Notation, 135
GENERATE SUBROUTINE POOL
  background, 325
  Use, 45
Generic data type
  background, 296
Generic programming
  background, 309, 324
  use, 312
Generic typing
  background, 296
  example, 297
GET
  background, 304
  Program execution, 53
GET REFERENCE
  dynamic access, 321
Global class
  Local declaration, 169
  Naming convention, 103
  use, 221
Global data object
  background, 260
  Naming, 110
  Naming convention, 107
Global declaration
  Arrangement, 124
  Example, 126
  Top include, 125
Global declaration part
  Background, 124
Global exception class
  Naming convention, 103
Global interface
  Naming convention, 103
Globalization
  product standard, 329
  Product standard, 35
Global variable
  use, 224
GT
  Notation, 135
GUI status
  use, 300

GUI title
  translatability, 332

H

Hashed table
  background, 273
  table type, 274
  use, 276
Hash key
  background, 276
  use, 278
Header
  dynamic memory object, 318
Header comments
  Use, 118
HEADER LINE
  Obsolete, 345
Helper variable
  declaration, 230
  example, 231
  Example, 148
  Use, 147

I

IF
  Complexity, 149
IMPORT
  Notation, 136
IMPORTING
  background, 289
  Naming convention, 107
  use, 290
IN
  Notation, 135
Include program
  Background, 130, 132
  Example, 134
  Multiple use, 133
  use, 222
  Use, 131
INCLUDE STRUCTURE
  background, 226
  use, 227
INCLUDE TYPE
  background, 226
  example, 227
  use, 227

Indentation
    Comment, 121
    Use, 86
Index table
    table type, 275
    use, 276
INDX
    Use, 209
Information message
    Use, 193
Inheritance
    ABAP Objects, 42
    Background, 166
    Reuse, 166
    Rule, 166
INITIALIZATION
    background, 304
    use, 305
INITIAL SIZE
    background, 280
    example, 281
    use, 280
INPUT
    Obsolete, 358
Input parameter
    background, 289
INSERT REPORT
    background, 325
Instance component
    Background, 162
Instance component selector
    Naming, 109, 110
Instance constructor
    Background, 171
    Use, 163
Instantiation
    ABAP Objects, 42
Integer
    background, 250
    use, 250
Interface
    ABAP Objects, 43
    Naming, 96
    Use, 167
Interface component selector
    Background, 167
    Example, 168
    Use, 167
Interface parameter

Naming, 96
    Naming convention, 112
Interface pool
    Program type, 51
    Rule, 53
    Use, 54
Interface reference variable
    Background, 167
    Example, 168
Interface work area
    example, 301
    use, 300
Internal procedure call
    background, 298
Internal table
    background, 273
    dynamic data object, 313
    fill, 281, 283
    loop processing, 286
    memory requirement, 280
    output behavior, 284
    secondary key, 276
    table type, 274
    use, 314
International development
    Development language, 61
Internationalization
    background, 329
    Product standard, 35
INTO
    READ TABLE, LOOP AT, 285
Invalid value
    background, 243
    example, 244
IS ASSIGNED
    Notation, 135
IS BOUND
    Notation, 135
IS INITIAL
    Notation, 135
IS REQUESTED
    Obsolete, 349
IS SUPPLIED
    Notation, 135

J

Java convention
    Use, 82

K

KISS principle
  Background, 32
  Example, 33

L

Language
  text environment, 333
LE
  Notation, 135
LEAVE
  Obsolete, 348
LEAVE PROGRAM
  Use, 194
LEAVE TO LIST-PROCESSING
  Background, 195
LEAVE TO TRANSACTION
  Program execution, 52
LENGTH
  Notation, 136
LIKE
  background, 230
  rule, 230
  use, 230
LIKE LINE OF
  rule, 230
LIKE reference
  Obsolete, 344
Line end comment
  Background, 115
  Use, 120
Line type
  background, 273
Line width
  Background, 89
  Example, 90
  Use, 90
List
  Background, 195, 204
  Use, 197
Literal
  background, 233
Literal operator
  Example, 91
  Use, 90
LOAD
  Obsolete, 346

Loader
  Use, 214
LOAD-OF-PROGRAM
  background, 304
  use, 305
LOCAL
  Obsolete, 351
Local class
  Declaration, 125
  Global class, 169
  Naming, 110
  use, 221, 300
  Use, 153, 200
Local data type
  Global class, 169
Local declaration
  Arrangement, 128
  Background, 127
  Example, 129, 130
  use, 221
  Use, 169
  Validity, 129
Locale
  text environment, 333
Local interface
  Declaration, 125
  Global class, 169
  Naming, 110
Localization
  Product standard, 35
Local name
  Naming, 109
Locator
  use, 316
Logical database
  Program attribute, 56
  Rule, 56
Logical Database
  Use, 57
LOOP
  Complexity, 149
LOOP AT
  background, 284
  rule, 285
LOOP AT dbtab
  Obsolete, 362
LOOP (dynpro)
  Obsolete, 358
Lowercase

Example, 88
LT
  Notation, 135

M

Macro
  background, 288, 306
  example, 307, 308
  use, 307
Main program
  background, 299
  Background, 130
  Source code modularization, 131
Main program group
  background, 299
MAJOR-ID
  Obsolete, 361
Mathematical notation
  background, 247
  use, 248
MAXIMUM
  Obsolete, 359
Memory Inspector
  Memory test, 37
  use, 317
Message
  Background, 191
  Code Inspector, 73
  Exception text, 193
  Extended program check, 69
  translatability, 331
  Use, 174
MESSAGE
  background, 192
  Use, 174
Messages
  Background, 173
Message text
  Exception text, 181
Message type
  Background, 192
Method
  background, 287
  Naming, 97
  use, 300
Method call
  Example, 142
  Long form, 142

Notation, 141
  Short form, 141
MINIMUM
  Obsolete, 359
MINOR-ID
  Obsolete, 361
Mixed case style
  Example, 82
  Use, 81
Modern language element
  Background, 62
  Example, 64
  Use, 63
MODIFY
  example, 286
  rule, 285
MODIFY dbtab
  Obsolete, 362
Modularization
  Background, 157
MODULE
  background, 304
Module pool
  Program type, 51
  Rule, 53
  Separation of concerns, 24
  Use, 55
MOVE
  Example, 144
  Use, 143
MOVE PERCENTAGE
  Obsolete, 350
Multilingual development
  Rule, 60
MULTIPLY
  Use, 143
MULTIPLY-CORRESPONDING
  Obsolete, 352

N

Name
  Example, 100, 105
Named data object
  Background, 217
Namespace prefix
  Use, 104
Naming
  Abbreviations, 98

Background, 91, 94
Digit, 99
Example, 105, 112, 113
Namespace, 108
Prefix, 111
Program object, 106
Repository object, 101
Shading, 108
Suffix, 111
Naming convention
  Background, 92
  Check, 365
Naming language
  Background, 92
  Example, 93
Native SQL
  Background, 210
  Use, 211
Nesting depth
  Background, 149
  Example, 150
NEW-SECTION
  Obsolete, 359
nmax (predefined function)
  Use, 150
nmin (predefined function)
  Use, 150
NODES
  background, 232
  interface work area, 300
  use, 233
NOT
  Notation, 135
Notation
  Example, 136, 137
Number specification
  background, 247
  example, 249
Numeric literal
  background, 234
  example, 235
  use, 234
Numeric text
  background, 243
Numeric type
  background, 249
  rule, 250

O

Object generation
  Use, 162
Object header
  dynamic memory object, 319
Object orientation
  Design, 155, 162
  Use, 157
Obsolete language element
  Background, 62, 341
  Example, 63
  Use, 63
OCCURS
  Obsolete, 345
ON CHANGE OF
  Obsolete, 350
Online Text Repository -> see OTR, 180
OO transaction
  Program execution, 52
  Use, 54
OPEN DATASET
  rule, 337
Open SQL
  Background, 210
  chained statement, 140
  Use, 211
Operator notation
  Use, 143
Original language
  Background, 60
Orthogonal concept
  ABAP Objects, 43
OTR
  Exception text, 181
Output parameter
  background, 289

P

PACK
  Obsolete, 351
Package
  Background, 101
  Naming, 95
  Naming convention, 103
Package check
  Syntax check, 67
Package concept

Use, 29, 104, 166, 209
Package interface
  Naming, 96
PACKAGE SECTION
  Rule, 157
PACKAGE SIZE
  use, 316
Packed number
  background, 250
  use, 251
PAI module
  Use, 200
Parameter interface
  background, 289
PARAMETERS
  Background, 195
  use, 225
Pass by reference
  background, 260, 292
  example, 261
  use, 293
Pass by value
  background, 292
  example, 261
  use, 261, 293
PBO module
  Use, 200
PERFORM
  Obsolete, 348
Performance
  Product standard, 36
Performance test
  Code Inspector, 73
PERFORMING
  Obsolete, 360
PERFORM ... IN PROGRAM
  background, 299
PERFORM ON COMMIT
  Use, 44
PERFORM ON ROLLBACK
  Use, 44
Persistency
  Background, 208
  Rule, 208
  Separation of concerns, 29
Pointer
  use, 323
Polymorphism
  Use, 167

Pragma
  Extended program check, 70
  Use, 70
Predicate
  Notation, 135
prefix namespace
  Name, 101
Pretty Printer
  Background, 86
  Case sensitivity, 81
  Example, 83, 85
  Use, 86
Primary key
  background, 273
  example, 279
Print list
  Background, 204
Print parameter
  Obsolete, 359
PRIVATE SECTION
  Global class, 169
Procedure
  background, 287, 288
  Complexity, 150
  exit, 302
  Naming, 97
  use, 300
Procedure call
  background, 298
  Program execution, 52
Procedure volume
  Background, 150
  Example, 151
Processing block
  background, 287
Product standard
  Background, 35
  Example, 38
Program
  Executable, 24
Program attribute
  Background, 55
  Rule, 56
Program generation
  background, 325
  example, 327
  use, 326
Program group
  background, 299

Programming style
  Background, 79
Program object
  Naming, 106
Program structure
  Background, 79
Program type
  Background, 51
  Rule, 53
PROVIDE
  Obsolete, 356
Proxy service
  Separation of concerns, 29
Pseudo comment
  Code Inspector, 73
  Example, 75
  Extended program check, 70
  Use, 70, 73
PUBLIC SECTION
  Rule, 157

R

RAISE
  Use, 175
RAISE EXCEPTION
  Use, 176
RAISING
  MESSAGE, 192, 194
RANGES
  Obsolete, 346
READ
  Obsolete, 355
READ DATASET
  Notation, 136
READ TABLE
  background, 284
  rule, 285
READ TABLE dbtab
  Obsolete, 362
Redefinition
  Background, 166
  Use, 163
REFERENCE INTO
  dynamic access, 321
  use, 285
Reference semantics
  use, 323
Reference sematics

dynamic access, 321
REFRESH
  Obsolete, 356
REFRESH FROM dbtab
  Obsolete, 362
REJECT
  use, 303
Remote-enabled function module-> see
RFM, 54
REPLACE
  Notation, 136
  Obsolete, 353
REPLACE ... ALL OCCURENCES
  Use, 150
Report, 24
  Classical, 26
  Separation of concerns, 29
Repository object
  Naming, 101
RESUMABLE
  Use, 180
RESUME
  Use, 176
RETURN
  background, 302
  example, 303
RETURNING
  background, 289
  Naming convention, 107
  use, 290
Return value
  background, 289
RFC
  Use, 44
RFM
  Example, 24
  Use, 54
ROLLBACK WORK
  Use, 194
Rounding error
  background, 253
  example, 254
RTTC
  use, 326
RTTI
  use, 325
RTTS
  use, 325
Runtime analysis

Performance test, 37
Runtime error
  background, 257, 311
  example, 258

S

SAP buffering
  Background, 213
SAP GUI
  Background, 195
SAP List Viewer -> see ALV, 204
SAP namespace
  Name, 102
SCI -> see Code Inspector, 72
SEARCH
  Obsolete, 353
Secondary key
  example, 279
  use, 277
Security
  Code Inspector, 73
  Product standard, 36
SELECT (dynpro)
  Obsolete, 357
Selection screen
  Background, 195
  Example, 202
  Use, 197
Selection screen event
  Use, 45, 200
SELECT-OPTIONS
  Background, 195
  use, 225
Separation of concerns, 23
  Example, 28
SET EXTENDED CHECK OFF
  rule, 70
SET LOCALE
  example, 334
  text environment, 333
Shared buffer
  Use, 214
SHARED MEMORY
  Background, 213
  Use, 214
Shared Objects
  Background, 213
  Example, 215

Use, 214
Sharing
  background, 236
  details, 293
Singleton
  Background, 162
  Example, 164
  Use, 162
SLIN
  Extended program check, 69
SOA
  Separation of concerns, 24
SORT
  use, 282
SORTED BY
  background, 281
  use, 282
Sorted key
  background, 276
  use, 278
Sorted table
  background, 273
  table type, 274
  use, 275
SPLIT
  use, 336
Standalone data type
  Background, 218
  Example, 220
Standard comment
  Use, 87
Standard selection screen
  Use, 202
Standard table
  background, 273
  table type, 274
  use, 275
START-OF-SELECTION
  background, 304
  Program execution, 53
  use, 305
  Use, 45, 55
Start value
  background, 238
  example, 239
Static class
  Background, 161
  Example, 164
  Polymorphism, 163

Use, 162
Static component
  Background, 162
Static constructor
  Use, 163
Status message
  Use, 193
STOP
  use, 303
Streaming
  use, 316
String
  background, 236
  dynamic data object, 313
  dynamic memory object, 315
  use, 314
String header
  dynamic memory object, 318
String literal
  background, 234
Structured programming
  Background, 157
  Use, 158
STRUCTURE typing
  Obsolete, 343, 345
Subclass
  Background, 166
  Use, 166
Subfield access
  background, 258
  use, 336
SUBMIT
  Program execution, 52
  use, 305
SUBMIT VIA JOB
  Use, 45
Subroutine
  background, 287, 288
  use, 300
  Use, 45
Subroutine pool
  Program type, 52
  Rule, 53
  Use, 54
Substructure
  background, 226
  example, 228
SUBTRACT
  Use, 143

SUBTRACT-CORRESPONDING
  Obsolete, 352
SUMMARY
  Obsolete, 358
SUMMING
  Obsolete, 359
Superclass
  Background, 166
SUPPLY
  Obsolete, 362
Surrogate area
  background, 336
sy
  background, 262
sy-index
  use, 265
sy-mandt
  Use, 212
Syntax check
  Background, 65
  Example, 68
  Severity, 66
  Use, 67
Syntax cleansing
  ABAP Objects, 43
Syntax error
  Background, 65
Syntax warning
  Background, 66
  Example, 68
  Priority, 66
SYST
  background, 262
System codepage
  text environment, 333
System field
  access, 262
  actual parameter, 268
  background, 262, 264
  evaluation, 265
  example, 263, 264, 266, 269, 271, 272, 273
  operand position, 272
  use, 262, 264, 265, 268, 270, 272
  user interface, 270
System text
  background, 329
sy-subrc
  background, 267

example, 267, 268
use, 265, 267
sy-tabix
  use, 265, 279

T

Table body
  background, 286
  dynamic memory object, 315
  use, 287
Table header
  dynamic memory object, 318
Table index
  background, 273
TABLES
  background, 232
  interface work area, 300
  Obsolete, 342, 344
  use, 225, 233, 291
Table type
  background, 273
  rule, 275
Table work area
  background, 232
Technical scientific notation
  background, 248
Technology access
  ABAP Objects, 44
Termination message
  Use, 194
Terminology
  Rule, 62
Text environment
  background, 333
Text field
  example, 237
  use, 237
Text field literal
  background, 234
Text file
  example, 338
Text string
  background, 236
  example, 238
  use, 237
Text symbol
  use, 330
Time field

background, 243
Timestamp
  use, 244
Top include
  example, 225
  Global declaration part, 125
Transaction
  Program execution, 52
Translatability
  example, 331, 332, 333
TRANSLATE
  Obsolete, 354
Transport Organizer
  ATC, 77
Truth value
  background, 239
  example, 240, 241
TRY
  Background, 185
  Example, 189
TYPE
  background, 230
  rule, 230
Type group
  Background, 220
  example, 222
  Program type, 52
  Rule, 53
  use, 222
  Use, 55
Type pool
  Program type, 52
TYPE-POOLS
  Obsolete, 343
TYPES
  background, 220
Typing
  background, 296
  rule, 296

U

UI service
  Separation of concerns, 29
Underscore
  Example, 82
Unicode check
  Example, 58
  Program attribute, 56

Rule, 56
Use, 56
Unicode program
Background, 56
Example, 59
Use, 56, 341
Unilingual development
Rule, 60
Update function module
Use, 54
Usability
Product standard, 36
User interface technology
Background, 195
Encapsulation, 199
USING
background, 289
use, 290

V

Validity area
Naming convention, 111
Valid value
background, 243
example, 244
VALUE
DATA, 238
Value range
background, 258
Value semantics
dynamic access, 321
use, 322

Variable
background, 224
Naming, 96

W

Warning
Code Inspector, 73
Extended program check, 69
Use, 193
Web Dynpro ABAP
Background, 196
Example, 198
Use, 196, 207
WHILE
Complexity, 149
WHILE VARY
Obsolete, 350
WITH BYTE-ORDER MARK
OPEN DATASET, 337
WRITE
Background, 195
WRITE TO
Obsolete, 356
use, 254

Z

Zero division
background, 255
example, 255

Tools for performance analysis:
Code Inspector, runtime analysis,
performance trace, and more

Performance aspects in development:
SQL queries, internal tables, buffer,
data transfer

Application design: general
performance and parallelization

Hermann Gahm

ABAP Performance Tuning

This book for ABAP developers details best practices for ABAP
performance tuning. Covering the most critical performance-relevant
programming issues and performance monitoring tools, this book will
show you how to best analyze, tune, and implement your ABAP
programs.
Starting with a description of the client/server architecture, the book
moves on to discussing the different tools for analyzing performance.
Programming techniques are then analyzed in detail, based on numerous
real-life examples. This book will help you ensure that your ABAP
programs are tuned for best performance.

348 pp., 2009, 69,95 Euro / US$ 69.95
ISBN 978-1-59229-289-9

Tools for performance analysis:
Code Inspector, runtime analysis,
performance trace, and more

Performance aspects in development:
SQL queries, internal tables, buffer,
data transfer

Application design: general
performance and parallelization

Hermann Gahm

ABAP Performance Tuning

This book for ABAP developers details best practices for ABAP
performance tuning. Covering the most critical performance-relevant
programming issues and performance monitoring tools, this book will
show you how to best analyze, tune, and implement your ABAP
programs.
Starting with a description of the client/server architecture, the book
moves on to discussing the different tools for analyzing performance.
Programming techniques are then analyzed in detail, based on numerous
real-life examples. This book will help you ensure that your ABAP
programs are tuned for best performance.

348 pp., 2009, 69,95 Euro / US$ 69.95
ISBN 978-1-59229-289-9

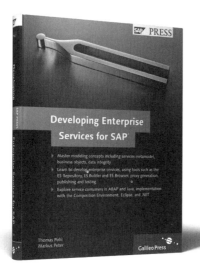

Modeling: Services meta model, enterprise services repository, ARIS

Development: proxy generation, inbound services, synchronous and asynchronous communication

Usage: consumer proxies in ABAP and Java, security, error handling

Thomas Pohl, Markus Peter

Developing Enterprise Services for SAP

This book is a developer's guide to programming enterprise services. After reading this book, you will be able to develop enterprise services in ABAP and in Java, and you'll then be able to integrate these services into larger applications.
You will be guided through the modeling process, the development of services, and finally to the implementation of the service. Using numerous screenshots of the Workbench and Eclipse, and showing numerous code listings, this book will help you understand how to develop enterprise services.

396 pp., 2009, 69,95 Euro / US$ 69.95
ISBN 978-1-59229-291-2

>> www.sap-press.com

Interested in reading more?

Please visit our Web site for all
new book releases from SAP PRESS.

www.sap-press.com